ENCYCLOPEDIA OF THE
Animal World

Vol 14   Moose — Otoliths

Bay Books Sydney

1070

MOOSE VERSUS LOCOMOTIVES. During the rut bull moose bellow, challenging rival males and attracting females. At one time the whistles of Canadian trains happened to imitate this bellow and locomotives were sometimes attacked by bull moose, who have poor eyesight. Eventually the whistles had to be changed to prevent accidents. When a cow moose hears a bull bellowing she responds and he comes to find her. Indian hunters used to imitate the cow's call with a birch-bark trumpet to lure the bull within range. They also used wooden whistles to imitate the calls of young deer to call up the does. This was a dangerous method of hunting as it also attracted wolves. A more bizarre form of lure was employed in Africa where a hunter would bite the tail of a baby crocodile. Its cries attracted adults to the spot.

MORAYS, a family of *eels.

MORGAN, T. H., 1866–1945, an American trained as an embryologist who became the founder of 20th century genetics and Nobel prizewinner for medicine in 1933. In 1909 while Professor at Columbia University, Morgan decided that *mutations should provide a profitable means of testing the many imponderables in the new doctrine of genetics. His search for a suitable experimental animal led him to the Fruit fly *Drosophila melanogaster*; a portentous meeting, for the work of the Morgan school with this animal led to enormous strides in the study of genetics. *Drosophila* has been called 'fruitful fly' and it has been said that 'God created the fruit fly especially for Morgan'.

By subjecting his flies to extreme temperatures, unusual diets, chemical agents, radioactivity and other 'unusual' influences, Morgan had produced 40 mutants by 1911. Some were without wings, hairs or eyes, others had unusual colouration or abnormal wing veins. Further breeding established that the *white eye* mutation only occurred with *yellow wing*; *pink eye* only with *ebony body*; and *vestigial wing* only with *black body*. Thus three chromosomes were indicated, but *Drosophila* has four: three large and one small. However, in 1914, *bent wing* was discovered. It was unconnected with the other groups and, after another five years' work, *eyeless* and *shaven* were found. They were linked with *bent wing,* so there were four groups of mutations which corresponded with the four chromosomes. The chromosomal nature of inheritance was therefore, established.

But what of the fact that *white eye* only occurs in males? How does this 'sex-linkage' occur? Morgan showed what is now common knowledge, that one of the male chromosomes is slightly different from its female equivalent and that this difference is responsible for sex determination and the characters linked with it.

MORPHOLOGY, the study of form and structure in animals and plants, especially of superficial features. The word is also used loosely to describe the form and structure themselves.

MOSAIC EVOLUTION, the term given by Sir Gavin de Beer to a mode of evolution involving the complete transformation of some organs to a new form while others remain unchanged. His discoveries arose from studies on transitional forms of fossils intermediate between the five different classes of vertebrates. *Archaeopteryx* (Jurassic) has a number of characters that are purely reptilian: a simple brain with a small cerebellum, a long tail of 20 elongated separate vertebrae, simple 'draughtsman' articular facets of vertebrae, a short pelvic girdle, free fingers and toes and simple thoracic and abdominal ribs. At the same time it has a number of characters which are purely avian: feathers and their arrangement on wings, fused collar-bones forming a 'merry-thought' and big toes opposable to the others which is an indispensable condition of perching on a branch. The transition from reptile to bird was effected, not by a gradual transformation of all organs, but by a complete transformation of some to the new form while others remained unchanged in the old form, like pieces of a mosaic. Comparable conditions are found in the transition from fishes to amphibians, from amphibians to reptiles and from reptiles to mammals. One of the most important examples of mosaic evolution is shown by the

Female mosquito *Aedes aegypti* with its blood-sucking mouthparts puncturing human skin.

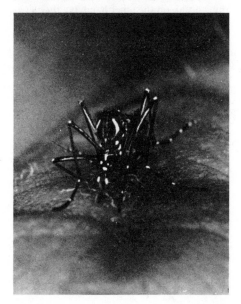

australopithecines, the man-like apes ancestral to man. The small brain-volume, massive projecting jaws and large molars are purely ape-like; while the smooth rounded forehead (in the young), the curved arch of the teeth, the type of wear in molars (human method of chewing), the delicate forelimbs, and the shape of the pelvic-girdle and thighbones, indicating vertical stance on two legs, are purely human.   G. de B.

MOSQUITOES, two-winged flies belonging to the family Culicidae with some 3,000 known species. The females of many species feed on vertebrate blood. They have their mouthparts drawn out into slender stylets which, except when feeding, are enclosed in a sheath forming a long proboscis. During blood-feeding the sheath is drawn back and the bundle of stylets is inserted through the skin into a small blood vessel. This type of feeding is known as capillary feeding. It contrasts sharply with the mode of feeding of other groups of biting flies. These have shorter mouthparts which are used to excavate a small pit, or sump, into which the blood flows and from which it is imbibed, a mode of feeding known as 'pool feeding'.

Four larval stages and a pupal stage are passed through in the course of development. The larvae are found in water of almost every imaginable kind. Besides absorbing oxygen through the general body surface they take in air at the surface of the water through a pair of breathing pores or spiracles situated at the tip of the abdomen. In the tribe Anophelini the spiracles are flush with the surface of the abdomen. Anopheline larvae consequently rest parallel with the surface film to which they adhere by means of rosette-like hairs. In the larvae of the other tribes (Toxorhynchitini, Sabethini, Culicini) the spiracles are situated at the tip of a tubular respiratory siphon. In these only the tip of the siphon is flush with the surface film from which the larvae hang downwards at an angle.

The pupae of the different tribes differ only in detail. They breathe, in all cases, by means of paired respiratory trumpets situated on top of the thorax. The tip of the abdomen is furnished with a pair of paddles, used, in most cases, like a lobster's tail to propel them through the water. The larvae mostly swim by means of a jerky side to side movement of the body, but some culicines employ a curious vibratory motion presumably adaptive to progression through the thick sludges in which they breed. The larvae of most species have a pair of dense hair tufts, known as mouth brushes, at the front of the head. These are used for sweeping food into the mouth but they can also be used for propulsion with the body held rigid. This type of locomotion is seen particularly in certain species breeding in tree holes or

Pupa and larvae of *Culex pipiens* suspended from the surface film through which their breathing tubes protrude.

plant pitchers and with the body covered with dense rosettes of stiff spines thought to be protective against predation. Finally, the larvae of some sabethines, breeding in water collecting in the leaf bases of broad-leafed plants, can crawl rapidly over moist surfaces and thus are able to migrate from one leaf base to another.

Among other structural modifications the most conspicuous are those affecting the respiratory siphon which assumes an extraordinary variety of shapes and sizes. In most species it is relatively short but in some it is greatly elongated and in one species of *Culex* it attains several times the length of the abdomen. In the genera *Mansonia* and *Coquillettidia* it is modified for penetrating the air spaces in the underwater tissues of aquatic plants to which the larvae are permanently attached. In this as in most, but not all, other cases modification of the larval siphon is accompanied by a comparable modification of the respiratory trumpets of the pupa.

The eggs may be laid singly or compacted into a floating ribbon or raft or, in some cases, a more or less symmetrical egg mass attached to the underside of floating vegetation. Raft-forming species necessarily rest on the surface of the water while depositing their eggs. Some Anophelini and Toxorhynchitini, on the other hand, lay their eggs on the wing. In at least one species of *Sabethes,* breeding in tree holes with very small apertures, the eggs are projected with remarkable accuracy into the interior of the tree hole while the mosquito hovers outside. Species of *Toxorhynchites,* breeding in the joints of bamboos, probably inject their eggs in a similar manner through the small boreholes made by beetle larvae. In contrast to this, species of *Aedes* and related genera lay their eggs on dry or damp surfaces. Those breeding in tree holes or other container habitats generally lay them just above the water line. Those breeding in temporary ground pools insert them into small crevices in the soil. One species, breeding in crab holes, attaches them to the legs of the crabs. Other species, breeding in swamp habitats, may attach them to dead leaves or other vegetation subject to periodic inundation. In all these cases the eggs are highly resistant to desiccation and the larva contained in the egg can survive long periods of cold or drought in a state of suspended animation.

Although the larvae show striking modifications adaptive to particular types of breeding place, the situations in which they find themselves are determined mainly by the behaviour of the ovipositing females. Running-water habitats are favoured chiefly by certain anophelines which lay their eggs in situations such as the edges of slowly running streams where standing or overhanging vegetation affords shelter from the current. The behaviour-patterns of the adults ensure that the eggs are laid in a favourable situation and the reactions of the larvae ensure that, after hatching, they remain within the limits of safety. Contrary to former belief little or nothing is left to chance.

Two main categories of still-water habitats can be distinguished comprising, respectively, ground water and container habitats. Ground-water habitats range from temporary pools, subject to rapid desic-

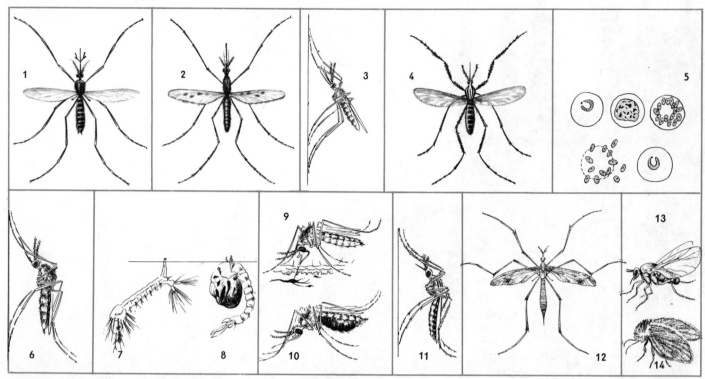

Mosquitoes and disease. Top row, left to right: 1. the Common mosquito *Culex pipiens* 4.5–6 mm long, 2. the Malarial mosquito *Anopheles maculipennis* 6–8 mm long, and 3. the same seen in side view to show how its abdomen is tilted upwards when the insect is at rest, 4. the Yellow fever mosquito *Aedes aegypti* 4–8 mm. Finally, in this top row, human blood corpuscles 5, infected with the Malarial parasite *Plasmodium vivax*. First a cell containing a trophozoite which breaks up into merozoites that are liberated into the blood. It is at this stage that antidotes to malaria can be effective, before the merozoites re-enter other corpuscles to assume the sickle-shape and start the cycle all over again. Bottom row: 6. Common mosquito at rest, with body horizontal. 7. A larva and 8. a pupa of this mosquito, both aquatic, breathing, suspended from the surface film. Two Common mosquitoes, 9. the one above feeding, 10. the one below gorged with blood. Next is 11. the Yellow fever mosquito, resting, seen in side view, with the body horizontal, as in the common mosquito. Finally, 12. the large but harmless Crane fly *Tipula gigantea*, 13. the small blackfly *Melusina maculata* and 14. the midge *Clytocerus ocellaris*, relatives of the mosquitoes.

cation, to permanent bodies of water with dense aquatic vegetation. Temporary pools may be filled directly by rain or by overflow from streams or rivers or the encroachment of tides, under estuarine conditions, or, finally, in the case of arctic *Aedes* by melting snow. Arctic *Aedes,* which occur in enormous numbers, overwinter in the egg. The eggs are laid on that side of the future breeding place which will be exposed first and longest to the spring sunshine. Various species of Anophelini and Culicini breed in brackish pools under estuarine conditions and a few Culicini are found in sea-shore breeding places sometimes with a salinity in excess of sea water. High mineral content is also a feature of desert pools and pools in volcanic regions. One species of *Aedes* breeds in volcanic pools hot enough and alkaline enough to take the skin off a foot incautiously inserted into them. Organic pollution is lethal to many species but favourable to some. Huge increases in *Culex fatigans,* the urban carrier of the disease known as Bancroftian filariasis, have occurred in recent years in consequence of the pollution of tropical cities by domestic and industrial waste.

Among container habitats already mentioned are the leaf bases of broad-leafed plants. A good example is furnished by the plants known as bromeliads which grow in great numbers on the trunks and branches of forest trees in the New World tropics. These provide breeding places for a great variety of anophelines, culicines and, particularly, sabethines, often far above the ground in the forest canopy. Broad-leafed food plants such as banana, pineapple and yam are favoured

by some Old World species such as *Aedes simpsoni,* an important carrier of rural yellow fever in Africa which owes its wide distribution in that continent, in part, to the dispersal of such plants as articles of commerce. Plant pitchers are favoured by some Sabethini with larvae able to resist the digestive juices which these contain. Such larvae often have powerful jaws with which they feed on the corpses of other insects trapped in the pitchers. Artificial containers are a principle source of the urban Yellow fever carrier, *Aedes aegypti,* with stacked motor tyres forming a particularly prolific breeding ground and one which is difficult to treat adequately either by emptying or with insecticide. Other container habitats with a varied and interesting fauna include, as has already been mentioned, split, bored or cut bamboos and rot-holes in trees or fallen logs. Other breeding places in the same category, but with a much more restricted fauna, are snail shells, cup fungi, fruit husks and the rotting pith of soft-stemmed, tree-like plants such as paw-paw. Rat-bored coconuts are a particularly important source of the major carrier of Bancroftian filariasis in the Pacific islands, *Aedes polynesiensis.*

Up to the end of the Second World War mosquito control was effected largely by the elimination of breeding places by drainage or other measures or by treating them with insecticides, such as oil or Paris green. Knowledge of larval biology grew accordingly. Growth in our knowledge of adult biology has been more recent and has accompanied the development of insecticides such as DDT and dieldrin which can be sprayed on the inside walls of houses leaving

A male mosquito C. pipiens just emerged from the pupa at the surface of water.

a long-lasting deposit lethal to mosquitoes resting on it. However, the substances are now prohibited in some countries.

Emergence from the pupa is followed by a resting period lasting from a few hours to a day or more depending on the species and the environmental temperature. During this time the wings expand and harden and flight becomes possible. After this the mosquitoes disperse. Forest species probably disperse only for comparatively short distances at ground level but those which fly up into the canopy to feed may be caught up in ascending air currents and dispersed more widely, an important consideration with respect to the dissemination of forest mosquito-borne viruses. At the other extreme salt-marsh mosquitoes often achieve dispersals of the order of 20 miles (32 km) or more and wind assisted flights of over 100 miles (160 km) have been recorded.

Mating takes place in certain genera (*Opifex, Deinocerites*) while the female is emerging from the pupal skin. In widely dispersing species it may take place both at the time of dispersal and later. Such species commonly form large male swarms in which mating takes place with any females which enter and are recognized by the sound of their wing-beats. Opinions differ as to the proportion of all mating taking place in such swarms. After emergence the male claspers rotate through 180°. Mating cannot take place until this rotation is largely completed. The delay is, however, partly offset by the fact that males usually emerge before the females. Many species possess the ability to mate in small cages (stenogamy) and so can

be readily colonized in the laboratory. Others lack this ability, although some of them can be colonized by selecting stenogamous strains genetically. The timing of such activities as emergence, dispersal, swarming and feeding is controlled, in general, by an internal 'clock' set by the daily change from light to dark. This may be overridden if conditions are unfavourable.

Only the females feed on blood. Male mosquitoes feed on sugary substances such as the nectar secreted by flowers. Such substances also form an important part of the diet of the females of many species, the blood meal serving mainly to provide additional resources for developing the eggs. Some genera are incapable of taking blood. Both sexes of Toxorhynchitini have the proboscis modified for feeding on flowers. In the genus *Malaya* it is modified for feeding on the regurgitated food of ants. All the main groups of backboned animals are attacked except for the fishes. Only one of these, the mudskipper, which spends much of its time out of water, is known to be attacked by mosquitoes. Many birds and mammals harbour blood parasites, ranging from viruses to single-celled Protozoa, such as the Malaria parasites, and parasitic worms, such as those causing filariasis. Particular species of mosquitoes may transmit such parasites to man as happens in the case of many virus diseases, Brugian filariasis and, occasionally, Monkey malaria. Other mosquito-borne diseases, such as Bancroftian filariasis and the four different kinds of human malaria, are confined to man.

Attempts at the control or eradication of

mosquito-borne diseases have received a serious setback from the development of insecticide resistance. The mode of inheritance of this kind of resistance has been intensively studied giving rise to a rapidly growing science of mosquito genetics. At the same time alternative methods of control have received increasing attention. Among these is the 'sterile male technique' which involves the release of large numbers of sterilized male mosquitoes sufficient to mate with the females to the exclusion of normal males.

Mosquitoes have many natural enemies other than man. Some of these have already been used for purposes of control and others are being studied for use in the future. Fishes have been widely employed and one of these, the North American topminnow *Gambusia affinis* has been used throughout the warmer parts of the world so that it probably now has the widest geographical range of any freshwater fish. Some of the very large, brightly coloured mosquitoes of the genus *Toxorhynchites*, the larvae of which feed on those of other mosquitoes, have been introduced into islands in the Pacific with a view to controlling species of *Aedes* transmitting filariasis. Unfortunately, however, their slow rate of reproduction, and propensity for feeding on larvae of their own species, makes them only moderately effective. Among parasites of mosquitoes, the fungus *Coelomomyces* has been successfully established in another group of islands, while another species of the same genus is being studied with a view to controlling the worst of the African malaria carriers, *Anopheles gambiae*. Certain parasitic worms (Mermithidae) are also being studied with a view to use against this species and parasitic protozoans (Microsporidia) are also being investigated.

Assessing the effectiveness of these and other measures is a complicated matter demanding, in itself, an intimate knowledge of mosquito biology. Among the sampling methods employed are the use of traps, such as entry or exit traps fixed to the windows of dwellings or experimental huts; artificial outside resting places, such as pits or earth-lined boxes; and traps with human, or other animal, bait. Such devices can only yield reliable information if allowance is made for the bias inevitably introduced by the reaction of different kinds of mosquitoes to the trap and by the particular environment in which the trap is set up.

An especially important factor determining whether a particular mosquito population is dangerous or not is the life expectancy of its members. A mosquito which does not live long enough for the disease causing agent to reach maturity presents no danger even if it becomes infected. The proportions of mosquitoes with different life expectancies in a given population can be estimated by dissecting the ovaries of captured females and ascertaining the number of ovipositions which each has performed. If the interval between successive ovipositions, at the prevailing temperature, is known, the age of the individual at the time of capture can be estimated.

It used to be said that to control mosquito-borne diseases we had to learn to think like a mosquito. This is still true but in addition we are having to learn to think like a population of mosquitoes. FAMILY: Culicidae, ORDER: Diptera, CLASS: Insecta, PHYLUM: Arthropoda.   P.F.M.

MOSQUITO EGGS. The eggs usually receive little attention in the study of insects and one does not think of insect eggs as having protective devices. Yet Professor H. E. Hinton has shown that the minute eggs of *Culex* mosquitoes have two forms of protection. Like many seabirds and fishes, the floating mosquito eggs are dark above and pale below, so that to an aerial predator they merge with the dark water and to an underwater predator they merge with the brightness of the sky. The pale underside of the egg is produced by a thin film of air in the egg membrane that acts as a mirror. The second protective device is a small drop of fluid on the pole of the egg which repels insect predators. Insect eggs are preyed on by ants when they are stranded by a falling water level. Professor Hinton showed that the ants tend to leave mosquito eggs alone or spend more time cleaning themselves, if they do touch them, than if presented with blowfly eggs or sugar paper.

MOSQUITOFISH *Gambusia affinis,* a small freshwater fish from North America belonging to the live-bearing group of toothcarps. Its common name derives from its food of mosquito larvae. The mosquitofish occurs in Trinidad and other Caribbean islands and is widespread in the southern parts of the United States. The female closely resembles the female guppy but can be distinguished by the presence of small black spots on the tail. The male resembles the male guppy in shape but lacks the bright colours of that fish, the body being olive-brown with occasional spots. The mouth is directed upwards and the fishes swim just below the surface, feeding on mosquito larvae or other small animals. Since the mosquitofish is able to destroy its own weight of mosquitoes in one day, it became the most important fish to be introduced into countries where malaria-carrying mosquitoes were prevalent. Unfortunately, its virtues blinded public health authorities to the fact that it also preyed on the eggs and young of other fishes to such an extent that

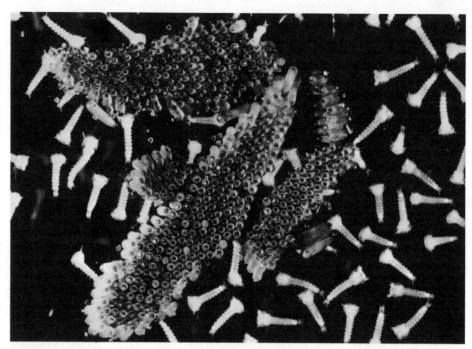
Eggs of *Culex* mosquito float in rafts on water. Around them are newly hatched larvae.

local species often became rare or were destroyed altogether. In Bangkok (Thailand) the native panchax *Aplocheilus panchax* has now become rare and the unique little *Phenacostethus,* which was known only from there, has disappeared. In the streams near Laguna de Bay in the Philippines, the mosquitofish flourishes but *Gulaphallus* has gone. *Micropanchax schoelleni* of the lower Nile cannot now be found, while the mosquitofish flourishes. Dr G. S. Myers, who has done much to point out the dangers of the mosquitofish, first encountered the problem when the staff at a hatchery for Black bass reported that the mosquitofish, introduced as a 'forage fish' for the bass, were in fact destroying a large proportion of them. In his own goldfish pond, Dr Myers discovered that the total weight of goldfish increased threefold over a period of seven years compared with the weight that had existed when the pond was stocked with both goldfish and mosquitofish. FAMILY: Poeciliidae, ORDER: Atheriniformes, CLASS: Pisces.

MOSS-ANIMALS, a popular name for the *Bryozoa.

MOSS MITES, also commonly referred to as oribatids or Beetle mites, are minute, free-living arachnids occurring in great diversity and abundance in the upper layers of the soil, in organic debris and clumps of moss. More than a hundred families of mites are included in this order, and the group is usually characterized, at least in the adult stage, by the complete or almost complete sclerotization, or thickening, of the body surface which is often dark-coloured, brown or black. With very few exceptions, Moss mites possess a

pair of prominent, specialized sensory setae inserted in cup-shaped pits on the upper surface of the body. Apart from a few primitive groups, the body shows little evidence of segmentation, although it is often divided into two parts, an anterior prosoma and a posterior hysterosoma, by a transverse furrow between the second and third pair of legs. These two regions of the body are immovably fused together in most oribatids, but in the 'box-mites', or Phthiracaroidea, the prosoma can be reflexed against the hysterosoma to protect the soft parts of the body and legs, in a manner reminiscent of that of the armadillo. A distinctive feature of certain families is the presence of a pair of lateral, wing-like expansions on the hysterosoma; these structures, which are called pteromorphs, are large, hinged and capable of movement in some cases, notably in the family Galumnidae.

The body surface of many oribatids is delicately sculptured and patterned, particularly on the upper surface of the prosoma, with accessory plates or lamellae and, not uncommonly, the skins of previous moults remain attached to the upper surface of the hysterosoma. The mouthparts, which are housed in a cavity at the anterior end of the body, are of the typical arachnid type, namely a pair of 'jaws', or chelicerae, and a pair of leg-like sensory palps. In most cases, the chelicerae are heavily developed as toothed cutters, each with a pair of opposable articles; occasionally they are elongate and stylet-like.

Although frequently the most abundant of the soil arthropods, these arachnids are easily overlooked for they are small, ranging in size from 0·2 mm to 1·5 mm, slow-moving, dark-coloured and often globular, like the soil particles and organic debris which surrounds them and with which they sometimes adorn their bodies for camouflage. Nevertheless, they are often counted in hundreds of thousands per square metre in grassland and forest soils, although they flourish best in highly organic, undisturbed woodland soils, and are much less successful in regularly cultivated agricultural soils. As a general rule, Moss mites require humid conditions and rarely stray far from the protection of the soil or dense vegetation. However, a few species have become adapted, through the development of a waterproof body surface, to drier conditions, and characteristically occur on the leaves and bark of trees. At the other extreme are species adapted to an aquatic mode of life, some to freshwater, others to the marine habitat. A truly cosmopolitan group, oribatids also occur in hot dry deserts and in the bleak rock crevices of Antarctica, in situations where few other arthropods can survive.

Some species of Moss mites can reproduce parthenogenetically, but in many cases fertilized eggs are produced. Although adult females are usually slightly larger than males and, in some families, there are marked secondary sexual differences, more often than not the two sexes are practically indistinguishable. Rarely is copulation a preliminary to sperm transfer; usually the male produces spermatophores, each consisting of a globular packet of sperm carried at the tip of a rigid stalk. The stalk is deposited vertically on the substratum, and the sperm packet is taken into the genital tract of the female as her body passes over it. Eggs are laid through an extensible tube, or ovipositor, which probes into sheltered crevices in the soil, leaf litter or under bark. The life-cycle is basically similar in all Moss mites, development to the adult involving four active immature stages, namely a 6-legged larva, and three 8-legged nymphs, the protonymph, deutonymph and tritonymph. The immatures contrast with the adults in being pale-coloured, and differ from the latter in several other respects, as a rule. For example, in addition to having only three pairs of legs instead of the four pairs possessed by other active stages, the larva also lacks a genital aperture; the number of body setae often varies from one developmental stage to another, and the pteromorphs of the 'winged' mites only develop in the adult. The duration of the life-cycle is long, compared with other groups of mites, and under natural conditions in temperate regions the majority of species probably produce one, two or three generations per year, but rarely more than this.

Most Moss mites are unspecialized feeders, at least as nymphs and adults, and will eat whatever is available in the way of organic material. Fungal hyphae and spores frequently form a large proportion of the solid food present in the gut, and the heavy chelicerae, with their opposable cutting surfaces, are ideally suited for clipping this fungal material into short fragments. These mouthparts are also useful for tearing and fragmenting large pieces of moist, decaying plant material, another popular item of the diet, A predilection for woody tissue is shown by some of the box-mites which burrow in woody twigs, producing a gallery system in which all stages of the life-cycle may be found. Although instances have been recorded of Moss mites attacking the growing stems, roots and fruits of potatoes, strawberries, cherries and grasses, they are rarely important pests of cultivated crops; many of the species which live on the aerial parts of growing vegetation feed mainly on algae. Feeding habits have not been investigated fully, in many cases, and this is particularly true of those with stylet mouthparts incapable of dealing with solid food; these groups may

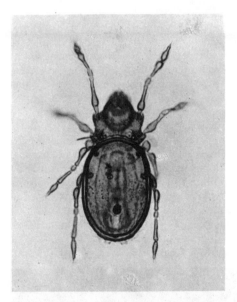

Moss mites live in large numbers in moss.

feed on the liquified products of plant decay or on bacterial colonies. The mouthparts of the larva are less strongly developed than those of later stages, and early instars often feed on the faeces of the adults. Faecal-feeding, or coprophagy, is fairly common, and by no means restricted to the larval stage.

Moss mites of pasture soils have attracted considerable attention since the discovery that members of at least half a dozen families serve as intermediate hosts for certain sheep and cattle tapeworms belonging to the genera *Moniezia*, *Anoplocephala*, *Cittotaenia* and *Bertiella*. The eggs of these parasites are ingested by the mites after they are dispersed in the soil. The choice of these arachnids as intermediate hosts is a fortunate one, as far as the tapeworms are concerned, because the mites often migrate during the day from the soil on to the stems and leaves of grasses, where they are easily ingested by grazing animals, and a cestode infection is initiated. Mites known to be potential hosts include several common and widely distributed species, such as *Scheloribates laevigatus*, *Liebstadia similis* and large-winged mites of the family Galumnidae. ORDER: Cryptostigmata, CLASS: Arachnida, PHYLUM: Arthropoda.   J.A.W.

MOTHER CAREY'S CHICKENS, the name bestowed by seamen on the *Storm petrels which flutter low over the surface of the water and pick up plankton and frequently follow ships for scraps. The name is derived from Mater Cara, the Virgin Mary.

MOTHS, closely related and similar in appearance to butterflies and with them constituting the order Lepidoptera. The order is divided into nine 'superfamilies', eight of which comprise moths and one, butterflies.

White ermine moth *Spilosoma lubricipeda*.

The distinction between moths and butterflies is, to a considerable extent, one of degree, rather than of kind. Butterflies nearly always, though not invariably, fly by day and rest with the wings raised over the back, while moths fly either by day or by night, more frequently the latter, and generally rest with the wings outspread or wrapped around the body, though quite a number raise them like butterflies. The antennae of butterflies nearly always end in a knob. This is rare in moths and when that condition does occur in them the fore- and hindwings are held together in flight by a catch or 'frenulum' on the underside. That mechanism is usual in moths but absent from practically all butterflies. Thus these two features taken together do provide a distinction between the two groups.

Most moths, though not all, possess large

internal ears which, curiously enough, vary in their position: they may take up about $\frac{1}{3}$ of the thorax, or about the same amount of space in the larger abdomen. They are not found in butterflies which, nevertheless, can certainly appreciate sound, though by a means not fully understood. A large proportion of nocturnal moths is attracted by a light, mainly its short-wave component, but curiously, this stimulus affects only the males. The long-range scent perception of certain moths, by which the males can detect the female 1 mile (1·6 km) or more away, is unknown in butterflies and is probably unique in nature. To achieve it, the area of the scent-perceiving organs, the antennae, has to be much increased by great numbers of side branches. It will be appreciated that these occur only in the male sex and never in butterflies. The existence of such brush-like antennae is a certain indication of acute olfactory powers.

Numerous species of moths, about 100 in Britain, have, since the middle of last century become black or blackish in the industrial areas and a comparable situation has been reported from Japan, Europe and the USA. The change has affected caterpillars as well as perfect insects. It involves not only their colour, tending to protect them from bird predation on the blackened trees of manufacturing districts, but may also alter their physiology so that they are hardier than previously. The condition is noteworthy as a striking evolutionary change which has taken place fast enough to be studied by observation and experiment. See Lepidoptera. ORDER: Lepidoptera, CLASS: Insecta, PHYLUM: Arthropoda. E.B.F.

MOTH REPELLENTS. The theory of 'Spontaneous generation' held that animals could arise from inanimate objects. Thus mice were supposed to develop from piles of dirty linen and Horsehair worms from horsehairs that fell into water. According to the 16th century writer Bartholemew 'a Moth is a worm of clothes, and is gendered of corruption of cloth, when the cloth is too long in press and thick air, and is not blown with wind, neither unfolded in pure air'. This is an excellent description of conditions liable to lead to infestation by moths and Bartholemew's prescription of laurel leaves to prevent moth attack is sound. Laurel leaves contain cyanide and are sometimes used for killing insects. A century later, Thomas Muffet, father of Little Miss Muffet, claimed that kingfisher skins or lion pelts kept moths away.

MOTIVATION. An animal does not always make the same response to two identical stimuli; the difference in its behaviour on the two occasions is attributed to changes in its motivation. Motivation, therefore, is a theoretical concept which refers to the internal state of the animal and which can be measured as differences in response to a particular stimulus.

If food is placed near the tentacles of a Beadlet anemone *Actinia equina* the animal discharges its stinging cells (nematocysts) and sticky cells (cnidoblasts) on the tentacles contacting the food; these convey the food to the mouth which opens and ingests it. An anemone which has just been fed, however, does not respond to food in this way. The tentacles show no reaction and the mouth does not open, whereas an anemone which has been starved for some time will even swallow unpalatable substances such as cotton wool or filter paper. The motivation of its feeding behaviour is said to be low when it shows little or no response to food and high when it accepts unpalatable substances.

The motivation of hunger is normally related to an animal's metabolic needs. The psychologist N. E. Miller discovered that damage to the ventro-medial nucleus of the hypothalamus of the brain of a rat resulted in the animal having an insatiable appetite so that in time it became grossly obese. In this experiment Miller had damaged the mechanism which lowers hunger motivation when the rat has eaten an adequate amount of food.

In addition to hunger and thirst a number of other motivations have been described, sexual motivation being one. A male chaffinch *Fringilla coelebs* copulates with a female in the breeding season but cannot be induced to do so in the winter. Treatment with a male hormone, or androgen, however, alters his sexual motivation so that he copulates with a female even in winter.

Individuals of the same species frequently vary considerably in their aggressive motivation, some having a high motivation to attack an opponent whilst others show a low motivation and are unaggressive or timid. Previous experience also influences the aggressive motivation. House mice *Mus musculus* which have lost a number of previous fights show a much lower motivation to attack their fellows than those which won earlier encounters.

Some animals have evolved ways in which they can communicate information to members of their own species regarding their motivational state. Some fish can change colour and the work of the Dutch ethologist G. P. Baerends showed that the colouration of the guppy *Lebistes reticulatus* indicates the likelihood of a male attacking, taking to flight or showing sexual behaviour towards a female. Social Primates such as monkeys and apes can indicate their current motivational state by bodily posture and facial expression. This form of communication is valuable in promoting social harmony and cooperation within the group.   T.B.P.

MOTMOT, common name for the eight tropical, forest-dwelling birds of the family Momotidae. They are confined to the New World, occurring from Mexico south to northeastern Argentina, but most of them are found in Mexico and in northern Central America.

Motmots vary in length from $6\frac{1}{2}$–$19\frac{3}{4}$ in ($16\frac{1}{2}$–50 cm) and have short and rounded wings, a long tail and a large bill, which is broad and somewhat decurved with serrated

The Polyphemus moth *Telea polyphemus*, of north America, is 12.5 cm across the spread wings.

The Blue-crowned motmot, noted for perching for long periods, calling monotonously.

The nestlings are naked when hatched and are brooded and fed by both parents. FAMILY: Momotidae, ORDER: Coraciiformes, CLASS: Aves. F.H.

MOTOR PATTERN, the pattern of movements made by an animal, especially as regards their nervous control.

An animal may have a relatively limited number of motor patterns which it utilizes in different contexts and various sequences to produce patterns of behaviour suitable for feeding, mating, escape from enemies, as well as the smaller activities. It is possible to use these movements in the analysis of the animal's behaviour. Thus, it is convenient to divide the locomotion of a horse into walking, trotting and galloping. But galloping towards a stimulus, for example, food or a mate, and galloping away from a possible danger will have different behavioural significance, so we see that the orientation of the motor pattern is of considerable importance.

Locomotory movements can be analyzed into sequences of contraction and relaxation of the muscles, such as Weiss did for the movements of the forelimb of the salamander during a single step. The determination of stepping patterns of a salamander, the body movements of a fish and other locomotory movements is through nervous control from the central nervous system. There are two possibilities for the origin of such patterns; there may be an internal rhythm with the nervous system responsible, or a sensory input from the limbs or other parts of the body may control by *feedback. Experiments have been performed in which frogs with their brain removed had, in addition, all the sensory nerves feeding into the spinal column severed. Being without brains these animals had no other sensory input to the cord. Their stepping rhythm disappeared. But if only a few of the sensory nerves were left intact, the rhythm was retained. This showed that sensory input is necessary for the carrying out of these complex motor patterns.

Many of the motor patterns which are characteristic of particular species seem to be able to develop even when the animal is brought up in isolation. Partly this is the result of maturation of the nervous system as the individual grows and nervous connections are established, but what connections are made must be largely genetically determined. The complicated behaviour of beavers by which they fell trees and make dams develops normally in isolation as does the elaborate courtship pattern of male Jumping spiders.

Motor patterns are often remarkably unaffected by learning. This is very well demonstrated by experiments on rats where the opposing muscles of the limb were transposed. After this operation if the extensor muscle contracts it will retract the limb, and the retractor's action will also be

edges. In most species the tail is graduated and in typical motmots the two central tail-feathers are much longer than the others and in the subterminal parts the barbs are loosely attached and fall off when the bird preens them. This results in part of the vane becoming naked while at the end of the vane the barbs remain intact leaving a racquet or spatula tip.

Most motmots are greenish, olive or rufous brown with some bright colours on the head and a dark spot on the breast. They live in dark forests and, because of their blending plumage, are difficult to locate among the foliage even when they call constantly. They feed mainly on insects and berries which are snapped off in flight.

The Blue-crowned motmot *Momotus momota* has the widest distribution of all, occurring from northeastern Mexico south through Central and South America to Argentina. It is green above and brownish below. Its crown is black, the forehead cobalt blue with an ultramarine band behind the crown and a black area around the eyes. On the breast is a small black spot edged with pale blue. This is the only species of motmot found in the Guianas where it is not uncommon in dark forests. It often sits motionless for long periods, not very high up on a branch of a tree, uttering its peculiar and rather loud call—a rhythmical and staccato 'jootoo, jootoo'. Two birds often sing in duet. When sitting they sometimes swing their long tails like a pendulum from side to side.

Motmots nest in holes which they dig with their strong bills in the ground, either in a bank or in the level ground of the forest floor. The entrance pipe can be long and even curved and at the end is a chamber where the eggs are laid. Usually the nests are very difficult to find. The eggs are roundish and pure white. The best known species lay three or four eggs. Both sexes incubate and the incubation period is from 21–22 days.

reversed. Despite the disruption of limb movements which results it is impossible to retrain the animals to use the muscles in a different way, the extensor continues to contract when the limb should be thrust forward even though the very opposite effect results.

The basic motor patterns used in behaviour seem therefore to be the most rigid part of the action patterns which distinguish species-specific behaviour. But they may nevertheless be incorporated in adaptive learned behaviour, so that when a rat learns a maze, it still uses these fixed patterns in its locomotion.   J.D.C.

MOUFLON *Ovis musimon,* the smallest of the sheep, native to Corsica and Sardinia. See sheep, mountain.

MOULTING, the shedding of the skin or external covering of animals. This process is often under hormonal control, as in the insects and crustaceans. It may be a seasonal occurrence, as for example, the loss of feathers in birds and fur in mammals. See also sloughing.

MOULTING IN BIRDS, the regular, periodic shedding and renewal of the feathers. In some species, other epidermal structures such as bill plates, as in the puffin, are also moulted. It is of vital importance to a bird that its feathers are maintained in good condition, hence the considerable amount of care given to the feathers and their replacement at least once a year. In most birds there is a post-nuptial moult which renews the worn feathers after the rigours of the breeding season and prepares the plumage for its winter functions of waterproofing and heat retention. In a number of species there is also a partial prenuptial moult which improves the plumage display features by adding brighter colours or special plumes. This moult is more common in males. A very few species also moult a third time. The ptarmigan *Lagopus mutus,* for example, has a third, partial moult in autumn when it assumes a brown plumage between the grey of spring and the white of winter. The male old-squaw or Long-tailed duck *Clangula hyemalis* has an unusual moulting sequence with different breeding, eclipse and winter plumages.

In cranes the flight feathers of the wings are moulted in alternate years only, but one of the most unusual patterns of moult is that of the cocks of the domestic breed of fowl known as the Longtailed yokohama. After the first two moults while the bird is immature, the moult of the tail feathers is somehow stopped and the tail continues to grow throughout the bird's life, which may be 12 years or more, and may reach a length of over 25 ft (7.6 m).

In general the post-nuptial moult sequence involves the loss of feathers equally from both sides of the bird, beginning with the flight feathers of the wing, then of the tail and then the body feathers. In the duck family Anatidae all the flight feathers of the wings are shed together during eclipse of the males, which then become temporarily flightless. There is also a simultaneous moult of the wing feathers in other groups such as the divers and grebes. The penguins moult their feathers in irregular patches and are unable to swim during the moulting period. Thus they are forced to fast during the moult.

A localised moult is seen in brood patches which, are sometimes developed at the beginning of the breeding season by the loss of feathers in special areas on the underside of the body together with the increased blood supply to the skin of those areas.   P.M.D.

MOUNTAIN CHICKEN *Leptodactylus fallax,* a large frog of the family Leptodactylidae which includes many of the smaller frogs of the New World. Native to the West Indies, where it lives on the mountainsides, it is large and an important item of diet to the peoples of that region, hence the name 'Mountain chicken'. All frogs of this family reproduce by laying eggs in frothy nests built close to water but not in water as in most frogs. FAMILY: Leptodactylidae, ORDER: Anura, CLASS: Amphibia.

MOUNTAIN GOAT *Oreamnos americanus,* one of the most peculiar hoofed mammals; not a goat, but a goat-antelope and a distant relative of the European chamois. It is an animal specialized to live on steep, wet, and usually snowcovered mountains, where chilling snowstorms are not absent even in summer and where winter reigns for up to eight months of the year. The Mountain goat has massive, muscular legs which terminate in large, broad hooves. It is a methodical climber, not a jumper, and resembles a bear when moving. Only exceptionally is it found away from steep, broken cliffs. Its white coat is made up of thick, long underwool and long guard hairs. There is a hair ridge on the neck, withers, and rump, and long hair parts on hind and front legs. The underwool tends to be greasy to the touch. Males and females are almost identical in appearance and both have large chin beards, narrow pointed ears and short, recurved, black horns. The males carry large glands behind the horns, which swell during the rutting season.

The Mountain goat is most striking in its social adaptations, its adaptable, diverse food habits and its ability to cope with snow. Although tied to cliffs, it eats almost anything that grows on them; herbs, grasses, twigs or conifer needles. Its broad hooves and flexible, strong forelegs are superb tools for removing deep snow from the vegetation

Mountain goat; not a goat but a goat-antelope.

it covers, or for carrying the goat over snow crusts that any Mountain sheep or human would break through. Winter or summer, Mountain goats roam at high elevations, sometimes feeding among rubble that appears to defy plant growth.

The social adaptations of goats stem from their sharp and very dangerous horns, which function as weapons only. In combat, Mountain goats jab their horns into the opponent's haunches, belly, groin, or chest, wherever they can land a blow. Unlike most ruminants, they do not catch and neutralize an opponent's attack with the head. This would be quite impossible for Mountain goats since their skulls are thin and quite fragile. Instead, they have reduced their bloody, or even fatal, combat to the very minimum, and evolved a thick hide as a protection. Since in combat most blows land on the opponent's rear, here large males have a skin up to 1 in (2.5 cm) thick.

The possession of sharp, dangerous horns forces the female to protect her offspring whenever it gets into an aggressive interaction with another Mountain goat. Hence, females tend to be not only good, protective mothers, but also the most aggressive goats. They also dominate the slightly larger adult males. The males readily withdraw not only from aggressive females, but also from juveniles and even kids. In the early rutting season, the males court the females by crawling to them on the belly. At first, the males are threatened away but they persist, and eventually the females accept them. For about two weeks of the year, the males dominate females and mate with them. Then females revert to the dominant position, and most males leave the female ranges. Outside the rutting season which is late in November, the males tend to live alone, while females live in groups with their offspring. During the rut, one male and a female form a consort, unless deep snow forces rutting goats into groups on the few areas of thinner snow. The males dig rutting pits and are often distinguished by their dirty belly and haunches. They roam extensively between mountain ranges.

The kids are born in seclusion after a gestation period of about 180 days. Twins are not uncommon. In early summer, goats tend to congregate about salt licks. At this time they shed the long winter hair, and long strands of white goat wool decorate the shrubbery along goat trails.

Mountain goats are distributed from Wyoming to southeast Alaska and the Mackenzie Mountains of northern Canada. They are most abundant in the wet, cold mountain ranges such as the coastal ranges, Selkirks, or the western slopes of the Rocky Mountains. Here they reach much larger sizes than in dry mountains. Large males in wet mountains may weigh over 260 lb (118 kg), but will only be about 140 lb (64 kg) in the dry, southern Rockies. Little is known about the goat's life expectancy, its parasites or diseases. We do not know how important predators are in checking the growth of goat populations. The steep, dangerous terrain, favoured by goats, and the readiness of this rather nervous, though apparently phlegmatic animal, to ascend high cliffs if a wolf howls, appear to protect it sufficiently.
FAMILY: Bovidae, ORDER: Artiodactyla, CLASS: Mammalia. V.G.

MOUSE, a term applied rather loosely to almost any small rodent, especially if it has a long tail, and there is no sharp dividing line between the smaller species normally called mice and the larger ones normally called *rats. Also, small mice with long tails may belong to any of a considerable number of families of rodents. The great majority, however, fall into two groups: the Old World mice, family Muridae, and the New World mice which belong, along with other groups like voles, lemmings, hamsters and gerbils, to the family Cricetidae.

Mice belonging to these groups are characteristically very active animals that do not hibernate. They are short-lived but are prolific breeders, and they are distinguished structurally from most other families of rodents by the possession of only three cheekteeth in each row. Mice of these two families, Muridae and Cricetidae, may be extremely similar, but the Muridae are characterized by the presence of three longitudinal rows of cusps or tubercules on the molar teeth while in the Cricetidae there are only two such rows. This difference, although apparently trivial, is sufficiently constant to make it quite probable that these represent groups of mice that have evolved and produced their great diversity of species independently.

The Old World mice are found in great abundance and in great diversity throughout Africa, tropical Asia, New Guinea and Australia. They also occur, but with rather few species, in Europe and temperate Asia. This is the group that includes the familiar *House mouse *Mus musculus,* the European Wood mouse *Apodemus sylvaticus* and the Harvest mouse *Micromys minutus.* This family provides many of the climbers amongst the small rodents in contrast to the more terrestrial voles, lemmings, hamsters and gerbils.

Amongst the 300–400 species are some that are the most abundant and dominant mammals in their region, like the European Wood mouse, which is found in a great variety of habitats from forest to heathland, and others that are specialists, like the recently discovered Swamp mouse *Delanymys brooksi,* resembling a tiny Harvest mouse. It seems to be confined to a particular kind of sedge swamp in the mountains between Uganda and the Congo, and fewer than a dozen individuals have yet been found.

In Britain, the European Wood mouse, or Long-tailed field mouse as it is often called, is probably the most abundant and ubiquitous of all the mammals. In winter, especially, it sometimes enters houses where it is frequently mistaken for the House mouse. It is, however, a much more attractive animal than the House mouse, with large, bright eyes, larger ears, a rich yellow-brown fur above and pale silvery grey below with a little streak of yellow in the centre of the chest. Its extreme agility enables it, when it goes foraging at night, to travel over open ground away from the protection of grass and dense vegetation, to which slower and more diurnal species like the voles and shrews, are confined. The Wood mouse, for example, is the only species that will be found in woodland with a closed canopy and no undergrowth, but it is equally at home in gardens and hedgerows, shrubby sand dunes or on rocky hillsides. In spite of its alertness and agility the Wood mouse is far from immune from predation, and it forms a large proportion of the diet of the Tawny owl. The versatility of the Wood mouse extends to food as well as habitat. Seeds, buds and insects are all relished, and nuts are gathered in autumn for use in winter.

Close relatives of the Wood mouse, in the genus *Apodemus,* are found throughout temperate Asia as far as Japan. The only other member of this family in the temperate region is the *Harvest mouse which is much more of a specialist, spending its life climbing amongst the stems of long grass in which it builds a small, compact spherical nest. In spite of the hazards due to mechanization in the cornfields, the Harvest mouse survives well in Britain in hedgerows and reed beds wherever there is a dense stand of grass stems.

Long-tailed field mouse of Europe, also called European Wood mouse.

House mouse with young in the nest.

Tracks of a Harvest mouse *Micromys minutus*:
1. hindfoot, 2. forefoot; the tail is dragged.

The Pygmy mouse *Mus minutoides,* an African relative of the House mouse, is the smallest of all rodents, measuring only 2 in (5 cm) without the tail. It is found in the dry savannah areas of southern Africa. The African Striped mice, e.g. *Lemniscomys striatus* and *Rhabdomys pumilio,* are abundant grassland species that are amongst the most attractive of the Muridae, with parallel longitudinal rows of dark and light stripes or spots. Equally distinctive are the Spiny mice, *Acomys,* that occur in the drier regions throughout Africa and southwestern Asia. The entire pelage consists of stiff spiny hairs. Spiny mice are also unusual amongst the Muridae in having a long gestation period (about six weeks) resulting in a small litter, often only two, of unusually well developed young born with the eyes already open.

In southeastern Asia are several species of Tree mice, e.g. the Malay Tree mouse *Hapalomys longicaudatus,* most having extremely long tails and delicate prehensile feet. Australia has a great diversity of mice of this family belonging to endemic genera. Some, such as the species of *Leggadina* and *Pseudomys,* are rather typical mice with few peculiarities. Others, such as the Australian Hopping mice of the genus *Notomys,* are more like gerbils or jerboas than true mice. They have extremely long, slightly tufted tails and very large thin ears. They are capable of bounding bipedally at great speed on their long hindfeet, although their more

normal mode of progression is on all fours. This is another example of radiation in the Australian fauna comparable to that shown by the *marsupials in the absence of other major groups of mammals.

New World mice of the family Cricetidae show a similar abundance and diversity throughout North and South America and many can only be distinguished from their Old World equivalents by their teeth. The North American equivalent of the European Wood mice are the Deer mice of the genus *Peromyscus.* These are represented by a large number of species throughout North America and some are extremely similar in appearance, behaviour and ecology to the Eurasian species of *Apodemus.* The most widespread and best known species is the Long-tailed deer mouse *Peromyscus maniculatus,* which occurs in a great diversity of habitats from Alaska and Labrador south to California and Mexico. Like its European counterpart, it is a nocturnal, agile, versatile species. The North American Harvest mice, *Reithrodontomys,* are likewise rather similar to their Old World equivalents, the resemblance extending to the small spherical nests woven into the grass stems. But there is a greater diversity of species of Harvest mice in America than in Eurasia. The Grasshopper mice, *Onychomys,* occur in the more arid parts of North America. They have much shorter tails than most other mice of this group and are further distinguished by

their diet which consists almost entirely of insects. An alternative name, Scorpion mice, indicates another favourite item of their diet. Grasshopper mice have a remarkable high pitched squeal which they use very frequently, not only when molested, so that they can often be heard before they are seen.

In Central and South America there is a great diversity of species of mice belonging to this family, perhaps in the region of 200 species altogether. These vary from long-tailed arboreal mice to shorter-tailed species that tend to take the place of the voles, which are absent in the southern continent. Such, for example, are the species of South American Grass mice, *Akodon,* which are abundant throughout the continent. They are undistinguished little mice with soft brown fur and the tail a little shorter than the head and body, but they may be extremely abundant and play a dominant ecological role as grazers.

Some other groups of mice are superficially very similar to the murid and cricetid mice described above, but are placed in separate families because their internal structure, and especially their teeth, show that they have evolved quite independently. The northern Birch mouse of Europe *Sicista betulina* is a small mouse with a very long slender tail and a black stripe along the back, found in the birch forests of Scandinavia and Siberia. It represents the family Zapodidae, which is distinguished from the Muridae not only structurally, for example by the presence usually of an additional premolar tooth, but behaviourally in the habit of hibernating. The family is represented in North America by the Jumping mice, e.g. of the genus *Zapus,* found throughout most of the forested areas.

Another unrelated group of mice are the Pocket mice, Heteromyidae, of North America. The name refers to the cheekpouches which open on the outside of the cheeks and have a furry lining as in the related *Pocket gophers. The pouches are used to carry food which is stored and these mice, again unlike the murid and cricetid mice, tend to hibernate or at least become inactive and torpid during the winter. Pocket mice are found especially in the arid parts of western North America and some members of the family, the Kangaroo mice *Microdipodops,* show a very strong superficial resemblance to the Pygmy jerboas of the Old World, with a long tail, long hindfeet for bipedal hopping and greatly enlarged auditory capsules in the skull. Kangaroo mice are desert animals and can survive without drinking water even on relatively dry food, like seeds. Their water comes mainly from oxidation of food, and a store of fat that forms a swelling around the centre of the tail is probably part of the animal's water conservation equipment. The kidneys also play their part in water conservation by producing urine with up to 25% urea, compared with 6% in man. FAMILIES: Cricetidae, Heteromyidae, Muridae, Zapodidae, ORDER: Rodentia, CLASS: Mammalia.   G.B.C.

MOUSE REMEDIES. Topsell in *Fourfooted Beasts* (1607) gives an excellent recipe for preserving teeth. 'Of the heads of Mice being burned is made that excellent powder for the scouring and cleansing of the teeth called tooth-soap. For the rottenness and diminishing of the teeth, the best remedy is to take a living Mouse, and to take out one of her teeth . . . and hang it by the teeth of the party grieved . . . and he shall presently have ease and help of his pain'. Another author suggests that 'Mice dirt bruised with vinegar keepeth and saveth the head from falling of hair'. This is probably no worse than some *modern remedies.

MOUSEBIRDS, a family of small, long-tailed and crested arboreal birds. They are similar to songbirds but assigned to an order of their own. They are found only in Africa, in areas south of the Sahara and in Abyssinia, where they occur in the more open tree savannahs and forest edge habitats. The six species are finch-sized and all have tufted crests and long, slender graduated tails. The plumage, particularly that of the head and neck, is soft and lax. It is generally dull in colour, overall brown or grey, at times with some fine transverse barring. The only distinctive colouring is on the head, which is red-cheeked on *Colius indicus,* white on *C. leucocephalus,* and blue-naped on *C. macrourus*. There is bare skin around the eyes and nostrils which may be red, blue or grey; and the bill may be black-and-white or red in different species.

In general appearance mousebirds are squat and large-headed, with a stout, short and curved bill. The legs are short and the feet are strong, with long sharp claws. The hindtoe can be reversed so that all four toes may point forwards, and the bird will frequently hang from a twig, tail downwards, with the toes hooked over the perch; but on a flat surface both the outer toe and hind toe may point back to give a zygodactyl foot. The birds tend to rest back on the whole tarsus when moving or resting, but can shuffle and clamber about the branches of trees in a variety of acrobatic postures, and hop or run on level surfaces. The shafts of the tail feathers are stiff and lend some support. The birds clamber rapidly about on trees and bushes, feeding mainly on fruit, but also eat other parts such as leaves, and occasionally take insects.

Flight is usually direct and fast, but usually used for short movements between trees. A more irregular flight of alternate bursts of flapping and gliding may also be used. Mousebirds are extremely sociable, usually living in small parties and huddling close together when resting and roosting. They sleep in tightly huddled hanging clusters and frequently preen each other. They appear to be non-territorial and tolerant of other individuals near the nest. Their notes are simple calls—harsh buzzing notes, twittering, trills, and clear whistles. Softer subdued conversational notes are also used.

The nests are shallow cups, built of a great variety of material, coarser outside and finer within. The eggs, up to four in a clutch, are cream-coloured or white with brown streakings in different species. Incubation starts with the first egg and the young in a nest may vary in size. Both parents take part in incubation and care of young, and during incubation fresh leaves for nest lining may be added by the relieving bird. Young of earlier birds may at times assist with the feeding of later broods. FAMILY: Coliidae, ORDER: Coliiformes, CLASS: Aves.

MOUTH-BROODERS, fishes in which the fertilized eggs are taken into the mouth and incubated there. This type of parental care fulfils two functions: it protects the eggs from predators and it provides them with a constant stream of well oxygenated water. The eggs are brooded either by the male or by the female, but rarely by both. Once the eggs have hatched, the fry are often kept in the mouth for a further period during which they make short excursions as a small shoal, returning to the parent's mouth if danger threatens. In rearing these eggs in the laboratory, an artificial 'mouth' can be made from a glass funnel with a slight flow of water passing through.

The family Cichlidae has many members that practise mouth-brooding. It is found, for example in the African genera *Tilapia* and *Haplochromis* and the South American genus *Geophagus*. The eggs are usually laid in a shallow depression excavated by the male after a nuptial display by him. In most species the female then scoops up the eggs into her mouth together with sperm from the male. In *Tilapia heudelotii* the male incubates the eggs, while in *Pelmatochromis guentheri* the male and female take it in turns. The eggs are held in the mouth and

Mousebird, of Africa south of the Sahara and Ethiopia, eating flowers of the Kaffir Boom.

Mouth-brooding cichlid fish with its young swarming towards its mouth for shelter.

throat, which may be somewhat expanded so that a brooding fish is noticeable on that account. Care of the eggs and young may last up to five weeks, during which time the parent cannot feed. In some species, however, methods of collecting microscopic organisms (diatoms, algae, etc.) involving a mucous stream or minute rakers on the gill arches may serve to provide a little sustenance.

The cichlid fishes produce fairly small eggs but in the Sea catfishes of the genus *Arius,* which are also mouth-brooders, the eggs are few and very large (up to 20 mm in diameter). They are brooded by the male and feeding is out of the question during the incubation period.

Blind cave fishes of the family Amblyopsidae are also believed to be mouth-brooders, eggs having been found under the gill covers.

MUCUS, the name given to practically any slimy or sticky liquid produced by animals. It generally contains a base of muco-protein or muco-polysaccharides and often other substances as well, various poisons for instance, but in many cases its composition is unknown.

MUD-DAUBER WASPS, solitary tropical insects, notable for the construction of clay or mud nests commonly attached to foliage or plastered on the walls of buildings. In some cases, the nest consists of a single chamber, resembling a miniature swallow's nest, fitted snugly into the angles of walls or the underside of eaves. One mud-dauber in particular, sometimes called the Potter wasp *Eumenes,* makes a beautifully fashioned clay pot attached to vegetation. Other mud-daubers produce tubular nests consisting of a series of cylindrical chambers lying one next to another. The nests are then provisioned with paralyzed spiders and insects, and a single egg deposited in each cell. The aperture to the cell is then closed with another daub of mud. FAMILY: Sphegidae, ORDER: Hymenoptera, CLASS: Insecta, PHYLUM: Arthropoda.

MUD DIVER, or Mud toad *Pelodytes* of which there are probably two species: *P. caucasicus,* the mountain form from Transcaucasia, and *P. punctatus,* from the lowlands of southern and western Europe. There is some doubt whether these are separate species or a single species with two sub-

species. The Mud diver belongs to the family Pelobatidae, which includes the Spade-foot toads. The Mud diver is, however, smaller than the spade-foots and measures around $1\frac{1}{2}$ in (3·8 cm) in length. It lacks the spade and is characterized by its habit of diving into the water at the first sign of danger. The body is rather warty and individuals are especially adept at changing colour. FAMILY: Pelobatidae, ORDER: Anura, CLASS: Amphibia.

MUDMINNOW, a name given to several species of fish of the genera *Umbra* and *Novumbra* found in the fresh waters of North America and parts of Europe. The European mudminnow *Umbra krameri* is a small fish found in moorland pools in western Austria and eastern Hungary. Despite their name they are not related to the minnows but are relatives of the pikes. The Alaska blackfish is the best known member of this group. FAMILY: Umbridae, ORDER: Salmoniformes, CLASS: Pisces.

MUDPUPPY, a name correctly applied to *Necturus maculosus* and by extension to other salamanders of the genus *Necturus.* In the southern United States, however, these salamanders are known as waterdogs and the name mudpuppy is reserved for the adults of the Mole salamanders (Ambystomidae). In the North, the name waterdog is commonly used for the *hellbender *Cryptobranchus alleganiensis*. Some authorities, to compromise with the folk usage, call the southern forms of *Necturus* waterdogs. However, since there is no biological distinction it is just as well to call all of them mudpuppies.

There are four species of mudpuppies with some regional variations that make a total of eight recognizable forms or subspecies. Their only near relative is the degenerate, cave dwelling olm *Proteus anguinus* of Yugoslavia.

Mudpuppies are long-bodied salamanders the largest a little over 19 in (48 cm), but the usual length is less. They have an oblong head with a rounded snout. The four legs are short and each has only four toes. The tail is about $\frac{1}{3}$ the total length and is flattened laterally into either a broad oval or a tapering blunt point, according to species. Eyes are small and without eyelids. The most prominent feature are the external gills, the three branches on each side of the neck dark stubby when the mudpuppy is in well oxygenated water, but developing into large dark red plumes in warm or stagnant water. Mudpuppies retain throughout life the external gills, normally found only in salamander larvae, and reproduce technically in their larval form, a

condition known as *neoteny. In contrast to other salamanders, such as the axolotl, they cannot be induced under any condition or treatment to assume any other form. They do, however, mature partially and when adult develop lungs, in addition to gills, and an adult tooth structure.

The colour varies considerably even within a species. When the group is taken as a whole, it can be anything from yellowish-brown to dark greyish-brown usually with varied arrangement of spots, small blotches or mottlings. There often is a dark bar through the eye.

Mudpuppies are found throughout the eastern half of the United States except the state of Maine, peninsular Florida and the ridge of the Appalachian mountains, and in southeastern Canada. They live in sluggish low gradient streams of the lowlands and in small lakes and ponds, preferring clear water with aquatic vegetation.

Mating takes place in late autumn. The male is reported to court the female actively and deposits a spermatophore. The female remains passive, but picks up the spermatophore. Fertilization is internal and egg laying does not begin until the spring of the following year. The female finds an appropriate site under a rock, or she may excavate a small nest usually with the entrance facing down stream. The eggs are attached singly to the underside of the nest's roof. The eggs are

globular, $\frac{1}{4}$ in (5 mm) in diameter and surrounded by a layer of jelly. The female guards the eggs during incubation which may take a month or two depending on the water temperature (longer in cold water) and may stay with the larvae until they leave the nest. At this point they are less than an inch long. The young begin to feed on small aquatic animals, worms, insect larvae and small crustaceans. Later, crayfish form the bulk of mudpuppy diet but they will take other animal food, even fish eggs, sometimes accidentally ingesting vegetable matter in the process. Growth is slow. They do not reach maturity until the fifth year.

Mudpuppies do not adapt readily to captivity. They often refuse to feed and slowly starve. When in this condition they are also susceptible to a variety of infections. They are nocturnal, spending their days among rockwork of the aquarium into which they blend so well that they are difficult to see. If the oxygen level in the water is low, they will wave their feathery gills and this movement gives them away. An occasional specimen acclimatizes well and may then survive for a few years.

The name mudpuppy supposedly originates from the salamander's reported ability to emit yelping or barking noises, a fact that many authorities dispute, pointing out the lack of voice-producing mechanism. Some experienced amphibian watchers claim, however, that mudpuppies on rare occasion may emit audible sounds. All mudpuppies in my personal experience have remained silent. FAMILY: Proteidae, ORDER: Caudata, CLASS: Amphibia.   E.L.J.

MUDSHRIMPS, also known as Burrowing shrimps, are shrimp-like but are closely related to Squat lobsters and Hermit crabs. They are softer bodied than true shrimps and have a smaller carapace and broader abdomen.

The claws are of equal size and relatively large and hairy. They are not used to seize food but prod and loosen mud during burrowing. The rear legs are fan-shaped and used for circulating water through the burrow rather than for swimming. The tail fan is small. The walking legs are used for moving up and down the burrow and a variety of other purposes. One pair is held up to balance the animal against the walls of the burrow. Another pair is very mobile and used for cleaning the body surface and gills, and the female uses these for cleansing and aerating the eggs when she is 'in berry'. The claws and first pair of walking legs are used to scoop up mud in burrowing. One American species makes horizontal galleries $1\frac{1}{2}$ ft (0·4 m) beneath the surface and about 3 ft (1 m) long. Usually, however, a network of tunnels is made interrupted at intervals by larger excavations where the mudshrimp can turn

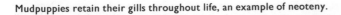

Mudpuppies retain their gills throughout life, an example of neoteny.

round, as for example, when carrying mud to the surface when excavating.

Upogebia deltura and *U. stellata* are comparative rarities of the intertidal and estuarine mud around the coasts of northwest Europe and the British Isles, but are probably more common offshore. Two species, common in sandy mudflats between tides and in estuaries along the west coast of America are known as ghostshrimps. Another, the Blue mudshrimp *Upogebia pugettensis*, ranges from Alaska to California. They live in pairs in a burrow. Their larvae are taken in plankton in spring and summer.

Mudshrimps are *suspension feeders. They draw a stream of water into the burrow and filter the particles in suspension. The first two pairs of legs are held out from the body so that their bristles together form a mesh or filter. The particles caught on the filter are then passed forward by the smaller front limbs to the mouth. The jaws are small since particulate food does not need to be masticated. Larger pieces of food are rejected and may be pushed out of the burrow. More often, however, they are put to good use by other animals who have crawled into the mudshrimps burrow for protection. The feeding current also aerates the burrow and it carries excreta to the outside.

Several small animals live commensally in mudshrimps' burrows. Some are occasional visitors, sheltering while the tide is out. Others are more or less permanently associated with the mudshrimps. A blind goby, for example, lives in the Blue mudshrimp's burrow. One of the Pea crabs is also a commensal of the Blue mudshrimps. The male Pea crab is smaller than the female so that it can easily visit the burrow containing a female to breed. Visored shrimps live with the Blue mudshrimps in pairs. All these animals devour any food which is dropped or rejected by the mudshrimp, so serving as scavengers.

There is a small clam which lies across the abdomen of the Blue mudshrimp and seamats encrust its carapace. Another small clam lives in the mud or sand adjacent to the deeper galleries with their tubular siphons opening into the burrow. This uses the mudshrimp's burrow as an extension to its siphons so that, despite its small size, it can go down as deep as the much larger clams. FAMILY: Upogebidae, ORDER: Decapoda, CLASS: Crustacea, PHYLUM: Arthropoda
W.A.M.C.

MUDSKIPPERS, a family of small goby-like fishes living in brackish waters and mangrove swamps of the Indo-Pacific region. Their common name refers to their habit of leaving the water and skipping across the exposed sand or mudflats at low tide. Their overall shape is similar to that of the gobies, with a steep forehead and tapering body, but the eyes bulge from the top of the head and the pectoral fins have become modified with a fleshy base so that they can support the body. In some species the pelvic fins are also modified in this way, although in others they are joined to form a sucker.

One of the most widespread species is *Periophthalmus koelreuteri* of the Indian Ocean. It spends a great deal of its time, when the tide has receded, perched on the edge of small pools in mangrove swamps with the tip of its tail just in the water. When disturbed it will skip to the next pool, often with jumps of 2 ft (60 cm), rarely missing its target. These leaps are made by curling the body and then straightening it suddenly. It can also leap along the surface of the water. This species grows to about 5 in (12 cm) in length but certain of the Indo-Malayan species grow to about 12 in (30 cm) and are dug up from holes in the mud by local fishermen.

The limb-like pectoral fins are provided with extra strong muscles and can be used for 'walking'. They are thrust forward, the rest of the body being dragged after. The mudskippers are able to absorb oxygen in two ways. The gill cavities can be filled with water before the fish emerges but exchange of gases can also occur in the mouth and throat, which are well supplied with fine blood vessels. Thus, gill-breathing probably takes place for the first part of their stay out of water, but after this the gills and throat must still be kept moist for air-breathing.

Because of their need for a moist atmosphere and their tendency to leap, these fishes are difficult to keep in aquaria, but apparently once these difficulties have been overcome the fishes become quite tame and will often feed from their owners. FAMILY: Gobiidae, ORDER: Perciformes, CLASS: Pisces.

MULE, a hybrid between a horse and an ass, especially the offspring of a male ass and a mare, that from a she-ass and a stallion being a hinny. Mules have the shape and size of a horse and the large head, long ears and small hoofs of an ass. They are favoured for their endurance and sure-footedness as draught or pack animals. They are usually sterile, but the hinny sometimes produces a foal.

The name 'mule' is sometimes used for hybrids between other species, and more especially by bird fanciers for hybrid offspring of canaries mated with other finches.

MULE DEER *Odocoileus hemionus,* a long-eared *deer of western North America.

MULLER, H. J., born 1890, a prominent American worker in the *Morgan school of genetics and participator in the work on linkage, crossover and multifactor analysis in Fruit flies, *Drosophila*. Muller has been Professor Emeritus at Indiana University since 1964. His most important work concerns the cause of mutational change. By exposing Fruit flies to strong doses of X-radiation, to cause the chromosomes to break, he increased the mutation rate 150

Mudskippers *Periophthalmus chrysospilos,* small goby-like fishes of Malaya, living in brackish water, on a muddy beach at low tide.

times. Mutations or 'microscopic accidents' are unusual in nature, which is one of the reasons why they are rare, and why the chromosomes are not equipped to repair or overcome them. Muller's work earned him the Nobel Prize for Physiology and Medicine in 1946.

MULLETS, a common name that is applied to two quite different families of Bony fishes, the Red mullets and the Grey mullets, both dealt with separately.

MUNTJAC *Muntiacus,* a small *deer widely distributed in southern and Southeast Asia.

MURRE, pronounced 'mur' as in 'murmur', the American name for the *guillemots of the genus *Uria,* and formerly used for the same birds in southwest England.

MUSCULATURE, the various types of muscle and the mechanical principles governing their arrangement in the bodies of animals.

The first type of muscle to be considered is that called striated or voluntary muscle. It is called voluntary because we use it for nearly all the movements we can control consciously: it works our limbs and jaws and is responsible for speech and facial expression. It consists of thin cells known as muscle fibres which are often several centimetres long and have striations running across them. The striations are 0·002 mm apart and can be seen with an ordinary microscope. Electron microscopes show that most of the fibre is filled with tiny filaments arranged parallel to the length of the fibre, in a regular pattern which explains the striations. There are thin filaments of the protein actin and thick ones of the protein myosin. The thin ones are threaded through partitions (Z-discs) which run across the fibre. When a relaxed muscle is stretched the filaments are not stretched but simply slide past each other. When it is stimulated to contract, projections on the sides of the thick filaments attach to the thin ones and then work their way along them, shortening the muscle. Striated muscles cannot exert much force when they are greatly extended or greatly contracted. If they are stretched too much few of the projections can attach to the thin filaments and the force is small. If they shorten too much the thick filaments press against the Z-discs and the force is again small. Most striated muscle fibres are arranged in the body so that the maximum length to which they are ever extended is not more than $1\frac{1}{2}$ times the minimum length. Some, such as the swimming muscles of fish, work over very small ranges of length.

There are two types of striated muscle fibre known as red and white fibres. They are easily distinguished in the flesh of fish such as the herring *Clupea harengus.* The band of dark

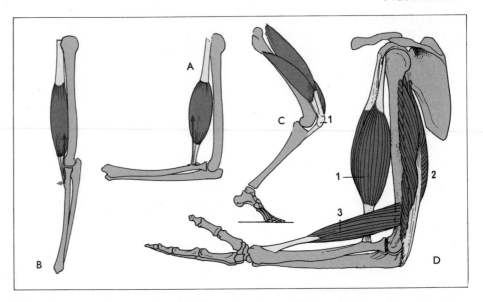

By muscle action a distinction is made between 'joint activity' (pressure in the joint) and 'rotation activity'. In A the first is low, the second strong; in B both actions are reversed. C Where the greatest strength is needed for a stretching movement, the rotation activity may be enforced by a sesamoid bone (1. D Muscles are only able to pull. The action of a muscle as a rule needs a second muscle to counteract it (antagonism) as in 1. and 2. When two muscles work together (1 and 3) it is called synergism.

flesh which runs along the side of the fish just under the skin consists of red fibres and the main bulk of the flesh consists of white fibres. The white flesh on the breast of a chicken consists mainly of white fibres but the dark flesh of the legs consists largely of red ones. Similarly, different muscles in mammals have different proportions of the two types of fibre. Red fibres use fat as fuel and can only work when they are supplied by the blood with sufficient oxygen. White fibres get their energy by converting carbohydrate to lactic acid and can work without oxygen for a while, but oxygen is needed eventually to get rid of the accumulated lactic acid. Lungs (or gills) can only take up oxygen at a limited rate. White fibres enable an animal to have brief spells of violent activity which would require an impossible rate of oxygen consumption if the oxygen had to be supplied at the time, and then recover over a relatively long period while the lactic acid is eliminated. Red fibres are apparently best for sustained activity and white ones for occasional violent activity. It has been shown by implanting electrodes in the muscles of fish that the red fibres alone are used for sustained swimming and the white ones for bursts of higher speed which cannot be sustained. Mackerel *Scomber scombrus,* which cruise about all the time, have far more red muscle than fish like the plaice *Pleuronectes platessa,* which spend most of their time resting on the bottom. Similarly domestic fowl spend most of their time running about, using the dark muscles of their legs, and only use the white breast muscles to flap their wings for occasional short flights. (The breast muscles are the main wing-flapping muscles and the dark muscles in the wing itself are only used for folding and

unfolding the wing and minor adjustments of its position.) Pigeons *Columba livia* can fly long distances and their breast muscles consist mainly of red fibres. Hummingbirds spend a lot of time hovering and their breast muscles are entirely red.

Insects have striated muscles with thick and thin filaments arranged as in vertebrates. The ones which flap their wings are peculiar. Each contraction of an ordinary striated muscle fibre is started by an electrical impulse arriving along a nerve (some arthropod muscles need several impulses) but insect wing muscles can be kept in a state of rapid oscillation by occasional nerve impulses (see flies). The wing muscle fibres of a blowfly which is beating its wings 120 times a second may only be receiving three nerve impulses per second.

The second main type of muscle is smooth, unstriated or involuntary muscle. There is smooth muscle in the walls of the gut which squeezes the food that is being digested slowly along towards the anus. Smooth muscle in the womb makes the contractions involved in human birth. Smooth muscle in the walls of small arteries is used to restrict the flow of blood to parts of the body where little is needed at the time, so that more may go to the organs which need it most. Smooth muscle has no striations. It contains actin and myosin, and thin filaments of actin can be seen with the electron microscope. There are thick filaments consisting of myosin and another protein in the smooth muscles of invertebrates but thick filaments cannot be found in vertebrate smooth muscles. The mechanism of contraction of invertebrate smooth muscle is presumed to be the same as for striated muscle, but the apparent absence of thick filaments makes one wonder whether the mechanism is different in vertebrate smooth muscle. Smooth muscles have no Z-discs and the filaments are not arranged in neat bands, which is why there are no striations.

Smooth muscles generally contract much more slowly than striated ones but they can contract much further. The smooth muscle fibres in the wall of the human bladder, which contract to expel the urine, are twice as long when the bladder is full as when it is empty. A common Sea anemone *Metridium senile* can distend itself with water until it is a large, very thin walled, cylinder but contracts when poked to a tiny knob of flesh with hardly any internal cavity. Its muscles are smooth, and some of them are four times as long when it is distended as when it is contracted.

The thick filaments of invertebrate smooth muscle are much longer than in striated muscle, so each has more projections to attach to thin filaments. This enables some smooth muscles to exert very large forces. For instance mussels *Mytilus edulis* attach themselves to stones by a bunch of elastic threads, the byssus. A group of muscles attaches the byssus to the inside of the shell. One of these muscles has been tested and found able to exert 5 times as much force as a frog muscle of the same dimensions, but it contracts at only $\frac{1}{32}$ of the speed of the frog muscle.

Smooth muscle uses less energy in resisting a steady force than striated muscle. One type known as catch muscle is particularly economical, using only about $\frac{1}{200}$ of the energy a striated muscle of the same size would need to do the same job. There is some evidence that catch muscle is locked at the required length by direct attachments between the thick filaments, so that though the thin filaments are involved in the process of shortening they play no part in maintaining tension. Bivalve molluscs have catch muscles to hold their shells shut. The two valves of the shell are joined by elastic material so that they can be closed by muscles but spring open when the muscles relax. So long as the shell is closed the muscles must be kept tense and a lot of energy would be wasted if they were not catch muscles. The muscle to the byssus of mussels, which has already been mentioned, is also a catch muscle.

Striated muscle is paralyzed if its nerves are cut but smooth muscle in a piece of the gut of a vertebrate can go on contracting rhythmically even after the piece is removed from the body. In the intact animal the nerves control the intensity of contraction but do not carry specific instructions for each individual contraction. The heart also goes on beating after its nerves have been cut. Heart muscle has striations but differs in so many ways from ordinary striated muscle that it is regarded as a separate type.

There is another type of muscle which has striations running round its fibres like a screw thread, instead of straight across. It contracts faster than smooth muscle but generally more slowly than striated muscle. The shell-closing muscle of oysters (Ostreidae) consists partly of this type of muscle, to close the shell quickly when danger threatens, and partly of catch muscle to hold it shut without wasting energy.

Two muscles with opposite effects are called antagonists. They may be made antagonistic either by a hydrostatic skeleton or by a jointed skeleton.

A 'hydrostatic skeleton' is not a skeleton at all, for the term is used of fluid-filled cavities which make muscles antagonistic to each other by transmitting pressures. An example is the series of cavities in the body of an earthworm. An *earthworm has an outer body wall and a central gut, but there is a fluid-filled space between the two which is partitioned so that each of the 80 or more segments has its own cavity. The body wall contains muscle fibres running circularly round the body and others running longitudinally along it. When the circular muscles in a segment contract the segment gets thinner, but since the fluid in its cavity cannot escape it also gets longer and the longitudinal muscle fibres are stretched. Similarly contraction of the longitudinal fibres makes the segment fatter as well as shorter. The circular and longitudinal muscles are thus antagonistic. The same principle applies to the movements of other soft-bodied animals including the flatworms, which have deformable tissue instead of fluid-filled cavities surrounded by their muscles.

Jointed skeletons are best developed in vertebrates and arthropods. They are made of bone or other rigid material and the principle making muscles antagonistic is very simple:

muscles acting on one side of a joint tend to bend it while those on the other side tend to extend it. The actual arrangement of muscles is often surprisingly complicated, and many muscles affect more than one joint.

The knee joint is a simple hinge joint so the only movements it can make are bending and extension. The hamstring muscles are attached at one end to the back of the thigh and the pelvis, and at the other end to the tibia by means of the tendons (hamstrings), which can be felt at the back of the knee. When they contract they bend the knee, but they also tend to swing the leg backwards at the hip. The quadriceps femoris is a group of muscles attached by a tendon to the kneecap, which is attached in turn by a ligament to the tibia. It straightens the knee and one of its constituent muscles, which is attached to the pelvis, helps to swing the leg forward from the hip. The use which is made of the two groups of muscles has been investigated by implanting electrodes in them. When a standing man sways forwards or holds a weight in front of his body the hamstring muscles contract, helping to prevent his body from toppling forward at the hips. If he sways back the quadriceps muscles contract and prevent his knees from bending. The two groups of muscles contract together as the foot strikes the ground in walking; this is at first sight rather puzzling but could doubtless be explained by a thorough mechanical analysis of the complicated process of walking.

There are two more muscles which affect the knee. The sartorius has the same effect on the knee joint as the hamstring muscles, but the opposite effect on the hip. The gastrocnemius runs from the femur to the heel, to which it is attached by Achilles' tendon, and so affects both knee and ankle. The sartorius has its fibres running lengthwise, with a short tendon at its attachment to the tibia, and each

Left: Diagram showing arrangement of actin and myocin in muscle (1), relaxed (2), beginning to contract (3) and fully contracted (4). Right: The knee, a simple hinge joint (1), with muscles fully extended and contracted (2). (3) and (4) show the mode of attachment of muscles to the tibia (3) and the femur (4).

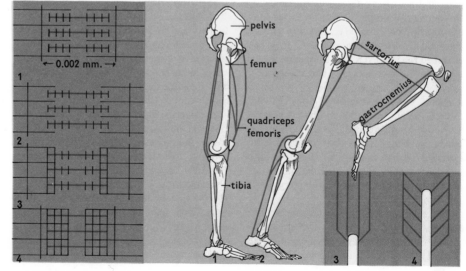

fibre is about 1½ times as long in the extended position as in the contracted one. The gastrocnemius has a pinnate structure with short muscle fibres running obliquely between two long outer tendons, attached to the sides of the femur and the central Achilles' tendon. The muscle as a whole is only about 1¼ times as long when extended as when contracted but the short fibres must change their length by a bigger fraction than this.

A muscle fibre can contract rapidly against a small force or more slowly against a large one, but it works most efficiently and delivers most power when contracting at moderate speeds against moderate loads. This is why variable gears are helpful on a bicycle. The pinnate gastrocnemius can exert larger forces than a parallel-fibred (sartorius-like) muscle of the same dimensions, because it has more fibres, but is cannot shorten so quickly or so far because the fibres are shorter. The pinnate arrangement ensures that the individual fibres contract at moderate speeds against moderate forces in walking and running. The same effect could have been obtained with a parallel-fibred muscle acting further from the joints, so that it had a longer lever arm and a bigger mechanical advantage, but this would have meant a very long heel and a gap between the muscle and the tibia. The pinnate arrangement is thus more compact. Pinnate muscles predominate in the slender legs of insects, where compactness is important. They have the additional advantage of being able to contract without swelling.

The same muscles in different animals often work at different mechanical advantages to suit different ways of life. Seals for instance use their hindlimbs for strong but necessarily slow swimming movements rather than the faster weaker movements of running mammals. These limbs are short and their muscles act well away from the joints, giving the required mechanical advantage.
R.McN.A.

MUSHROOM CORAL, a coral with an interesting life-history, the Mushroom coral *Fungia* is a large solitary animal. It is a true or Stony coral found on reefs and has a discoid skeletal cup or theca resembling a mushroom. Some species grow up to 3 ft (1 m) across the disc. The skeleton is calcareous and bears marked ridges or sclerosepta. The oral disc of the living polyp bears numerous short, retractile tentacles arranged in rings and the colour of the polyp varies from brown to yellow, green or even red-violet or pink. Symbiotic algae or zooxanthellae are present in the cells of the polyp. As in other members of the *Cnidaria, sexual reproduction leads to the production of planula larvae. These swim by means of cilia and settle on a suitable substrate, growing into a stalked coral with a broad oral disc. When the coral has developed into an adult the disc breaks free and the

Musk-oxen forming up into a phalanx for defence at sight of the photographer.

soft body of the coral grows across the place of detachment so that the calcareous skeleton now appears internal. On examination of the skeleton this site of detachment can be seen as a scar. The attached stump may then regenerate and grow another oral disc. Asexual reproduction may also occur with new polyps being budded off directly from the adult disc. Although the free, sedentary polyps do not have any obvious means of locomotion, they can alter their positions and are capable of living in water containing some silt. Movement, including removal of sand and debris falling on the oral disc, is brought about by the action of cilia on the surface of the polyp. ORDER: Scleractinia, CLASS: Anthozoa, PHYLUM: Cnidaria.
S.E.H.

MUSK DEER, three species of small *deer of central southern Asia, completely lacking antlers and hunted for their musk glands.

MUSK-OX *Ovibos moschatus,* heavily-built member of the family Bovidae from the Arctic of North America; not a true ox, but more closely related to sheep and goats. It is 44–60 in (110–150 cm) high, weighing at least half a ton (50 kg). The long guard hairs are blackish and the soft light brown underfur is dense, and is shed in patches in the summer. The stocky legs are white. There is a hump on the shoulder. For all their clumsy appearance, musk-oxen are agile. They are highly aggressive and during the rut the bulls even chase birds!

For most of the year, musk-oxen form herds of four or five or up to 100 or more; adult bulls are often solitary, young bulls herd together. The cow is sexually mature at four years, the bull at five or six. The rutting season may start as early as mid-July, but does not reach its peak until September. The

bulls give off a strong odour at this season, butt each other, bellow and try to mate with the cows. Finally a few dominant bulls emerge; each of these stands with his forefeet on a rock or mound, preparing to defend his cows; often a bull only manages to cover one cow, but sometimes large numbers. The smaller bulls, usually not yet full-sized, quickly learn to avoid the dominant ones. Calves are born in April or May, a single calf to each cow; it weighs on average 15½ lb (7 kg), and stands 18 in (46 cm) high. The mother protects her calf fiercely. Suckling continues for nine months; hence a female will calve only every other year. The calf moves along with the herd from its first day. Calves are heavily predated by wolves, and the herd's defence mechanism is to form a circle of adults around the calves, facing outwards showing a well-nigh impenetrable array of horns. Musk-oxen live for twenty years.

Musk-oxen have always been heavily hunted for their fur. Nowadays the fur is farmed and musk-oxen have been introduced into Norway and Spitzbergen. In 1930, after the Thelon Game Sanctuary in Northwest Territories (Canada) was set up, there were 9–10,000 in Canada, mostly on the arctic islands, and perhaps the same number in Greenland. Today there are at least twice that number, and most musk-ox populations are increasing rapidly. FAMILY: Bovidae, ORDER: Artiodactyla, CLASS: Mammalia.
C.P.G.

MUSK RAT *Ondatra zibethica,* or musquash, the largest of the voles, found throughout North America wherever the habitat is suitable. There is a second species *O. obscura* which is restricted to Newfoundland. Its total length is up to 25 in (63 cm) including a scaly rudder-like tail up to 10 in (25 cm) long. It weighs about 2 lb (0·9 kg). Its coat ranges in colour from silvery brown to almost black and is composed of a thick waterproof underfur overlaid with long glistening guard-hairs. Its feet are broad and flat, the hindfeet being webbed.

The Musk rat is aquatic, living in fresh-water or salt marshes, or by streams and rivers. In summer it lives among the water plants and in the winter it builds a house of stems and other vegetation which projects above the water-line. Sometimes it tunnels into the river banks and builds its nest there. It feeds mainly on water plants but will also take fish, frogs and freshwater mussels. It mates in the water and has 3–5 litters a year with an average of 5–7 young in each. The gestation is 19–42 days.

The Musk rat is valued for its fur and also because it helps to keep waterways clear of water plants. It has been introduced into Europe where it is kept on ranches. Many, however, have escaped and gone wild and caused damage to river banks. FAMILY: Cricetidae, ORDER: Rodentia, CLASS: Mammalia.

MUSQUASH *Ondatra zibethica*, alternative name for the *Musk rat.

MUSSELS, bivalve molluscs mainly living in the sea but with a few freshwater species. The best-known of the marine mussels is the Edible mussel *Mytilus edulis* which often occurs in dense communities near the mouths of estuaries or elsewhere on the shore where there is a suitable surface for attachment. The tissues are completely enclosed by the black-blue shell which may reach 3 in (7.7 cm) in length, and which is attached by means of a series of threads, the byssus threads, to the substratum. Each of the shell valves is the mirror-image of the other and can be closed very tightly by means of an anterior and a posterior adductor muscle which join the two valves transversely. As in other bivalves, the shell is made up of several distinct layers comprising an outer periostracum underneath which is a white prismatic layer and finally a mother-of-pearl layer. The periostracum gives the shell its characteristic colour. The shells of mussels which have grown rapidly are either smooth black or variegated ('pitch pine' mussels) whilst those living under crowded conditions have shells from which the outer periostracum has been worn away. This gives them a bluish colour and often they are encrusted with barnacles. In dead or dying mussels the shell gapes because the adductor muscles are no longer able to overcome the elasticity of the ligament which joins the valves at the hinge region.

As in many other bivalves, food is strained from a current of water drawn in by the activity of cilia on the gills filling much of the mantle cavity. The two gills are one on each side of the foot and each consists of two series of filaments loosely united by ciliary junctions. The two series of filaments alternate on each side of a central gill axis and each filament is very long and folded upwards at the tip so that the whole gill is W-shaped in cross section. The cilia responsible for creating the feeding current are located between adjacent filaments and cause a current to flow in through the inhalant part of the mantle cavity and out through an exhalant part. The particles in the water are meanwhile strained off by a sheet of mucus which covers the frontal surface of the gills. Such entrapped material is then transported by frontal cilia in sheets down to the tips of the gill filaments and to the free edge of the gill where it may be either rejected or transported towards the mouth. The rejected material is expelled from the mantle and accumulates in silt-like deposits between adjacent mussels. The mucous sheet is ideal for entrapping very fine particles but it is unselective. Other feeding mechanisms have been described in which particles are transported individually towards the mouth where they are transferred from the gill across ridged lips or labial palps. Here dense large particles fall into grooves and are rejected whilst finer particles are transported across the grooves and into the mouth. The presence of a mucous sheet has been observed by sealing a glass window into the shell of a mussel and it has been found that the mucus is secreted in response to the type of particles entering with the inhalant stream. Thus, when mussels were fed with suspended minute graphite particles, few of the particles were retained, but when supplied with living organisms (flagellates) of the same size as the graphite particles, the retentive capacity was increased by the secretion of a mucous sheet and most of the flagellates were retained.

The presence of suitable supplies of suspended food is of great importance in the commercial fishing of mussels. Specimens living on the shore are often stunted due to overcrowding and irregular food supplies. Such mussels may be removed and placed in brackish water where there is abundant planktonic food due to the drainage of nutrients from the land, and under these conditions spectacular increases in growth have been recorded. This method is the basis of the 'mussel bed' system of commercial culture. On some European coasts brush-wood supports are placed on the substratum and the mussels cling to these by the byssus threads and are then easily removed for market. This method is widely used in France where it is known as the 'fascine' or 'bouchot' system of culture.

Spawning in the Edible mussel occurs between March and early June with a series of peaks in breeding coinciding with new and full moons. The germ cells are shed freely into the sea and are sometimes so numerous that the water appears milky. The fertilized egg gives rise to a planktonic ciliated larva called a veliger (see larval forms), the cilia being principally borne upon a swimming lobe called a velum which gradually diminishes in size as the foot of the larva grows. Eventually after several weeks the larva can both swim by means of the velum and crawl by means of

Diagrammatic transverse section through the Edible mussel. Small arrows show the direction of movement of food particles. (Bottom left) Glochidium larva of a freshwater mussel. Edible mussels occur in dense communities near the mouths of estuaries.

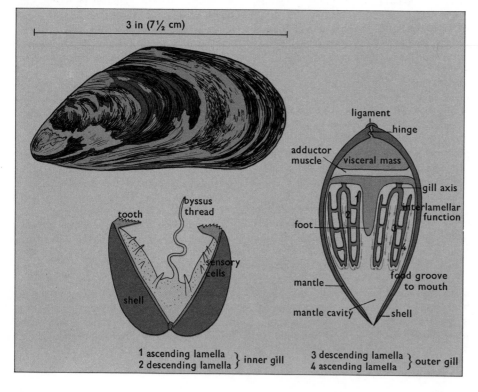

3 in (7½ cm)

tooth
byssus thread
sensory cells
shell

ligament
hinge
adductor muscle
visceral mass
gill axis
interlamellar function
foot
food groove to mouth
mantle
mantle cavity
shell

1 ascending lamella } inner gill
2 descending lamella

3 descending lamella } outer gill
4 ascending lamella

Edible mussels exposed at low tide. On rocky (or muddy) coasts they may total millions to the mile.

the foot and is called a pediveliger; at this stage site-selection and settlement occurs. However, such mussels do not attach permanently; instead they detach themselves after an initial period of growth and are transported by inshore currents and resettle in areas rich in niches such as are provided by banks of adult mussels. Although this behaviour ensures that the juveniles settle in an area suitable for adult life, dense settlement sometimes smothers the parents and often restricts the growth of the young mussels. Lowered salinities also reduce both the growth rate and the final size attained. Mussels are often heavily parasitized by the small red copepod *Mytilicola* which lives in the rectum of the mussel; the commensal Pea crab *Pinnotheres pisum* is commonly found in the mantle cavity.

Apart from the Edible mussel, other marine mussels belonging to the family Mytilidae include the North American Edible

mussel *Mytilus californianus*, the Mediterranean mussel *M. galloprovincialis*, the Horse mussels *Modiolus* and the Crenella mussels *Musculus*. There is also a newly described species called *Fungiacava eilatensis* which lives buried in the tissues of the coral *Fungia* and in certain closely-related genera. Of the 250 specimens which have been collected, most come from the region of the Gulf of Eilat, particularly from the northern tip of this isolated arm of the Red Sea. A few other specimens have, however, been found elsewhere where the coral *Fungia* or its close relatives occur. The Mediterranean mussel is, as its name suggests, confined to southwestern regions of Europe. It is also the dominant mussel on the north Devonshire coast of England and is rather similar in form to the Edible mussel. It does not, however, occur in estuaries and the edge of the mantle tissues are dark-coloured compared with the whitish-yellow mantle margin in the Edible

mussel. The Common horse mussel *Modiolus modiolus* is the largest of the two marine mussels and often reaches 4 in (10·2 cm) in length. It is sometimes found on the shore but is more common below low water mark. All Horse mussels tend to have horny processes on the shell, at least when young. In the Common horse mussel these processes are absent in the adult which may then be distinguished from the Edible mussel and Mediterranean mussel partly by its large size and partly by the fact that the edges of the mantle are not frilly; the shell, too, is of a rather different shape. The other Horse mussels are much smaller and retain the horny processes on the shell throughout life. The Bearded horse mussel *M. barbatus* never reaches more than 2 in (5·1 cm) in length and the horny processes are serrated on one side. These features distinguish it from the Bean horse mussel *M. phaseolinus* which is always less than $\frac{3}{4}$ in (2 cm) long and has no

Mediterranean mussels *Mytilus galloprovincialis* with limpets and acorn barnacles.

serrations along the horny processes on the shell. Finally there is *M. demissus* which is a North American Horse mussel which lives high on the shore. It is able to breathe air and survive for considerable periods of time out of water, especially under humid conditions such as occur on salt marshes.

The Crenella mussels are small green bivalves which are often difficult to find on the shore although they are widely distributed. The Marbled crenella *Musculus* (or *Modiolaria*) *marmoratus* has a smooth rounded green shell of about $\frac{3}{4}$ in (2 cm) length and is often found in deeper water embedded in the tests of Sea squirts (ascidians) or in the holdfasts of the Oarweed *Laminaria*. The Green crenella *Musculus* (or *Modiolaria*) *discors* has a bright green shell of about $\frac{1}{2}$ in (1·3 cm) in length. It is quite common on the shore amongst coralline algae. Finally, there is one other marine mussel which belongs to a different family from all the mussels cited above. The Fan mussel *Pinna fragilis* is a very large bivalve with a thin fan-shaped shell reaching as much as 1 ft (30·5 cm) in length and 6 in (15·2 cm) at its wide end. It is normally found below the low water mark in gravels but may occasionally be found on the shore.

The gill chamber of freshwater mussels is more complex than that of the marine mussels. Adjacent gill filaments, as well as the ascending and descending limbs of each gill filament, are united by tissue junctions which makes the whole gill a more solid structure than in the marine mussels. They feed, like the marine mussels, by straining suspended particles with the gill and transporting them to the mouth by ciliary tracts. Special lips or

labial palps also occur which transfer food to the mouth and also reject unsuitable material. The food passes into a crop which in common with other bivalves, including marine mussels, has a peculiar structure called a 'crystalline style'. This is housed in a diverticulum called the style sac and is a gelatinous rod which slowly rotates. Its end projects into the crop and continually dissolves liberating digestive enzymes in the process. Digested material is absorbed by the cells of a large digestive gland associated with the crop. All these features are common to both marine and freshwater mussels. However, freshwater mussels differ markedly in their breeding biology from marine mussels. Whereas the latter liberate planktonic larvae directly in the sea, these freshwater mussels practise a special form of brood-care. The sexes are separate and in the summer the eggs are fertilized in the exhalant chamber of the female. Then they become embedded in the outer lamella of each gill pair and develop there into tiny bivalved larvae called glochidia. Each valve is triangular and hinged along its base with the apex drawn out into a strong hook. There is a long sticky thread (the byssus) instead of a foot. The young glochidia are set free in the spring and further development requires a fish as a host. When a small fish passes over a glochidium, the young bivalve flaps its valves and drives out its byssus thread. This sticks to the fish and the glochidium then uses its hooks to hold onto its skin. The tissues of the fish then swell around the glochidium and a cyst is formed in which the parasite lives for some months absorbing nourishment from the fish. During this time the glochidium develops into a

young mussel and eventually escapes to lead an independent life. This life-cyle is especially interesting for it enables the mussel to be dispersed without the risk of the tiny larvae being carried downstream to the sea.

Common freshwater mussels include the Pearl mussel *Margaritifera margaritifera* which was used in the British pearl fisheries of Roman times. It is an inhabitant of soft waters in North America, Europe and North Asia and the glochidium larvae are parasitic on the gills of minnows, trout and the Miller's thumb *Cottus gobio*. Closely related to the Pearl mussels are the River mussels including the Painter's mussel *Unio pictorum* and the Swollen river mussel *U. tumidus*, both of which live in hard waters in western and central Europe. The second species also occurs in western Asia but neither occurs in the Mediterranean region. Other species of River mussels include the Swan mussel *Anodonta cygnaea*, the Duck mussel *A. anatina* and the Compressed river mussel *A. complanata*. All of these are large mussels of at least $3\frac{1}{2}$ in (9 cm) length.

Another group of freshwater mussels includes the Orb mussels and Pea mussels. The Orb mussels all belong to the genus *Sphaerium* and are relatively small globular bivalves. The Nut orb mussel *S. rivicola* is a western and central European canal-dwelling species with a shell length of about $\frac{3}{4}$ in (2 cm). The Horny orb mussel *S. corneum* is very common in clean moving waters in rivers and canals; the Lake orb mussel *S. lacustre*, on the other hand, can tolerate more stagnant conditions. Another species, the Oblong orb mussel *S. transversum* occurs in North America and Britain but has not yet spread into Europe. The Pea mussels are represented by at least 16 different species in Europe. All are less than $\frac{1}{2}$ in (1·3 cm) in length and are characterized by a broad and obvious hinge plate. All the species occurring in Britain are widespread either in North America, Europe and North Asia (holarctic distribution) or in Europe and North Asia (palearctic distribution). Their small size has probably played an important part in aiding their widespread occurrence because, for example, they can be easily transported on the feet of birds.

The Zebra mussel *Dreissena polymorpha* is a most interesting little mussel of 1–$1\frac{1}{2}$ in (2·5–3·8 cm) length and looking remarkably like the marine Edible mussel. The resemblance goes further than mere shell shape for the Zebra mussel has a planktonic veliger larva and the adult is attached to stones by byssus threads; unlike other mussels, however, there is a large long inhalant siphon and a shorter exhalant one. The shell surface is yellowish-brown with zig-zag bands. This mussel was known as a recent fossil in Britain, but until approximately 150 years ago its distribution area was restricted to S.

Russia. However in about 1824 it was discovered in the Surrey Commercial Docks, London, having probably been transported by shipping across from the Baltic, and by 1840 had spread through most of the canals of Britain. It now occurs throughout much of western and central Europe. FAMILIES: Mytilidae, Pinnidae, Unionidae, Dreissenidae, ORDERS: Filibranchia (marine), Eulamellibranchia (freshwater), CLASS: Bivalvia, PHYLUM: Mollusca.   R.C.N.

MUSSEL GOLD. At one time the byssus threads or 'beard' of the Fan mussel were woven into cloth which had a golden sheen. Articles made from this cloth, such as gloves, can now be seen in museums, but in bygone centuries this material, known as Cloth of Gold, was extensively used by the aristocracy, especially in southern Europe. The impressive but useless meeting outside Calais of the Kings of England and France in 1520 was known as the Field of Cloth of Gold from the amount of this material displayed there.

MUTATION, a change in the composition of a gene leading to a change in structure. See genetics and evolution.

MUTTON BIRD, the name given by seamen and others to various species of oceanic birds of the petrel family whose flesh is eaten, particularly the Sooty shearwater, *Puffinus grisea* of New Zealand, the Short-tailed shearwater *P. tenuirostris* of Australia and the Atlantic petrel *Pterodroma incerta* of Tristan da Cunha. Adults and young of these

Four-horned sheep, an example of a mutation, which has led to a change in structure.

species have long been collected at the breeding grounds for human consumption but it is now largely the young that are taken. The flesh of these birds is highly palatable, and they also yield a high-quality oil which may be used medicinally, as a lubricant or in oil lamps. FAMILY: Procellariidae, ORDER: Procellariiformes, CLASS: Aves.

MYNAH, the Indian word for birds of the family Sturnidae, of which the Common starling is perhaps the best-known member. This common name is shared by seven birds in the same family; five in the genus *Acri-*

dotheres two in the genus *Gracula* and one in the genus *Mino*. They are found in India, the Orient, Malaysia, and Indonesia. The Common mynah *Acridotheres tristis* and the Hill mynah *Gracula religiosa* are the best known of these birds.

The Common mynah was originally found only in Afghanistan, India, Pakistan, Nepal and Indochina but, like the House sparrow and starling, it has been successfully introduced into innumerable countries: Malaya, Natal, Australia, Hawaii, Seychelles, New Zealand and many other islands. It is a little larger than a starling, with a black head and neck, brown body and white underparts. The bill, legs and a patch of bare skin on the face are yellow and conspicuous white patches on the wings and tip of the tail show in flight.

Mynahs are well known wherever they are found because they live in association with man and make plenty of noise. They are as common a sight on the roadsides of pastoral New Zealand as they are in the dry hills of India. The food consists of fruit as well as insects, which makes them unpopular with fruit growers, though they are certainly blamed for a good deal of the damage done by less conspicuous birds.

In autumn and winter mynahs return at night to communal roosts, much in the manner of starlings, but apart from this they are very territorial birds. Both members of a pair can be found on the territory for most of the year. The song and calls consist of a variety of rather loud raucous, chattering and whistling notes, some parts of which are quite melodious. The nest is an untidy cup placed in a niche in a tree or building, and

Indian Hill mynah, famous 'talking' bird.

from four to seven pale blue eggs are laid. Incubation takes about a fortnight and the young spend as long again in the nest before fledging.

The Hill mynah or 'grackle' (not to be confused with the New World grackles, family Icteridae) is best known as a cage-bird and is perhaps the best mimic of them all. It is similar to the Common mynah, but has prominent yellow wattles pointing backwards from behind the eye. Its natural habitat is the forests of India, Ceylon, Pakistan, Burma, the Malay peninsula and Indonesia, where it feeds in noisy flocks in the canopy of trees. The food is said to be insects, fruit and berries, with nectar in season. Though they make excellent mimics in captivity they do not seem to imitate other sounds in the wild, but have a fantastically varied and noisy vocabulary of their own. The usual bulky mynah nest is placed in a hole in a tree and the clutch is two or three greenish-blue eggs with brown spots. See starling. FAMILY: Sturnidae, ORDER: Passeriformes, CLASS: Aves.   D.G.D.

MYOLOGY, the study of muscles. Recent work has concentrated mainly on various aspects of muscle physiology. Amongst the vertebrates, with the exception of man and some other mammals, comparative anatomical studies of muscles have proceeded less far than studies of any other system in spite of the fact that muscles account for up to one-third of the bulk of most vertebrates. In invertebrates the muscle system is generally simpler and muscles usually form a smaller proportion of the total weight but they are still relatively neglected.

Vertebrate muscle is divided into three main categories:

1 Smooth muscle, also called unstriated and involuntary muscle. This is found mainly in the gut wall and urinogenital organs. Each muscle fibre is a slender, spindle-shaped cell with a single central nucleus and no cross-banding; it contains a number of very fine, longitudinal fibrils. Contraction is initiated by nervous stimulation, by hormone action or by the contraction of neighbouring fibres.

2 Cardiac muscle. A peculiar type of muscle found only in the heart. The whole heart is made up of a continuous network of fibres which divide and rejoin. Each cell has a single central nucleus and shows cross-banding similar to that seen in striated muscle fibres; it forms a short section of the muscle network and is attached to adjacent cells by transverse discs called the intercalated discs.

3 Striated muscle, also called voluntary muscle. This forms the skeletal muscles. The fibres are complicated, large structures up to an inch (2·5 cm) or more in length; each is multinucleate, that is, it corresponds to several cells, has a thin outer membrane and shows a regular sequence of transverse bands or striations. As in the other types of muscle each fibre contains a number of longitudinally arranged fibrils. Striated muscle contracts by nervous stimulation which is often under conscious control.   Jo.G.

MYRIAPODA, an obsolete name for a class of many-legged terrestrial arthropods now divided into four separate classes. There are two large classes: the centipedes with nearly 3,000 species and the millipedes with 8,000 species, and two small classes: the Symphyla with just over 100 species and the Pauropoda with nearly 400. Centipedes and millipedes are encountered by most people, many of the species are quite large and conspicuous animals but the Symphyla are small and usually overlooked and the Pauropoda are all minute, the largest being under 2 mm long.

The important features common to myriapods are the single pair of antennae, the trunk composed of similar legbearing segments, the long tubular gut and the terrestrial habitat. Except for the Pauropoda which have no special structures for breathing, the myriapods have tracheae although the systems in centipedes and millipedes are not strictly comparable. However, the myriapods appear to have had a common ancestor, which probably also gave rise to the insects.

The two large classes of myriapods stand in striking contrast to each other and yet are often confused. Centipedes are swift-moving predators armed with weapons of offence, the poison fangs beneath the head. Millipedes, for the most part, are slow-moving animals feeding on dead vegetation and occasionally on the living parts of plants. They possess stink glands and the ability to curl-up on being disturbed. Millipedes are usually distinguished from centipedes in having two pairs of legs on each segment. The gardener's rule 'if it runs, let it; if it stays kill it' is a good rough and ready method of dealing out justice to the centipedes which might prey on garden pests and the millipedes which might eat his young seedlings.

Myriapods are among the commonest animals on the surface of the earth. A square metre of fertile soil in temperate regions will contain, on the average, several hundred millipedes and centipedes, and up to 1,000 symphyles. The Pauropoda are not sufficiently well-known to quote average figures but mean numbers of 450 and 629 per sq m have been recorded from woodland and grassland respectively. PHYLUM: Arthropoda.   J.G.B.

MYZOSTOMUM, external or internal parasites of *echinoderms, especially of brittlestars. The commonest species is found on the Feather star, *Antedon*. Although they are annelid worms, with a larva essentially polychaete-like, the affinities of the Myzostomaria with these worms would not be expected from their appearance.

The adults are flattened disk-shaped creatures with a number of short tentacles radiating from the rim. Those found on *Antedon* are usually on its disk, for the *Myzostomum* lives by robbing its host of part of its food before this reaches the mouth. Most of them are only a few millimeters across. Some *Myzostomum* species can move about quite actively but others hardly move at all and these can cause gall-like malformations on their hosts. The host tissues grow over or around where the *Myzostomum* takes up its position. The *Myzostomum* protrudes its reversible proboscis into the food grooves of the host or even into its mouth while it is feeding.

Apart from the short tentacles round the rim of the disk-like body there are a few reduced parapodia on the underside. The mouth opens at the rim of the disk but the anus is slightly inside the rim. These openings mark the anterior-posterior axis of the body. The parapodia on the underside are more or less papilla-like and betray the basically segmented pattern of the body which is clearly specialized. The parapodia are provided with grasping hook-like chaetae. Also on the underside is a series of sucker-like organs.

Like many parasities, *Myzostomum* is hermaphrodite, that is, both male and female. The male cells (sperm) mature first and then the female, so that self-fertilization is avoided.

That the Myzostomaria, though very specialized, have been derived from polychaetous annelid stock, is shown by the early development, the fertilized eggs developing into ciliated larvae with a bunch of long chaetae which are trailed on each side of the body when the larva swims. CLASS: Myzostomaria, PHYLUM: Annelida.   R.P.D

The term 'Myriapoda' is often applied to the four classes shown here. It used to represent a class but this has now been divided into four classes, but the term is still used loosely to signify a grouping of these four kinds of related arthropods.

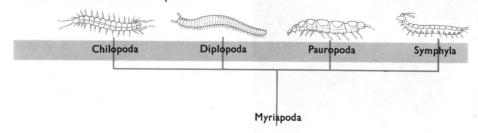

Chilopoda   Diplopoda   Pauropoda   Symphyla

Myriapoda

NAMING OF ANIMALS. The biblical legend of Adam giving names to all the animals (Genesis ii.19): 'whatever the man called every living creature, that was its name', was an attractive allegory devised to explain a fact of great importance, namely that there were so many different kinds of animals and that it was imperative for man to know them apart. Actually, it must have been some hundreds of thousands of years ago that Paleolithic man, dependent for his livelihood on hunting game, identified and named the various beasts against which he carried out collective hunts. With Neolithic man the necessity became even greater, for with the domestication of animals and their variation the number of forms to be identified and named became even greater. Primitive peoples today have astonishing powers of discernment of slight differences between varieties of common animals, each of which is given its own distinctive name.

From the point of view of modern science, the naming of animals may be said to have started in the 17th century, when the notion of kinds of animals, or species, became more precise. John Ray defined species as groups of organisms that resembled one another more closely than they resembled individuals of other groups, and bred among themselves, so that 'one species does not grow from the seed of another species'. The problem in plants was the same as that in animals. Animal nomenclature was put on a scientific basis by Linnaeus in the 18th century, who established a principle of practical importance which has been vital for the progress of biology. Names of animals in the 16th and 17th centuries had been diagnostic. Diagnosis means identification, which involves description, so as to distinguish the object of study, species, disease or function, from any other. In the case of species of animals, the diagnostic descriptions were written in Latin, and required many words to express, without any possible ambiguity, what the characters of the species in question were, so that the naturalist or physician could identify it and tell it apart from other species. But such a long description was very inconvenient when it was necessary to refer to a species by name, and Linnaeus established (he did not invent it) the principle of giving animals designatory names as labels for convenient use, the diagnostic features being obtainable in books of reference. Furthermore, as some species are found to resemble one another more than they resemble other species, such resembling species are grouped together under a genus and every Linnean specific name consists of two words, first the genus, beginning with a capital letter, second the species, beginning with a lower case letter: thus, *Homo sapiens*. This practice is in vogue today; generic and specific names are always printed in italic letters, and followed by the name, or identifiable initials, of the scientist who first described the species in question, in a published work.

International rules. The mention of the words 'first described' introduces the principle of priority. Until the middle of the 19th century, scientific journals were few in number and communications between different scientists were slow. This meant that two different names were often given to the same species and, conversely, that the same name was given to two different species, in good faith but in ignorance. It became increasingly apparent that, for the sake not only of science but of human affairs in general, there must be rules of nomenclature so that the identity of a species could be recognized by its name all over the world, not only because of the possibly useful characteristics of such a species, but also because of its possibly noxious qualities. The latter were first recognized in animals such as rats, but soon became identified as causes of disease, such as bacteria and viruses, and carriers of disease, such as mites, lice, mosquitoes or tsetse flies.

With the progress of biology and the enormous increase in number of species recognized, the situation became critical, because the names used for animals in advanced countries were in a state of chaos. The result was an attempt to draw up rules for zoological nomenclature under a code which it was hoped zoologists and taxonomists all over the world would accept and practise. The first such code was drawn up by Hugh Edwin Strickland in 1842, under the aegis of the British Association for the Advancement of Science. This was followed by other codes, but the problem reached the international level only after the Fifth International Congress of Zoology, held in Berlin in 1901, adopted the International Rules of Zoological Nomenclature and an International Commission was set up, under the Congress (convened at intervals of three years until the Second World War, then of five years), to interpret the Rules or the 'Code' as it is called.

The Code now in force is that adopted by the 15th International Congress of Zoology held in London in 1958 and published in 1961 in French and English. It contains 87 articles and five appendices including a code of ethics, latinization of words and general recommendations. The 'principle of priority' is defined in such a way that the valid name of a species is the oldest name applied to it… 'provided that the name is not invalidated by any provision of this Code'. The search for 'the oldest name' is an exercise carried on in libraries, and one often abused, as when a well-known name is found to have been preceded by another, which is already in common use for a different species. This situation has been remedied by two measures taken by the Code. The first stated arbitrarily that the starting point of zoological nomenclature was the 10th edition of Linnaeus's *Systema Naturae,* published in 1758 on a day determined as 1 January of that year. The date of publication of a name is of such great importance that at the present time, a printed journal containing the description and name of a new species is obliged to carry the publication date. The second measure adopted by the Code has been a decree that certain names, so well-known and anchored in zoological literature that to change them would cause more confusion than to retain them, should be kept as *nomina conservanda,* after decision by the International Commission.

The binominal system. The importance of

Linnaeus's work may be seen from the fact that when he published his *Systema Naturae,* it contained nearly 4,400 species, collected in 312 genera. The system of binominal nomenclature was adopted just in time to deal with the enormous increase in number of specific names resulting from the discoveries made by expeditions to all parts of the world, which would have led to inextricable chaos, as may be seen by the fact that today the number of species of animals already described and accepted approaches $1\frac{1}{4}$ million and increases at the rate of about 1,000 every year. The number of genera approaches $\frac{1}{4}$ million.

There is a further point of importance relating to the naming of animals. The Code decrees that for every species and every genus there must be a 'type', the specimen originally described and preserved in a museum or other institution where it is accessible to zoologists for study. Article 61 of the Code says: 'The "type" affords the standard of reference that determines the application of a scientific name' of a category of animals. This practice is responsible for what is known as 'typological thinking' in the concept and definition of a species: it is one specimen, kept somewhere for reference. This criterion of a species is obviously the only one possible when the specimens are few, very rare and obtainable only as a result of distant expeditions and also in the case of most fossils. But such a static method is at variance with what is now known of species since they are dynamic populations undergoing variation. To abstract one specimen and call it the species is arbitrary and an act of abstraction, whereas the reality is the totality of the living species and the measures of its variation around a mean (or more than one) in accordance with the concept of 'population thinking'. This adds to the definition of a species a biological conception based on the species as an inter-breeding unit of individuals which do not normally breed with individuals of other species. The species is then a 'gene-pool', so that a mutant gene occurring in any individual anywhere within the range of the species can, in principle, be transmitted by breeding to any other individual anywhere else in the species' range. The science of nomenclature is called 'systematics' and the concept of the species as a varying population is at the base of what is now called 'The New Systematics'. It has already allowed very valuable and important principles to be established, but, of course, the old systematics must continue for those groups to which the population concept cannot (yet) be applied.

Structure of classification. The naming of animals does not only involve nomenclature, as just described, but also taxonomy (or systematics, from Linnaeus's *Systema Naturae*) which is concerned with classification, arrangement of individuals within a species and of species within larger groups. Each category or group of organisms is called a *taxon* and it is found that they occur in an orderly system. Some species resemble each other more than any of them resembles other species and they are grouped together in a genus. Similarly, some genera, resembling each other more than other genera, fall naturally into a taxon of higher rank, the family (e.g. Hominidae, roman type, capital letter and ending -idae). Similarly, families are contained in orders (e.g. Primates), these in turn in classes (e. g. Mammalia) and these in phyla (e.g. Chordata), all phyla together constituting the animal kingdom.

It was pointed out by Darwin that this orderly hierarchical structure of classification, which is based on observation of nature, differs fundamentally from a random arrangement such as that of grains of sand on a beach and from an arbitrary arrangement such as that of stars in the heavens, grouped into constellations, which are figments of the imagination used to describe the stars in the relative positions which they occupy. The classification and the hierarchy of taxa are either an inexplicable accident of nature or they receive a consistent and rational explanation as a reflection of the path taken by the evolution of the various lineages. The most important taxon is the species, because it alone is a 'real' definable and objective unit. Every living organism exists in one species or another and every new gene-pool, produced as a result of heritable variation and natural selection, is a species. The time comes when, as a result of heritable variation acted upon by natural selection, change sets in and part of the population of a species becomes unwilling or unable to breed with the remaining parts of the population of that species. The result is the origin of new species and an old species from which a number of new species have branched off becomes a genus. The repetition of the same process turns an old genus into a family and this in turn into an order which may become a class or even a phylum if sufficient evolution takes place in its contained taxa to warrant its promotion in the taxonomic hierarchy to high rank. The important point to appreciate is that all higher taxonomic categories began as species. Whether any given species ultimately becomes a high-ranking taxon depends on many factors; some internal, such as the existence of sufficient heritable variability in the genetic endowment of the lineage; others external, such as the existence of great numbers of ecological niches into which they could fit (see evolution).

The result of these considerations is that the classification of animals takes the form of a tree, a genealogical tree, also called a phylogenetic tree, the branches and twigs of which represent the divergences achieved in evolution, while the points of branching show the community of descent from a common ancestor. There are still many points on the tree where further research is needed to clarify its shape and the way in which some branches are attached to each other, or to the original central stem, are imperfectly known. But there is already enough to show that the tree does reflect the progress of evolution and the hierarchy of rank of taxa receives its natural explanation. This is what

is meant by the endeavours of systematists to establish a natural classification.

The classification of animals. From what has been said above, it will be clear that the enormous number of taxa already recognized makes it utterly impossible to give a complete description of the classification of animals in anything less than several volumes. Here a brief survey will be given of the main groups and, to serve as a simple guide, a rough and schematic sketch of the shape of the animal kingdom will be described. It takes the form of a Y-shaped tree with a straight stem and two main branches. The stem is composed of the one-celled Protozoa and the lowest multicellular forms, Cnidaria. One of the two branches, with twigs for worms, snails, shrimps and spiders, leads to the Insecta, the most highly developed invertebrate forms. The other branch with twigs to lampshells, and starfishes, leads to chordates, and hence to vertebrates and man.

Protozoa is a phylum of unicellular animals which feed by ingesting food materials through the cell membrane. The whole organism, being a single cell, can be its own germ-cell and therefore protozoans are potentially immortal. They include the Mastigophora which move by means of a whip-like flagellum, many of which are parasites, like *Trypanosoma* in man. The Rhizopoda include *Amoeba* with a flowing ('amoeboid') movement of the protoplasm and some forms with a calcareous shell (Foraminifera). The Sporozoa are all parasitic, like *Plasmodium,* the malaria parasite. The Ciliata which includes *Paramecium,* the slipper-animalcule, the most highly developed Protozoa, are covered with hair-like cilia by the rhythmic beating of which they move rapidly.

Sponges. Parazoa or sponges are a lowly phylum which can be described as colonies of cells, very loosely organized and scarcely integrated together to form an organism. Some of the cells have flagella which create a current of water passing through the tubes and chambers of the sponge where food-particles brought in with the water are ingested by cells, as in Protozoa. Some sponges, Calcarea, have calcareous spicules; others, Hexactinellida, have siliceous spicules and others again, some of the Demospongiae, have soft horny skeletons, like *Spongia* the bath-sponge.

Cnidaria. The lowest true multicellular organisms (Metazoa) are generally held to be the Coelenterata (or Cnidaria). They take the form of hollow sacks consisting of an external protective layer of cells (the ectoderm) containing stinging organs or nematocysts, which can be shot out, and an internal digestive layer of cells (the endoderm) lining a gastro-vascular cavity which opens to the surrounding water through a mouth. The Hydrozoa contain the hydroid polyps such as *Hydra;* the Scyphozoa are jellyfishes like *Aurelia;* the Anthozoa contain the Sea anemones and the true corals with their hard, reef-forming calcareous skeletons.

At this point of the tree the stem may be said to divide into two main branches. In the first, or Protostomia, a number of features can be recognized. The mouth is formed from the blastopore or original opening of the hollow two-layered larva at the gastrula stage. This larva, in the more primitive classes, is formed from the fertilized egg by a special type of cell division called spiral cleavage. The larva has a ring of cilia in front of the mouth and the body of the animal has three layers of cells, the mesoderm coming between the ectoderm and endoderm. In all except the lowest forms, the mesoderm layer splits, giving rise to the body cavity or coelom (schizocoel) from the walls of which the germ cells are formed. By repetition of these pouches containing germ cells along the long axis of the body, this becomes divided into a number of more or less similar segments, the process known as metameric segmentation. Finally, in all except the lower forms (which have no skeleton), the skeleton is external, secreted by the ectoderm, as a substance known as chitin.

East African savannah with wildebeeste and zebra.

Platyhelminthes. The Platyhelminthes are the lowest phylum of Protostomia. Their body has the three layers of cells, but the mesoderm is not yet split to form a body cavity. They include the Turbellaria or flatworms; the Trematoda, all parasitic like the Liver fluke *Fasciola* and the Cestoda, also all parasitic like *Taenia* the tapeworm. At some not clearly defined spot on the stem of the animal evolutionary tree, not far from the Platyhelminthes, is a mixture of lowly forms to which the name Aschelminthes has been given. The most important class in this phylum is the Nematoda or roundworms, many of which are parasitic in plants, for example Wheat gall, *Anguina* and in animals, for example the Gape worm *Syngamus* in poultry, the Trichina worm *Trichinella* in pork and the Filarial *Wuchereria* worm in man.

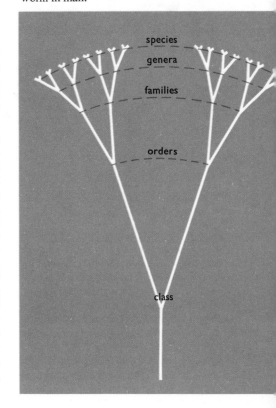

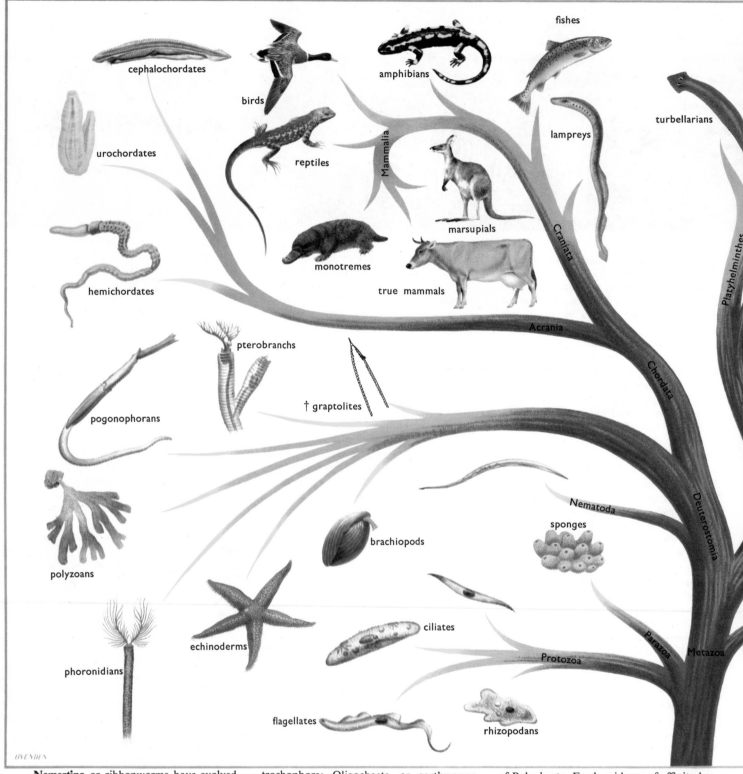

Nemertina or ribbonworms have evolved a body-cavity, but not metameric segmentation, in spite of the great length to which they grow, as exemplified by the Bootlace worm *Lineus*. Their larval form is the pilidium. Metameric segmentation can first be plainly seen in Annelida, the 'true' worms. They include Polychaeta or marine worms, each segment of the body of which has a rudimentary paddle or parapodium extending sideways, with a larval form known as a trochophore; Oligochaeta or earthworms like *Lumbricus;* and Hirudinea, leeches, many of which have evolved, like *Hirudo,* the specialized method of feeding by sucking animal blood.

Mollusca have long been known to be related to Annelida because the molluscan larva, the veliger, is so like the trochophore and many Mollusca develop from the fertilized egg by a process of spiral cleavage which is almost indistinguishable from that of Polychaeta. Fresh evidence of affinity has now come from the discovery of *Neopilina,* an obscure, limpet-like mollusc, which has metameric segmentation, for its body shows five pairs of tufted gills and six pairs of excretory organs. Other Mollusca, which show no metameric segmentation, must therefore have lost it. The classes of Mollusca are the Polyplacophota and Monoplacophora; the Gastropoda, characterized by a spirally-wound shell (sometimes lost),

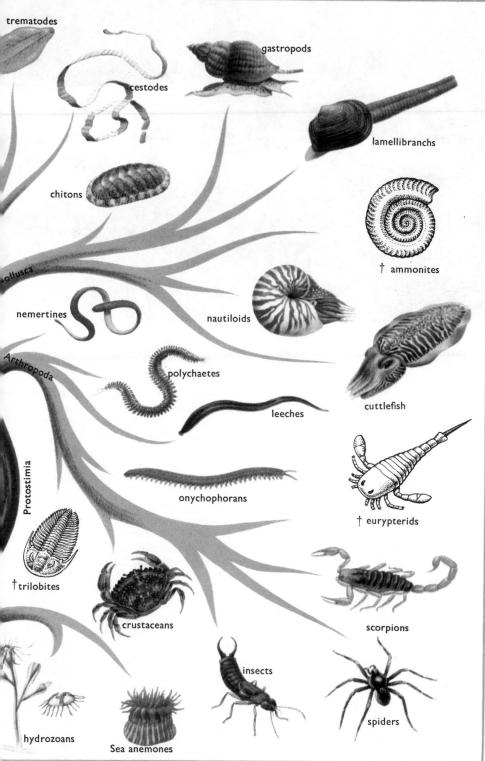

the legs could not move at all.

The most primitive class of living Arthropoda is the Onychophora, with *Peripatus*, a small segmented animal, exhibiting extreme discontinuous geographical distribution (South Africa, Australasia and South America) which is characteristic of old forms which have become extinct everywhere else. But the most characteristic forms of the Cambrian period (beginning 600 million years ago) are the Trilobita (all extinct by the end of the Carboniferous period) in which many zoologists have seen the ancestors of the Crustacea. The simplest groups of Crustacea are characterized by the nauplius larva, which could be derived by specialization from Trilobita. Crustacea include the Water flea *Daphnia*, the barnacle *Lepas*, and the lobster *Homarus*. Nearly all Crustacea are marine or freshwater animals, but the Wood louse *Asellus* is terrestrial.

The next three classes of Arthropoda are related and sometimes grouped together as Chelicerata. The Eurypteroidea, which flourished from the Ordovician to the Carboniferous period, are all extinct. They were large predatory animals holding the record size for Arthropoda—over 6 ft (2 m)—and exerting important selection-pressure by the danger which they represented to other animals. Next come the Merostomata, with the Horseshoe crab *Limulus*, a living fossil which has scarcely changed since the Jurassic period. The third class in this group is the Arachnida, with scorpions, spiders, and the mites and ticks.

The class 'Myriapoda' includes the millipedes and the centipedes. All are land animals and some, such as the millipede *Glomeris*, are of particular interest because they have a larval form with a head followed by a number of trunk segments, only the first three of which have pairs of walking legs, the fourth and following segments having only tiny rudiments of pairs of legs. It is from such a larval form that the class Insecta was probably evolved, by the mode of evolution termed *pedomorphosis.

The class Insecta contains over 850,000 already recognized species and probably about 3 million in all. It provides a good example of adaptive radiation, for after the colonization of land, these animals were able to fill the innumerable microecological niches which presented themselves. Their evolution coincided in time (Jurassic) with that of the flowering plants, and each group became adapted to the other in various ways, the plants providing food (pollen, nectar) and habitats, while the insects performed cross pollination. The flowers evolved coloured petals which attracted insects and where the co-adaptation was marked, the flowers assumed a bilaterally symmetrical shape, with labia' on which, as in orchids, the insects

with the whelk *Buccinum* and the Land snail *Helix;* the Bivalvia the body of which is protected by lateral (right and left) hard shells lined with mother-of-pearl, as in the oyster *Ostrea* the scallop *Pecten;* and the Cephalopoda in which the anterior region of the body is developed into eight or ten long sucker-bearing tentacles, as in *Octopus* and the cuttlefish *Sepia*. All Cephalopoda are marine, and their great size, power and highly developed nervous system and sense organs

make them the dominant group of marine invertebrates.

Annelida and Arthropoda. From the Annelida or their immediate ancestors it is easy to see that Arthropoda were evolved. Their name means 'jointed legs', a consequence of the fact that their legs, of which there is, primitively, one pair to each of the metameric segments of the body, are enclosed within a layer of chitin so hard (as in a lobster's claw) that were it not for the joints,

Naming of animals

landed to gather pollen or nectar and, in so doing, effected cross pollination.

The orders of Insecta are too numerous to mention, but these animals are well known, for their beauty as in butterflies, for their noxious characters as in lice, fleas, bugs and mosquitoes, vectors of parasites dangerous to man. All are characterized by possession of three pairs of legs, carried by the segments of the 'thorax', but the most primitive order, the Collembola or springtails, contains forms like *Campodea* in which the segments behind the thorax have vestiges of paired legs, reminiscent of the larvae of the millipede *Glomeris*. All Insecta other than the Collembola and related orders have two pairs of wings, one each on the second and third segment of the thorax. In the flies, Diptera, the hind pair of wings is modified into gyroscopic balancers, or halteres. In four separate groups of Insecta, termites, wasps, bees, and ants, there have evolved supra-organismal so-called social instincts, involving differences of structure and of behaviour in different individuals of the population which have become converted into a community, the preservation of which takes biological preference over that of the individuals. In all respects, the diversity and the complexity shown by Insecta and their enormous number of species, makes them the most highly evolved invertebrate animals.

The great divide. Returning now to the point on the stem of the tree of animal evolution where one branch became the Prostomia, the other branch gave rise to a number of related phyla which are together called the Deuterostomia, for the following reasons: in the larva the mouth aperture is a new opening, not formed from the blastopore of the gastrula and the ring of cilia is formed round the mouth, not solely in front of it; the division of the fertilized egg to form the larva is never by spiral cleavage; the body cavity or coelom is formed not by splitting in the layer of mesoderm, but as an outpushing from the gastral cavity or gut giving rise to a so-called enterocoel. Metameric segmentation, which does not occur in the lowest members of the Deuterostomia, is quite different from that found in Prostomia, for it concerns the muscle-plates at the sides of the body, primarily in the tail, which is the portion of the body extending back behind the anal aperture. Rythmical sinuous movements of the tail by waves of contraction of the segmental muscle plates passing backwards along it are the means of locomotion in water. The skeleton is formed of jointed plates, composed of carbonates or phosphates of calcium and is formed beneath the epidermis, which always covers it, as, for example, in the bones of the human skull. A curious feature of the Deuterostomia is that the primitive groups all have sessile or stalked adult forms, relying for nourishment

on particles of food in the water wafted towards their mouths by the action of cilia on the tentacles or other structures which surround them: the ciliary method of feeding.

Brachiopoda or lampshells have valves which recall those of bivalve molluscs, but differ from them in being beneath the ectoderm. Also, instead of being lateral, right and left, they are dorsal and ventral. Brachiopoda hold the record for the most persistent type, *Lingula* having scarcely evolved at all since the Ordovician period, 500 million years ago.

Echinoderms and chordates. Echinodermata, in the adult forms, have a pentamerous radial symmetry. Primitively they were stalked, as the Sea lilies, Crinoidea still are. The bodies have become detached from the stalks and in Sea cucumbers, Holothuroidea, Sea urchins, Echinoidea, starfishes, Asteroidea, and brittlestars, Ophiuroidea, lead a sluggish free existence. In the classes of Echinodermata there are very characteristic bilaterally symmetrical free-swimming larval forms, such as the auricularia which is important because it is from some comparable larval form that the phylum Chordata has in all probability evolved, by pedomorphosis.

Chordata are characterized in their more primitive groups by all the characters enumerated for the Deuterostomia, to which in many of the lower, and all the higher groups, there are added four more: gill-slits pierced through the side of the throat, through which water, which has been wafted into the mouth in the course of the ciliary method of feeding, goes out again; a dorsal hollow neural tube forming the central nervous system; a skeletal rod, the notochord, running along the back beneath the neural

tube, replaced in higher forms by the vertebral column; in higher forms metameric segmentation of the muscle-plates enabling sinuous movements of tail and body to be made when the animal moves in water an extension of the body behind the anus, as described above, which is not found in other groups.

In addition to the evolutionary connexion between Echinodermata and Chordata indicated by the similarity in plan of structure between the free-swimming bilaterally symmetrical echinoderm larva, such as the auricularia, and the higher Chordata, there are two additional facts. A group of Cambrian fossils, hitherto called the Carpoidea and included within the Echinodermata, have now been found to possess gill-slits, a stiffening rod or notochord, flanked by muscle plates and a tubular nerve cord in the stem and are, therefore, undoubtedly Chordata, now classified in the subphylum Calcichordata, of which an example is *Cothurnocystis*. These animals had a brain, not unlike that of the fishes giving off 'cranial' nerves, at the front end of the body, which moved by means of lateral flexures of the jointed stem. The skeleton is made up of closely fitting plates of calcite, each of which is a single crystal. The Calcichordata can be regarded as ancestral to all other subphyla of Chordata. Of these, the most primitive are the subphylum Hemichordata, containing the Acorn worms *Balanoglossus,* the larval form of which, the tornaria, is astonishingly similar to the auricularia larva of echinoderms. Also included in the Hemichordata are some degenerate forms such as *Cephalodiscus* and *Rhabdopleura,* the stalks of which may branch and so give rise to organically connected colonies of animals.

The subphylum Urochordata includes the

A herd of impala at a waterhole.

class Ascidiacea or Sea squirts, many of which live in colonies. It is now recognized that the Graptolithoidea or Graptolites, characteristic fossils of the Ordovician period, were ascidian-like chordates that lived in colonies. The classes Thaliacea, or salps, and Larvacea (which live permanently in the form of larvae) also belong to Urochordata which take their name from the fact that it is in the tail of the larva of Ascidiacea, the 'ascidian tadpole' and in the tail of the Larvacea that the notochord is found (as in the stem of Calcichordata).

The subphylum Cephalochordata, containing the lancelet *Amphioxus,* is also known as the Acrania, for these animals are clearly on the way to becoming vertebrates, but still have no skull. The notochord, flanked by metamerically segmented muscle plates, extends the whole length of the body, ventrally to the neural tube, of which the anterior end shows the rudiments of specialization into a brain.

Vertebrates. The subphylum Vertebrata is also known as the Craniata, for all its animals have a skull protecting the brain. Its lowest group is the class Agnatha (also called Cyclostomes because they have circular mouths without jaws). Here belongs the lamprey *Petromyzon,* the larva of which, called the ammocoete, still has the ciliary method of feeding, by means of an organ consisting of cilia creating a current of water into the mouth and a gland secreting mucus which, like a fly-paper, catches the particles of food in the in-wafted water. This organ, the endostyle, is converted into the thyroid gland in all vertebrates above the Cyclostomata, sometimes called Gnathostomata because their mouths are armed with jaws enabling them to catch and ingest large food

(macrophagy, taking the place of the ciliary method of feeding or microphagy).

The clear distinction is now made between the bony or true fishes and the cartilaginous fishes which include the dogfish, sharks and rays, these last, known as the Chondrichthyes or Selachii have a skeleton not of bone but of cartilage or gristle. The true fishes, known as Pisces or Osteichthyes have a bony skeleton.

The bony fishes include the Crossopterygii or fringe-finned fossils of the Devonian period from which were derived the Coelacanthini of which *Latimeria* survives today. The Dipnoi or lungfishes, so-called because the hinder pair of their gill slits has been converted into lungs into which swallowed bubbles of air pass thus enabling the fish to survive periods of desiccation, were also derived from them, as were the Amphibia and higher vertebrates.

Fishes. The fishes have two pairs of limbs in the form of fins, the web of which is supported by numerous skeletal struts or radials. In all Vertebrata above the fishes, the two pairs of limbs end in five digits, (i.e. the radials have become reduced to five and the web of the fin between them has been sliced down) forming feet, for which reason these vertebrates, colonizers of land, are called Tetrapoda. The colonization of land was an event of great importance for the Vertebrata, but it was accomplished quite simply, without any functional discontinuity, as will be shown after introduction of the class Amphibia, consisting of the Caudata or newts and the Anura or frogs. The fish breathes by taking water into its mouth, closing it, and raising the floor of the mouth, which forces the water down the throat and out of the gill slits. The frog breathes by

taking air into its mouth, closing it and raising its floor which forces the air down its throat into the lungs. The fish moves by passing waves of contractions of its muscle-plates alternately down each side of the body, which propel it forwards in the water. The newt moves by passing similar waves down the sides of its body, from which the limbs project at right angles, like oars, by means of which the animal 'rows' itself along the ground. The pentadactyl limb (five-toed foot) is an adaptation to life on land.

Amphibia. Although Amphibia colonized the land and radiated widely in Carboniferous times, they have never completely become adapted to life on land, for three reasons. First, the eggs and sperm must be laid in water, for the latter to swim to, and fuse with, the former; second, the fertilized egg must develop in water, for it would dry up and collapse on land; third, much of the respiration of an amphibian takes place through the skin, which must for that purpose be moist. Each of these problems has been solved by the next class, the Reptilia, which evolved from Amphibia in Carboniferous times. The necessity for water in reproduction was dispensed with by the development of copulatory organs, by means of which the sperms are inserted into the mucus-moist genital tract of the female, giving internal fertilization. The necessity of water for development of the embryo was avoided by the development of embryonic membranes (yolk sac, amnion, chorion and allantois), the amnion in particular containing amniotic fluid in which the developing embryo is bathed. With these adaptations, and a food-supply in the yolk-sac, the egg can be laid on land, protected by a shell until the embryo is hatched. This is the so-called cleidoic egg, which, however, requires one further adaptation to the conditions. The embryo lives, metabolizes and produces waste products. Of these, the nitrogenous are likely to be toxic, especially if, as in fishes and amphibians, they take the form of urea which is soluble. The problem here is that the blood-circulation of the embryo would intoxicate its own tissues if it transported the soluble urea. The problem was overcome by halting the breakdown of nitrogenous waste products at the stage of uric acid, which is insoluble, depositing it in the allantois (formed from the urinary bladder) and leaving it behind when the embryo hatches from its shell. Because of these embryonic adaptations, Reptilia, Aves and Mammalia are called amniotes, in contra-distinction to the Amphibia, or anamniotes.

There remains the further problem of respiration and this the Reptilia solved by bringing the ribs and intercostal muscles into use for expanding the lungs, which are then able to suck in air much more efficiently than in the Amphibia. To this may be added that instead of the belly being rowed along the surface of the earth by the limbs as in primitive Amphibia, in the Reptilia the legs lift the body right off the ground, with consequent speed in locomotion.

Reptiles. The evolutionary importance of the adaptations which enabled Reptilia to make the breakthrough onto dry land and to occupy the vacant and hitherto unoccupied ecological niches there, may be seen from the adaptive radiation which they underwent, from the Permian to the Cretaceous periods. On land there were Dinosauria large and small, Theropsida leading to Mammalia, Pseudosuchia leading to Aves. In the air were the Pterosauria and in the sea, as a result of secondary return to life in that medium, the Ichthyosauria, Plesiosauria, Thalattosuchia existed. At the end of the Cretaceous period, for reasons not yet explained, the majority of lineages of Reptilia became extinct. Today's survivals are represented by four orders; Testudines, the turtles and tortoises; Rhynchocephalia with only a single species, *Sphenodon punctatum*, living on an island off New Zealand; Squamata, the lizards and snakes; and Crocodylia, the crocodiles and alligators.

Birds. Aves or birds evolved from pseudosuchian reptiles and in the Jurassic form *Archaeopteryx they produced an animal which was perfectly intermediate between reptiles and birds and a good example of *mosaic evolution. It could climb up trees with the claws on its wings and glide down with the help of the air resistance provided by its feathers which, on the wings, were identical in form and in arrangement with those of modern flying birds; but *Archaeopteryx* was incapable of active flight. Feathers, which are characteristic of all

birds, were probably evolved first as a body covering, formed from frayed scales, which protected the animal from loss of heat, a feature of great importance as the birds had evolved a constant hot temperature, under which conditions their physiological functions were all more efficient.

The flying birds, sometimes called Carinates, give, in the large numbers of their orders, another example of adaptive radiation in the medium in which they are supreme. There are also some flightless birds, sometimes called ratites, such as the ostrich *Struthio* and some huge extinct forms like *Moa* and *Aepyornis,* but the structure of the cerebellum of their brains, their wing skeleton and tail skeleton, show that they were evolved from flying birds and have lost the power of flight.

Mammals. Mammalia are the highest class of vertebrate. They are characterized by a number of features: mammary glands secreting milk to feed the young; hair on the skin acting as a heat insulator and preserving a hot constant body temperature; a brain with a superficial cortex of grey matter; seven neck vertebrae; teeth differentiated into incisors, canines and molars, replacing once; non-nucleated red blood corpuscles; a single left aortic arch and a four-chambered heart; a muscular diaphragm; and a chain of three auditory ossicles between the tympanic membrane and the fenestra ovalis of the ear. The line between the theropsid Reptilia and the Mammalia, to which they gave rise, is drawn arbitrarily from the condition of the hinge of the lower jaw. In Reptilia the quadrate of the skull articulates with the articular bone of the lower jaw; in Mammalia the squamosal bone of the face articulates with the dentary bone of the lower jaw. On this showing, the Ictidosauria are the most mammal-like reptiles and it is certain that many of the features which have been listed above as characteristic of mammals were already present in the reptiles which were evolving in their direction, including viviparity (birth of live young). Only in the subclass Prototheria among Mammalia, in the Monotremata with the duckbill or platypus *Ornithorhynchus* does development take place in an egg laid in a shell. In the subclass Theria development of the embryo or foetus takes place inside the genital duct, or uterus, of the mother, by means of the embryonic membranes enumerated above, of which the yolk-sac, allantois and chorion produce an organ of physiological interchange between mother and embryo for supply of food and oxygen and removal of excretory products (now urea, not uric acid). This organ is the placenta and after the birth of the infant the placenta is voided as the after-birth. In the infraclass Metatheria, in the Marsupialia the intra-uterine development has become greatly shortened and the young is born in a con-

dition so immature that it becomes organically attached to the mammary glands of the mother inside the marsupial pouch, where it completes its development. In the infraclass Eutheria, true placental Mammalia, intra-uterine development is sufficient for young to be born, mostly in a condition to feed itself. But this is not true of Primates. The adaptive radiation of the placental mammals is a result of the greater efficiency with which they occupy ecological niches, after turning less well-adapted forms out of them.

Of the numerous orders of Eutheria, 12 contain well-known forms with which the reader will be familiar. It will therefore be sufficient here to name them and give examples of the animals they contain. Insectivora (which also eat other things besides insects) contains the hedgehog *Erinaceus,* the shrew *Sorex* and the mole *Talpa,* which are representatives of this primitive order. Chiroptera, with membranous wings spread over the fingers, are the bats, like *Pipistrellus* which have found a small niche for themselves in the air but do not really compete with birds. Edentata (not all toothless) contains the sloths, such as *Bradypus,* of which extinct forms like *Megatherium* reached large sizes and armadillos such as *Dasypus,* of which, again, extinct forms like *Glyptodon* were large. Lagomorpha contains the hare *Lepus* and the rabbit. Rodentia (with gnawing front teeth) include the squirrel *Sciurus,* the mouse *Mus,* and the Guinea pig *Cavia.* Cetacea are Mammalia which have returned to life in the sea, with the dolphin *Delphinus* and the Blue whale *Balaenoptera,* the largest mammal. Carnivora, flesh-eaters, includes the dog *Canis,* the bear *Ursus* and the cat *Felis.* Related to them are Pinnipedia with the seal *Phoca.* Proboscidea constitutes the elephants, the largest land mammals. Perissodactyla or the odd-toed hoofed mammals contains the horse *Equus,* the tapir *Tapirus* and *Rhinoceros.* Artiodactyla or the even-toed hoofed mammals includes the pig *Sus,* the camel *Camelus,* the giraffe *Giraffa,* the ox *Bos* and the sheep *Ovis.*

Primates, the 'first animals', contains man and his relatives: the tarsier *Tarsius, Lemur,* the marmoset *Callithrix,* the (African) monkey *Cercopithecus* and the great apes (gibbon, orang-utan, chimpanzee and gorilla). The Pleistocene form *Australopithecus,* or man-like ape, gave rise to *Homo erectus* (sometimes called Pithecanthropus), the ape-like man, and he to *H. sapiens,* modern man.

In these pages we have reviewed the animal kingdom, beginning with the simplest forms and ending with the most highly organized animals, with man highest of all. It was Linnaeus in his *Systema Naturae* of 1758 who used the name *Homo sapiens* or wise man. In view of the way man has treated his environment the name is ironic.   G. de B.

NARWHAL *Monodon monoceros,* a Toothed whale, probably the prototype of the fabulous unicorn. Even its name is strange, being of Scandinavian origin and meaning corpse-whale. The teeth are completely absent in both sexes except for the single specialized left-sided tusk in the male. Sometimes the tusk may be on the right-side and rarely there are two tusks, one on each side of the head, but the spiral always turns the same way regardless of which side of the head it is on. The body may be some 15 ft (5 m) and the tusk half as long. The function of the tusk is quite unknown. The narwhal is an arctic species that feeds on a wide variety of food which it catches effectively in spite of its toothless mouth. All the Toothed whales have asymmetrical skulls and that of the narwhal shows this feature to a considerable extent. This is not only on account of its tusk but is particularly associated with asymmetry in its nasal passages, probably related to needs of sonar sound production.

We are unlikely to see narwhals because they live in the north polar seas, high up in the Arctic in the waters around the North Pole, although single narwhals have sometimes come as far south as about latitude 58°N. This is, however, a very rare event. It is not that narwhals are themselves scarce. They usually go about in what are called pods, of anything from 5 to 50. Sometimes as many as two or three thousand will be seen all together in one pod and some people claim to have seen as many as 10,000. Although narwhals in the flesh are unfamiliar most of us have a fair idea of what they look like because in former times they were very much better known. This was because the early Viking explorers sent their tusks back from the Arctic to Europe in the belief that they represented the horn of the unicorn. Indeed, the narwhal used to be known as the Sea unicorn. Narwhal tusk was believed to have unusual virtues the most notable of which was that it would show whether food was poisoned or not. In those days of long ago

when nobody could trust his neighbour and killing a rival by poisoning his food was a common practice, anything that helped in this way was almost beyond price, worth its weight in gold.

The biggest puzzle about the narwhal is, however, what does the male do with its tusk? Some people have said that it uses it to poke holes through the ice so that it can breathe. Others claim that male narwhals fight each other with their tusks using them as rapiers. The third view is that the tusk is used to stir up the seabed when the narwhal is looking for food. Clearly, these must be wrong because the obvious question to ask is how does the female get on without any tusk to help her breathing or her search for food or as a weapon of defence? The only thing we can suppose is that the narwhal tusk is like the antlers of a stag, a male adornment with little use apart from impressing a female.

One strange feature of the narwhal is the large amount of Vitamin C which it appears to store in its skin. This is reported to be of the order of 31·8 mg per 100 gm of skin, the same amount as in many vegetables and fruit. This fact has been long appreciated by Eskimos who are otherwise short of this vitamin in winter and who have hunted the narwhal especially for its skin which they chew. Like that of the *White whale the skin makes excellent leather, a rare feature among Cetacea. See Toothed whales. FAMILY: Monodontidae. ORDER: Cetacea, CLASS: Mammalia. K.M.B.

NARWHAL HORN. When narwhals were first discovered in arctic seas it is not surprising that they were thought to be sea-unicorns and that their horns would have the same property of *unicorn horns in detecting poisons. The sailors under Sir Martin Frobisher even tested this theory. This was an unusual step in an age that tended to accept statements without question. They put some spiders in the hollow centre of

a broken horn and they 'presently died'. Unfortunately their experimental technique was poor and they did not perform a control experiment with non-poisonous animals of similar size.

NATIVE CAT *Dasyurus quoll,* one of the few living carnivorous marsupials, so called because it is about the size of a domestic cat to which it is quite unrelated. See Marsupial cat.

NATURAL SELECTION, the most important process in the origin of species by which individuals less well adapted to their environment are eliminated, leading to what used to be commonly called 'the survival of the fittest'. See evolution and Darwin.

NAUPLIUS LARVAE, see crustacean larvae.

NAUTILUS, or *Pearly nautilus, a cephalopod mollusc with a pearly gas-filled external shell. It is restricted to the Indian Ocean.

NAVIGATION. A great deal of interest has been shown recently in the methods by which animals manage to steer themselves when on long-distance journeys. Much of the mystery of bird migration, for example, has lain in how the birds find their way over thousands of miles of ocean; the mystery largely remains. Plainly, any animal which can both distinguish and learn visual landmarks will be able to use them in order to navigate (see homing) but many animals travel their first journeys without previous experience and without an elder to guide them.

Honeybees can return to their hives even if they are set down in surroundings offering little or nothing in the way of visual landmarks. They utilize the pattern of polarized light from the blue sky, being able to guide themselves by it when only a small proportion of the sky is showing through cloud. The pattern is one of percentage of polarization and direction of polarization; at two points in the sky, there is no polarization. It is directly correlated with the sun and thus as the sun moves so does the light pattern. A piece of polaroid (which polarizes light) held over a bee dancing on the horizontal alighting board of a hive may cause it to change its direction. (See bees, for description of dance.) This can be traced under the proper conditions to alteration of the light pattern from above to that of another part of the sky; the bee now orientates its dance with respect to this part

Sun navigation in ants. If a homing ant returning to its nest on a course at right angles to the sun, is held captive at point A while the sun shifts 40 degrees, it will on release still maintain a course at right angles to the sun and will thus steer 40 degrees away from the nest.

as if it were overhead being misled by the changes brought about by the polaroid filter. Other experiments have shown that the polarized light pattern is received through the upper part of the eyes whose detailed structure (similar to that in many other arthropods) suggests that each ommatidium can act as an analyzer of polarized light.

Bees are also able to allow for the movement of the sun (see rhythmic behaviour) and can dance showing the correct angle between food direction and the sun some hours after having returned to the hive.

Other arthropods are also able to utilize the polarized light sky pattern. One example is the sandhopper *Talitrus* which will move seawards from the drier parts of the upper shore. It can go in the correct direction at any time of the day, and therefore, like the honeybee, must be able to adjust for the sun's movement.

There seems little evidence that vertebrates can use this sky pattern; though there are indications that some lake fish may utilize it for homing. But there is much evidence that birds use the sun in other ways to guide them on both homing and migration journeys. For young birds making their first journey the task is not difficult. All they need to do is to maintain a fixed direction and they do so even when transported sideways from their normal route, showing none of the adaptability of adult birds. Such orientation, as this might correctly be called, needs no more than sun-compass behaviour. In this the animal maintains the sun at a certain angle as it moves; for it to go in a straight line, the angle has to change continuously as the sun moves across the sky. Many animals are known to be able to do this. See rhythmic behaviour.

However, it is less easy to suggest how a bird transported to a strange place can return home. This can be explained on the hypothesis that the bird uses the sun in the following way (in the northern hemisphere). By observing the sun and comparing its position with the one it would occupy at home the bird can, in human terms, tell whether it is to the west or east of its home (if to the west, the sun will be less far across the sky than the home sun; if to the east, farther across the sky). This requires that the bird's internal clock is set at home time and is unaffected by the local conditions.

The rate of change of elevation of the sun might give the clue to whether the bird should fly towards or away from the sun (i.e. whether it is to the north or south of home). The nearer the equator the bird is the faster the sun climbs or drops; again the bird must have a memory of the home conditions. In this way a bird could locate itself in relation to its home and select the correct direction in which to fly. This is true navigation and some authors use the term exclusively for this kind of behaviour, that is, 'the ability to initiate and maintain directed movement independently of learned landmarks'.

Though this theory may explain navigation by day, it is unfortunately true that many birds migrate by night. Radar observations have shown how well directed their movements are and in what quantity the birds move. Garden warblers were hand-reared indoors so that they had no experience of the sky by night or day. Yet when placed in the open at night in small cages when other warblers were on their autumn migration these birds' intention movements indicated that their orientation was similar to that of the free-flying birds. Experiments in a planetarium showed that rotation of the sky pattern caused the birds to change direction. Thus there seems little doubt that birds can maintain a direction guided by some clue from the night sky though this does not appear to be the actual pattern of constellations. Firm evidence that birds can navigate by the stars from an unknown place is still lacking.

The crucial experiments to put beyond any doubt the way in which the sun is used for navigation are very difficult to carry out. But at least there is much to support the use of the sun by birds and arthropods. The navigational abilities of fish are even more difficult to investigate (indeed with deep-sea fish well-nigh impossible). How is it, for example, that Atlantic salmon which wander very far from their home river can nevertheless find its mouth once again? Chemical clues in the water may serve to identify the home stream but such clues could hardly be expected to function after the confluence of the tributary streams, and certainly not over thousands of miles of ocean. Nevertheless it has not been necessary thus far to postulate any unknown sense, such as an ability to respond to the earth's magnetic field, to explain the navigational ability of animals. Before proposing such explanations it is as well to look very carefully at the development of what might be called the traditional senses and try to explain the remarkable navigational powers in that way.   J.D.C.

NEARCTIC FAUNA, the animal population of one of the six major zoogeographical regions, comprising all of the North American continent, together with the arctic islands to the north, Newfoundland, and Greenland. Southwards, it extends slightly below the Tropic of Cancer to include the high, cool Mexican plateau.

Like the Palearctic region, the northern fringe of the Nearctic region is covered by tundra, which southwards changes to coniferous forest and in turn to deciduous forest. Farther south, and especially in the USA, the climatic zones are complicated by the effects of the Rocky Mountains, which run north-south through the western half of the continent. The Rockies themselves bear strips of forest but are mostly arid. Immediately to the east of them, extensive grasslands cover the sediments laid down by the erosion of the Rockies. The rainfall of this region is low. Farther east, the rainfall progressively rises towards the Atlantic coast, and most of eastern North America was originally covered by deciduous or mixed forest.

As a result of these geographical and climatic features, there are two types of faunal zonation in the Nearctic region. The first, and most important, is a north-south zonation similar to that found in the Palearctic region. The fauna is most diverse and numerous in the warmer southern regions but gradually diminishes northwards

Map of the Nearctic region which includes most of North America, Greenland and most of the Caribbean islands.

as different groups in turn reach the limit of their climatic tolerance. Cold-blooded vertebrates, such as the amphibians and reptiles, therefore, become progressively less common as one travels northwards (or into higher altitudes in the Rockies), and are there represented mainly by their most hardy and widespread members—*Bufo, Rana* and *Hyla* among the frogs, skinks among the lizards, and colubrine snakes. Not only do these groups become more common and varied towards the south, but the fauna also becomes enriched by the appearance of more warmth-loving forms such as the land tortoises *Gopherus,* the Soft-shelled turtle *Trionyx,* the geckonid, teiid and iguanid lizards, the boa-constrictor, the Coral snakes, the mockingbirds and the peccaries.

The east-west zonation caused by the Rocky Mountains is, similarly, more marked in the cold-blooded vertebrates, which find more difficulty in tolerating or crossing climatically inhospitable regions. These forms, such as the freshwater fishes, salamanders, turtles and snakes, are in general more common in the moister, warmer eastern part of North America, though lizards are more diverse in the west.

Relatively few animals are found only in the Nearctic region. The Bowfin fish *Amia,* and a primitive type of frog *Ascaphus,* are relict species. The Gila monster *Heloderma,* which is the world's only really poisonous lizard, is found only in the southwestern part of the region. Other exclusively Nearctic forms are turkeys, the Pronghorn antelope and the sewellel (Rodentia). In addition, the plethodontid salamanders and the peccaries are basically North American forms which also extend into South America.

Another category in the Nearctic fauna is made up of animals which are mainly South American (the Neotropical region), but which have spread northwards. Animals have travelled in both directions along the Panama Isthmus, which is the best example of an existing land bridge. In general, there has been an approximately equal exchange of freshwater fishes and amphibians, more types of reptile and mammal have extended southwards than northwards, and more types of bird have extended northwards than southwards. Thus only three types of mammal (the opossum, the armadillo and the New World porcupine) found today in the Nearctic have spread there from South America, but many more members of the Nearctic bird fauna are immigrants from the south, parrots, jacanas, ibises, hummingbirds and New World vultures.   C.B.C.

NECKLACE SHELLS, a group of marine snails characteristic of sandy beaches and specialized for burrowing and feeding on burrowing bivalve molluscs. Necklace shells, Moon shells and Sharks' eyes are common names for them in different parts of the world and may refer to the large globular shells, with few whorls and a very smooth surface. This smoothness is particularly seen in Sea snails in which the shell is covered either by the mantle, as in the cowries, or by the foot, as in this family. The front end of the foot extends into a large flap, the propodium, which is the organ mainly used in digging, and also protects the front of the shell from sand grains. At the sides of the foot are two parapodia and behind there is a metapodium, so that the shell is almost completely covered with flesh. There are no eye-stalks, another distinguishing feature, and the eyes are embedded in the body wall.

Necklace shells are found in almost all parts of the world on sandy beaches, both intertidally and in shallow waters. Their egg masses are unmistakable and known as sand-collars. This describes their appearance exactly as they are broad bands of sand

cemented by a gelatinous secretion, into which the eggs are incorporated, and curved into an incomplete circle. They are moulded into shape by the large foot and so are characteristic of the species. The eggs hatch in two or three weeks. One of the most familiar European species is the Large necklace shell, *Natica catena,* with an almost spherical buff-coloured shell about $1\frac{1}{2}$ in (3·8 cm) in diameter.

Necklace shells feed mainly on bivalves such as Sunset shells, Carpet shells and Venus clams which live in the same habitat, burrowing in sand. Like *Rock shells they bore a hole in the shell of the prey through which the specialized proboscis is inserted so that the toothed radula can scrape out the soft parts. For a long time there has been disagreement on whether boring was by chemical or mechanical means. This is particularly difficult to decide with an animal like the Large necklace shell which will only bore when buried in sand. Most research on the method of boring has therefore been done with surface-living Rock shells. In Necklace shells there is no acid secretion and boring seems to be mostly mechanical by the action of the radula. There is, however, a boring gland on the underside of the proboscis, which has a softening effect on the shell of a mollusc, and may perhaps act on the organic material in the shell. Boring is a slow process and may take several days for a thick-shelled Venus clam, but perhaps only an hour or two for a thinner Sunset shell, the bivalve being held enveloped in the large foot all the time. A shell bored by a Necklace shell can be recognized by the curved sides of the hole; holes made by Rock shells and Dog whelks are straight-sided. FAMILY: Naticidae, ORDER: Mesogastropoda, CLASS: Gastropoda, PHYLUM: Mollusca.   E.D.

NEEDLEFISHES, an alternative name for *garfishes.

NEKTON and plankton together form the group known as pelagic animals—marine animals which live in the open sea, that is to say not intertidally or on the sea floor. Planktonic animals are small, with limited powers of locomotion, and consequently their movements are largely at the mercy of the ocean currents. Members of the nekton, on the other hand, can swim well and so can move about independently of the prevailing currents. The chief members of the nekton are the cephalopods (e.g. squids), the pelagic fishes and the whales.

Animals of the nekton feed either on one another or on animals in the plankton (the zooplankton). The Baleen whales and fishes, such as the herring, feed on plankton. Plankton-feeding fishes in turn provide food for other fishes, for the squids, and for the Toothed whales.

Squids and cuttlefishes are cephalopod molluscs. They are active swimmers and can move at very great speeds, in short bursts, by a sort of jet propulsion. They have excellent eyes and highly developed brains. Some squids live close to the sea bed and so may hardly be considered members of the nekton, but others are truly pelagic. Their numbers may often exceed what might be deduced from net hauls, for their good vision and active movements doubtless make them adept at evading capture by nets. The largest squids (e.g. *Architeuthis*) may be up to 50 ft (15 m) in length (including the two long tentacles, which extend beyond the other eight arms). Squid feed largely on fish, and are themselves taken by other members of the nekton such as the Sperm whale.

The nekton contains innumerable species of pelagic fishes, some of which occur in such large numbers that they support commercial fisheries. Herrings, for example, congregate in enormous shoals for spawning. The very young fishes are virtually planktonic, as their powers of swimming are slight, but as they mature their movements become pronounced, and they will congregate in areas rich in zooplankton, upon which they feed. Herrings feed mainly on planktonic copepod crustaceans, and are in turn 'eaten' by fleets of drifters.

Whales are prominent members of the nekton in certain areas. Some whales, such as the Sperm whale are toothed. They feed by preying on other members of the nekton (squids and fishes). Other whales bear sheets of baleen within the mouth cavity, which sieve off enormous numbers of planktonic animals such as the euphausiid crustaceans ('krill').   A.E.B.

NEMATOCYSTS, although called 'stinging cells' or 'nettle cells,' they are not cells but organelles secreted by cells called nematoblasts. Each nematocyst is a capsule, generally rounded at one end, pointed at the other, containing a coiled tube or hollow thread fastened at the narrower end and continuous with the capsule wall at this point. This end of the capsule is covered by a lid or operculum. There are two sorts of nematocysts, true nematocysts and spirocysts. Spirocysts are all alike and are found only in Sea anemones and corals. They are thin-walled capsules which stain with acid dyes and contain a long, spirally-coiled tube without any projections or barbs along its length. True nematocysts are thick, double-walled capsules which stain with basic dyes and which are impermeable to water, except at discharge. The wall of the capsule is composed of a protein similar to collagen. The construction of the inner, coiled tube is very varied and generally bears some spirally-arranged barbs, of 17 different types.

The development of nematocysts has been studied using the electron microscope. They

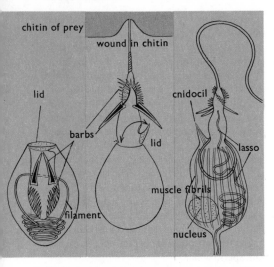

Large penetrating type of nematocyst of *Hydra*. (left) undischarged, (centre) discharged, (right) discharged but retained within its capsule.

arise from small undifferentiated cells known as interstitial cells. These start to divide and the daughter cells, instead of separating, remain attached to each other by a narrow neck of cytoplasm until about 18 cells in cytoplasmic continuity are formed. These constitute a 'battery' of nematocysts which develop synchronously. The cells cease dividing and the capsule and thread are secreted within the cell, the thread developing externally to the capsule at first and then being inverted, that is, pulled in like a glove finger, in an unknown way.

The developing nematocysts accumulate at certain sites, for example, the tentacles, and require a double stimulus to bring about their discharge. Light mechanical stimulation such as something touching the tentacle will cause the nematocysts to be discharged, and many nematocysts have a small spike-like projection, known as cnidocil, which acts as a trigger when touched. In addition, the presence of lipoprotein molecules given out by a prey species in the surrounding water brings about discharge. The lid of the capsule comes off and the thread is everted, its advancing tip rotating in a counter-clockwise direction, like a drill, to penetrate the prey and inject a toxin contained in the capsule into the prey, paralyzing it. It is thought that the thread in the capsule is in a dehydrated state and that when the lid comes off the capsule the thread is progressively hydrated, generating energy to bring more dehydrated thread up to the water molecules. The considerable increase in the size of the thread is probably attained by expansion of the thread, which has been shown to be pleated internally. Nematocysts are used only once and are replaced by new 'batteries'.

Nematocysts are present only in species of *Cnidaria except for one species of *Ctenophora *Euchlora rubra*.   S.E.H.

NEMATODA, a class of slender, threadlike worms, also known as *roundworms because the body is more or less circular in cross section. It includes the remarkable *thunderworm. CLASS: Nematoda, PHYLUM: Aschelminthes.

NEMERTINA, one of the phyla of elongated wormlike invertebrates, sometimes known as the Nemertea or the Rhynchocoela. They are given the common name of *ribbonworms because many of their members have flattened bodies and although very slender may be several feet (1 m) long.

NÉ-NÉ *Branta sandvicensis,* or *Hawaiian goose, an offshoot of the Canada goose which has been the subject of one of the more remarkable efforts in wildlife conservation.

NEOGAEA, alternative name for the *Neotropical Region.

NEOPILINA. On 6th May, 1952 the Danish deep-sea research ship 'Galathea' trawling at a depth of 1,945 fathoms (3,570 metres), collected 10 specimens and 3 empty shells of *Neopilina galathea,* a representative of a class of molluscs, the Monoplacophora, believed to have been extinct since the Devonian period, 350 million years ago. *Neopilina* has a small, fragile, limpet-shaped shell almost 1 in (2·5 cm) in length, with its apex near the front end. Its fossil relatives in the order Tryblidioida had a very similar shell, on the inner surface of which a series of up to eight muscle scars can be seen. Now that the soft parts of *Neopilina* have been studied, it can be seen that this pairing of muscles represents a true metameric segmentation of the body, as in annelids or ringed worms. This means the body is composed of a series of repeating parts, with a head and 'tail' outside the series. Those systems which show segmentation most clearly are the muscular system with eight pairs of foot retractors, the nervous system with a series of ten pairs of nerves radiating to the sides of the foot, and the gills and excretory organs, nephrida, there being five pairs of each. The head is well marked, but has no eyes or retractile tentacles. The mouth is on the underside, surrounded by mobile lips and with broad tentacles behind it. There is a radula, the tongue-like structure characteristic of molluscs, which is similar to that of chitons.

Since the discovery of *Neopilina galathea,* three further species have been found, all in deep water between 1,500 and 3,500 fathoms (2,752–6,431 metres) and all off the Pacific coast of America, within 15 degrees of the equator. The sea bed here is covered with greenish oozy mud rich in organic material with remains of microscopic plants (diatoms) and animals (radiolarians and foraminiferans). The temperature is almost

constant 34°–36°F (1°–2°C). Nothing is known of the breeding habits of *Neopilina* nor of the development of its eggs. Embryological knowledge would be very important to the understanding of the relationships of the Monoplacophora with other molluscs, and also with other invertebrate phyla. The sexes are separate, which suggests the population must be quite dense, though probably very patchy. This is also indicated by the fact that only one trawl of the 'Galathea' contained *Neopilina,* and that ten specimens.

As to *Neopilina's* habits and way of life there can only be conjecture. One of the later expeditions to bring back specimens also took some photographs of the sea bed in the region and these show deep furrows in the mud with *Neopilina*-shaped lumps at one end. This, together with gut contents and faecal pellets of the animal (containing bacteria like shapes, diatoms, radiolarians, foraminiferans and sponge spicules), seems to indicate that *Neopilina* ploughs its way through the mud, swallowing it indiscriminately and digesting the organic material.

The great zoological importance of the discovery of *Neopilina* is that it provides a definite link between the true worms (Annelida) and the Molluscs. Previous to its finding, a relationship was thought possible on the grounds of the similarity of development in the two phyla, but a more probable ancestor for molluscs was thought to be a flatworm. The discovery of a segmented mollusc shows that the mollusc line must have branched off

Schematic representation of the relationship of *Neopilina* (inset) to other molluscan classes. The definite traces of segmentation in *Neopilina* indicate its primitive nature, suggesting a link with the annelid worms, and mark it off sharply from other molluscs living today.

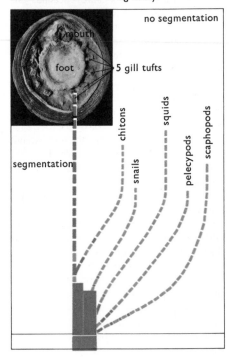

at a higher level than previously thought, after a flatworm ancestor had evolved into a segmented primitive annelid. FAMILY: Tryblidiidae, ORDER: Tryblidioida, CLASS: Monoplacophora, PHYLUM: Mollusca.
E.M.D.

NEOTENY, the retention of larval characters at sexual maturity. The word was first used by Kollmann in 1883 for certain salamanders which never undergo a complete metamorphosis and so retain at least some larval characters when sexually mature. Larval characters commonly retained are external gills, gill-slits and tail-fins. In addition skull bones are often suppressed. These neotenic amphibians are aquatic and typical examples are *Necturus, Proteus, Typhlomolge, Siren, Cryptobranchus, Megalobatrachus* and *Amphiuma.* None of these can be made fully to metamorphose by artifical means, but one form, the axolotl, given the right treatment, will metamorphose and produce a form known as *Ambystoma tigrinum* which displays no larval characters at all. Experimental work indicates that the action of the thyroid gland is crucial in this but the fact that in other neotenic forms metamorphosis cannot be induced would seem to indicate that genetic factors are at work aside from the level of thyroid activity; probably the pituitary gland is also involved.

Some authorities refer to temporary neoteny in contrast to the permanent neoteny of the forms referred to above. It occurs in newts, frogs and toads and takes the form of prolongation of the larval stage, possibly as an adaptation to winter survival. It is probably better regarded as overwintering and should be described as such.

Although neoteny was first described in the tailed amphibians the term has come to be used more widely in groups where parallel cases occur. Neoteny of a kind occurs in a number of invertebrate animals and is often described under the heading of pedogenesis, which means reproduction by immature or youthful individuals. A well known case is that of the Gall midge *Miastor* where the female produces four or five huge eggs which give rise to larvae which produce another generation of larvae internally from precociously developed eggs. These larvae burrow their way out and in turn form larvae internally. After several generations of larvae have been produced a stage is reached of larvae which pupate in a normal way and adult flies are produced. In this process parthenogenesis is also involved. Larval pedogenesis also occurs in the beetle *Micromalthus,* and pupal pedogenesis in the chironomid fly *Tanytarsus.*

Neoteny has obviously arisen several times in the course of evolution in the tailed amphibians and some writers on evolution theory, particularly Garstang and de Beer,

have suggested that neoteny has been one of the important means of evolutionary change in several groups. For example it has been suggested that the line which produced the earliest vertebrates may have been derived from animals with a life-history like that of the modern Sea squirt. The latter has two phases, a motile larva and a sedentary sexual form. If the larva, or ascidian tadpole, developed gonads and carried out pedogenesis the sedentary form could be eliminated from the life-history. In brief the neotenic larval form could be a means of evolutionary change. It is possible that some such change did give rise to the ancestral forms of the vertebrates, although any proof is unlikely. See pedogenesis.
R.W.W.

NEOTROPICAL REGION, one of the six major zoogeographical regions, comprising the whole of the South American continent including Tierra del Fuego, Central America as far north as the lowlands of Mexico, and also the island of Trinidad.

Most of the Neotropical region is covered by forests. The Amazon valley includes the largest area of swamp forest and evergreen tropical rain-forest in the world. Uruguay and much of Argentina are covered by grasslands—the 'pampas'. Down the western edge of the continent run the Andes, the western slopes of which are covered with mountain forest and grassland, but the eastern slopes of which are far more arid, including some areas of desert.

South America has been isolated from other land masses for longer than any other continent except Australia. In the absence of competition from new groups evolving over the wide areas of North America, Eurasia and Africa, those types of animal which have from time to time colonized South America were able to undergo a great adaptive radiation there, though they often became extinct elsewhere. As a result, much of its fauna is composed of a variety of forms belonging to a few groups which are found nowhere else.

This is particularly true of its mammal fauna, since much of mammalian evolution took place during the Lower Tertiary Period, at a time when there was no continuous land bridge along the Panama Isthmus. Five mammalian groups nevertheless reached South America during or before this time. These groups were the marsupials, the xenarthran edentates, some very primitive types of ungulate, the caviomorph rodents and the New World monkeys. Adaptive radiations of these groups formed the only mammalian fauna of South America until the Upper Pliocene to Pleistocene. At that time the final establishment of the Panama Isthmus allowed members of the more advanced placental mammal groups, such as the Carnivora, Perissodactyla (horses, rhinoceroses, tapirs)

The Neotropical region includes the whole of South and Central America and the island of Trinidad.

and Artiodactyla (deer, antelopes, cattle etc), to enter South America. Competition from these mammals led to the extinction of all the primitive South American ungulates and many of the xenarthrans and marsupials. The modern survivors of these groups include a few marsupials (the opossums and opossum-rat) and xenarthrans (the armadillos, tree-sloths and anteaters) and a variety of New World monkeys and caviomorph rodents, the latter undergoing an extensive radiation to give the capybara, the Guinea pig and the New World porcupines. All of these forms are characteristic of South America, though the opossum, the armadillo and the porcupines have spread into North America.

Two other mammals found only in the Neotropical region are the Vampire bats and the llamas. Llamas and the South American tapirs are both *relict species, the closest relatives of which are to be found today in Asia. The remainder of the mammal fauna is similar to that of North America, consisting of such widespread groups as the canids, felids, bears, deer, rabbits and squirrels, as well as more specifically North American forms such as raccoons and peccaries.

The Neotropical region has an extremely rich bird fauna; nearly half of the 67 families of land and freshwater birds found in the region are exclusive to it, or are centred there even though a few members extend northwards into the Nearctic region. These characteristically Neotropical families total more than 1,500 species—more than $\frac{1}{6}$ of all the known species of birds. The most important are the Furnarioidea (including the ovenbirds and antbirds), the American flycatchers, the hummingbirds, the cotingas, the manakins, the toucans, the New World vultures and the flightless rheas.

Few of the amphibians and reptiles of the Neotropical region are found only there, the only important group being the caimans (a type of crocodile). Two relict groups are the leptodactylid frogs, found today only in South America and the Australian region, and lepidosirenid lungfish, found today only in South America and Africa.   C.B.C.

NEPHRIDIA, the excretory organs of annelids. They consist of coiled tubules, typically two to each body segment. Each nephridium begins as a funnel, the nephridiostome, which connects to a narrow tube that passes through the septum into the next body segment where the remaining portion of the tubule lies. It empties through the body wall via the nephridiopore. See excretion and excretory organs.

NEPHTHYS, a pearly or creamy-white *polychaete worm found in sand or muddy sand on the seashore. Without obvious pigment apart from the reddish colour of the blood, these muscular worms burrow vigorously back into the sand when dug up and are carnivorous in habit. They vary in length from 2–3 in (50–75 mm) to perhaps 10 in (250 mm). They burrow into the sand by repeated eversion of the large muscular proboscis which is thrown out as a result of fluid pressure and is retracted by strong strap-like muscles.

The parapodia are all much the same: foliaceous with fans of slender chaetae and an inverted sickle-shaped gill between the main lobes. The prostomium (the extreme front end) is rather small and the tentacles and other sense organs not prominent. When the worm lies in the sand a respiratory current is maintained by cilia and flows between the main parapodial lobes across the sickle-shaped gills. This channel is maintained by the chaetae which are spread out on each side. These worms form only temporary burrows and are often found in relatively 'clean' sand subject to some wave action which other worms find untenable. Their ability to respire and to quickly rebury themselves are no doubt adaptations to these conditions.

Nephthys swims well; better than the *ragworm, Nereis.* The body is lashed from side to side, the foliaceous parapodia acting as paddles. CLASS: Polychaeta, PHYLUM: Annelida.

NERVE IMPULSES. In nearly all animals, there are cells which are specialized for carrying electrical messages from one part of the body to another, to keep the various organs in touch with one another. These nerve cells are basically long cables which pass information from one end of themselves to the other. It has been possible to put fine electrodes into nerve cells and to amplify the electrical events inside the cell during the

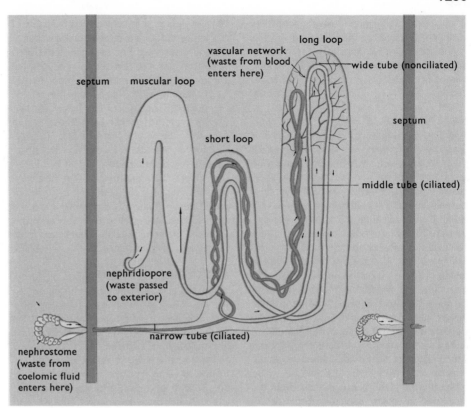

Nephridia are found in earthworms. They are slender coiled tubes and occur in pairs in all segments of the body except the first three and the last. Each opens at the surface by a small nephridiopore.

passage of a nerve impulse. The signal is then displayed on the screen of a cathode ray tube, which is basically similar to a television set. From this, it has been found that the nerve either transmits a full-sized electrical pulse or it transmits none at all (the so-called all-or-none response), so that the strength of a stimulus such as sound is not represented in the nerve by the size of a pulse, but by the number of identically-sized pulses. That is, the more impulses in the nerve, the more sound we hear.

A nerve impulse, travelling down an axon as the main 'cable' of the cell is called reaches the end of the cell where the receptive branches (dendrites) of another nerve cell are situated. This next nerve cell then starts to transmit an impulse. However, the cells do not actually touch, and the impulse does not jump the gap, or synapse, in the form of electricity. On the axon side of the synapse are sacs of chemical, which burst when an impulse reaches them. The chemical (it varies in different types of animal) diffuses rapidly to the next cell, and causes it to transmit an impulse. Since axons have the chemical, and the dendrites do not, impulses can only travel one way. Most nerve cells cause the next cell to become excited and transmit an impulse, but some cells inhibit the next cell and stop it being excited by the other nerve cells also making synaptic contact with it.

Nerve cells can be of various sizes and types. For example, a nerve to a human toe muscle runs a distance of about 3 ft (1 m)

from the lower part of the spinal cord to the muscle. These long nerve cells are associated in bundles of fibres which are easily visible; these are 'nerves' as the term is used in everyday speech. At the other extreme, the cells of the visual areas of our brains are perhaps $\frac{1}{16}$ in (1·5 mm) in length. Some cells have many dendrites, so that they can receive impulses from many other cells. Inhibitory cells are generally small and their effects localized.

These basic units are built into a nervous system in various ways. In the simplest instance, a sense organ (such as a heat receptor) may be joined by nerves to a muscle. If too much heat is received, messages are sent along the nerves to the muscle, which then contracts to move that part of the body away from the excess heat. This is a reflex, and is found in all animals with nervous systems. A reflex action is just what is implied by the term; it is quite automatic. If our hand touches a flame, a reflex jerk of the arm muscles pulls the hand away. We do not have to think about it and the whole action is performed without any conscious control. Simple animals may work entirely in this way.

Generally, however, nerve fibres are aggregated together, for there needs to be some correlation between reflexes. Thus, for example, if an animal moving reflexly towards food is also disturbed by extra light which causes reflex withdrawal it must have some means of controlling to which stimulus it responds, or at least avoiding remaining in one place, because of equal but opposite pulls. Such control above the individual reflex level is achieved by inter-connection between the various reflexes, and this is organized in a strand of nerves running down the body, joining up to the various reflex circuits. In invertebrate animals, this is called the nerve cord; in vertebrate animals it is called the spinal cord. Masses of aggregated nerve cells constitute a 'central nervous system'. Such inter-connection allows complex series of reflexes to occur. For example, if we tread on a pin, we raise the injured leg rapidly. At the same time, we move the other leg, and the arms, to preserve balance. Thus one stimulus sets off a number of reflexes of different types, all working in a co-ordinated fashion via the spinal cord.   G.E.S.

NERVOUS SYSTEM, co-ordinates the activities of an animal's body (such as the contractions of muscles) with each other and also relates these activities to the external world sensed through the sense organs. It is essentially a means of transmitting information about the body. Some of this information will concern the external world, and the rest will be about the state of the internal parts of the body. The nervous system has a sensory side and a motor one. The latter being the way in which 'orders' are carried to muscles and glands. But between these two sides in most animals is a co-ordinating centre where incoming information (carried by the sensory system) is analyzed and correlated.

The nervous system is typically composed of nerve cells, which are specializations of whole cells, and will only, therefore, be found in metazoan animals. In protozoans, there are conducting fibrils which seem to have many of the functions of the nervous system of higher animals. They may, for example, be responsible for co-ordinating ciliary structures in locomotion. Although the details of their structure vary in different groups, nerve cells essentially have a cell body, from which one or more prolongations extend, along which impulses are carried. The vertebrate nerve cell has short processes, the dendrites, on the cell body and one long axon leading from it. Transmission of impulses across the cell is from dendrites to axon, the latter making connection with a neighbouring cell. The axon may be extremely long, some, for example, stretching from spinal cord to the foot of an elephant. Yet axons are only about 20–50 microns thick and they may be even thinner. Vertebrate axons may be ensheathed in a variable amount of fat, those with very little are called non-myelinated, and those with a great deal are myelinated. The amount of fat is correlated with the speed of conduction, so that a 4 micron fibre of a cat nerve will conduct at 82 ft (25 m) per sec which is the same speed as that at which a 650 micron

squid giant nerve conducts. The cat's nerve has a thick layer of fat even though the fibre itself is very small.

Conduction of an impulse along a nerve cell probably occurs in the same way in all animals. The membrane bounding the cell is polarized from an electrical point of view because its outer surface carries a positive charge and its inner a negative one. Thus, electrodes placed one inside and the other outside the membrane of a resting nerve will show an electric potential of some 50 millivolts. When a nerve is stimulated, changes occur in the membrane's electrical state at the time that the impulse passes; indeed, these changes are the impulse. A wave of depolarization passes down the cell. Where the membrane is depolarized, local electric currents form to restore the polarized state of that small bit of membrane. As this involves changes in the neighbouring region, this in its turn becomes depolarized and the impulse passes along. These electrical changes can be explained on a basis of the movement of charged ions through the membrane. As in many other kinds of cell, the inside of an inactive nerve cell contains an excess of potassium ions compared with outside, but an excess of sodium and other ions outside the cell. The membrane is moderately permeable to potassium and chloride ions but less so to sodium ions. When a nerve impulse arrives this permeability is altered so that sodium ions can diffuse inwards, rendering the surface relatively negative and the inside more positive. Immediately after this, there is an outward diffusion of potassium ions the positive charge of which restores the polarization. During the subsequent refractory period, when the nerve cannot be stimulated again, sodium ions are pumped out of it and potassium is actively resorbed. When the original distribution of ions is restored so also is the polarization of the membrane, and the nerve is fully ready for action again.

The great majority of nerve cells make contact with their neighbours at synapses. Thus, where an axon ends close to the surface of another nerve cell, the two membranes do not fuse but come close together with a very narrow gap, measuring about 0·01–0·05 microns, between them. Impulses travelling down the axon have to pass across this space to continue along the next cell. As there is no physical contact between the membranes, some means of bridging the gap is necessary. This is done by the production of a chemical substance by the axon. In vertebrates this is very often acetyl choline. In electron microscope pictures very tiny vesicles can be seen within the ends of axons and they appear to discharge acetyl choline into the space of the synapse. However it is produced it is clear that the chemical functions as the bridge to the next cell. As a result of its action that cell is stimulated and a train of impulses passes

on. In vertebrates, acetyl choline and sympathin are the transmitter substances, as they are called, but in invertebrates other chemicals produced by the nerve cells have a similar function.

Synapses are extremely important for they permit nerve cells to connect together in all manner of combinations. Most cells in the central nervous system have many other cells connected to them, so that they receive many kinds of information. Some of these endings will be from nerve cells the action of which is to inhibit the activity of a cell while others stimulate its activity. By connections of this sort, integration and organization of the nerve paths of even the more complex animals, like vertebrates, is possible and here the number of cells acting as integrating units is very large indeed. It is their presence which permits the great range of behaviour which is possible in the highest vertebrates.

Primitive nervous systems

There is no sound evidence for the presence of a nervous system in sponges, the first type of system seemingly being the network of coelenterates. Typically, the nerve net lies beneath the ectoderm and above the endoderm. Each nerve cell consists of a cell-body and a number of branching fibres coming from it; most have two or three, a few have more. All are of equal importance and there is not one axon which can be differentiated from dendrites. Impulses travel down any of them to the cell-body from which they leave in all directions. Thus, this kind of nerve cell is not polarized, as is a vertebrate nerve cell, for impulses can go in any direction.

The tip of each process lies close to the tip of a process of another cell, the cells thus forming an irregular network. As the network is not polarized impulses travel in any direction over it. Indeed, in *Hydra,* for example, stimulation at one point radiates out from it in all directions. But as the impulses pass over the synapses they gradually disappear. This is connected with the resistance of the synapses to passing on information. The first impulse to reach a synapse may not pass it but may alter it so that a second impulse coming shortly after will cross the space. But this in turn may fail to pass a second synapse but will prepare it for the next impulse and so on. The more impulses there are following rapidly after each other, the farther the stimulation will spread. Since strong stimulation of the sensory cells produces a longer train of higher frequency impulses than a weak stimulation, it is the strong stimulation which will have the most widespread effect.

In other coelenterates, however, specialization of the nerve net leads to through-conduction paths along which impulses travel more quickly. For example, these paths ensure that there is co-ordination between the activities of various muscles in the closing response of anemones, allowing rapid contraction of the column if the animal is stimulated violently.

The evolution of nervous systems from this form of diffuse network is one of continuing concentration into a plainly marked central nervous system with the increasing development of an amalgamation of cells at the head-end to form a *brain (see cephalization). Usually the remainder of the central nervous system forms a cord running the length of the animal.

The early stages of this evolution can be seen in planarian worms. Here a brain of sorts is present and there are two to six longitudinal nerve cords. The nervous system of annelid worms shows the process well-established. These segmented animals have a brain and a double solid nerve cord running through the body on the ventral side. In each segment there is a collection of nerve cells which form a ganglion. From each of these ganglia, three or four nerves leave to supply the muscles of the body wall, the sensory structures on the skin and the gut, etc. The arrangement of cells in the cord allows for conduction in both directions, so that the activities of neighbouring segments can be co-ordinated and the worm when necessary can react as a whole.

It is in these annelids that giant cells first make their appearance. In an earthworm they lie in each segment sending processes to the very large giant axons in the dorsal part of the cord. These axons join to give rapid through-conduction paths which stretch from end to end of the worm. Thus, a noxious stimulation at the head-end excites the median giant axon, producing very rapid contraction away from the danger, while similar stimulation at the tail-end has the same effect via the lateral giant fibres.

The arthropod nervous system is arranged on a similar plan with well developed ganglia in each segment, although with a greater concentration of segmental ganglia in the head to form the sub-oesophageal ganglion. With the greater elaboration of sense organs, the supra-oesophageal ganglion or brain, becomes better developed than in worms. The segmental ganglia are themselves capable of initiating various behaviour-patterns. For instance, the pattern of sound made by a grasshopper rubbing its hindlegs against its wings is determined by the ganglion of the last thoracic ganglion. However, the brain exerts control over this, usually of an inhibitory nature (in this it differs from the function of the vertebrate brain). A decapitated insect can even learn simple actions, so that this learning must be taking place in the ganglia. A nerve cord removed from an arthropod's body and kept alive in the necessary nutrient solutions will show electrical activity, which is further evidence of the ability of the nerve cord to function without the brain.

Different arthropods show variations of this pattern of an elongated nervous system. Often further grouping together takes place, so that the nervous system is no longer stretched out through the body but the ganglia are drawn up together. Typical of this change of pattern are the nervous systems of the crab and the housefly. Despite their new position towards the anterior end of the animal, the ganglia still maintain their connections with areas which they normally supply.

In contrast to the invertebrates, chordate animals have a single, hollow nerve cord which is situated dorsally. It arises, in the embryo, as a tube which swells out at the anterior end to form the brain. Chordates are, of course, essentially segmented animals and, although most signs of this will have disappeared in the adult, the arrangement of the nerves coming from the spinal cord is segmental giving one of the few clues to the true nature of chordate organization.

There are no segmental ganglia, but each segment has a nerve on either side, and each nerve has two roots, a dorsal and a ventral one. The nerve itself is mixed for it contains fibres coming from sense organs (sensory fibres) and others (motor fibres) going to the muscles and glands which they control. The sensory fibres enter the cord through the dorsal root. Their cell bodies lie outside the cord in the swellings called the dorsal root ganglia. Thus, these cells have a long process leading to them without interruption from, say, a sense organ in the skin, and a short process making connections in the cord. The cell bodies of the motor fibres, on the other hand, lie in the ventral part of the cord and their axons pass out to the muscles etc, again without any synapse between cord and muscle. The simplest kind of interconnection between these two sets of nerves is shown in a spinal reflex arc. Here the sensory nerve makes direct connection with the motor cell in the cord, so that impulses travelling through the sensory nerve will set up impulses in the motor nerve. But more usually another cell, an internuncial neuron, is interposed between the sensory and motor cell. An increase in the number of these internuncials permits more elaborate cross connections to be set up and for reference to be made to the brain. A simple reflex response, such as the knee-jerk in humans, occurs without involving the brain.

In cross section a vertebrate spinal cord can be seen to consist of central grey matter (around the central canal) which spreads out into 'horns' which divide the outer white matter into three columns on either side. The grey matter consists of cell bodies while the white is made up of the axons of cells and is differentiated into columns which run along the cord each with particular connections in the brain or in other parts of the cord. These interconnections are the ones which permit

animals to carry out their, often complex, behaviour. Even the most ordinary, everyday activities involve large numbers of nerve cells in various parts of the brain and spinal cord.

So far we have been considering the part of the nervous system responsible for voluntary activity but closely associated with it is the autonomic (or sympathetic) system which carries out most of the unconscious control of the body's activities. This system is made up of cells gathered into ganglia lying away from the central nerve cord but connected to it by nerves. These contain fibres coming from the motor area of the cord and synapsing with the cells in the ganglion and other fibres which pass through the ganglion from an organ, say, the gut, to enter the spinal cord with the other sensory fibres in the dorsal root. In fact this system is divided into two, the sympathetic and the parasympathetic systems. Many organs of the body are innervated by both, one being excitatory and the other inhibitory. Thus, stimulation of the sympathetic nerves to the heart increases its rate of beat, while the parasympathetic will decrease it. This opposed action of the systems is used to control what might be called the 'unconscious' activities of the body. Autonomic systems have also been located in arthropods where they function to control the gut and so forth just as they do in vertebrates.

It has already been mentioned that nerves produce transmitter substances at their terminations and this stresses their ability to be secretory. Very often their secretory role is more strongly emphasized and the secretion acts as an endocrine substance (see endocrines). Much of the supraoesophageal 'brain' of polychaete worms is composed of neurosecretory cells; the hormones responsible for colour change in crustaceans are produced in cells in the brain. The neurohypophysis of the vertebrate pituitary gland stores hormones produced by neurosecretory cells of the hypothalamus and when they are released they play a part in the water balance of the body (anti-diuretic hormone) and in birth and suckling (oxytocin).

A distinction has often been made between the control of body functions by hormones and by the nervous system. While it remains true that quick short-term responses are mediated by the nervous system while slower longer lasting changes can be the result of endocrine action, the distinction between the origins of the two kinds of control is nowadays less clear for the nervous system has a double role; as a means of conveying impulses and as a producer of hormones.

J.D.C.

NEST-BUILDING, the behaviour involved in the preparation of a nest site, the collection of materials and the construction of a nest. Many species of animals build nests for the protection of eggs or young and some have

Nests of Weaver birds are built by the males from strips of leaves that are woven and knotted together to make a bag that is strong enough to withstand tropical downpours.

special sleeping nests. In some animals, such as social insects and many birds, nest-building is a very complicated process, being an adaptation to a highly specialized mode of life. In other species it is very simple indeed, involving a mere scrape in the ground in some birds, or the flattening of growing herbage in certain mammals. Winter nests are also of importance, particularly to those animals which go into deep hibernation.

The deposition of eggs and the maintenance of young in a nest is an advanced form of behaviour used by the more highly evolved groups of animals. Thus in the invertebrates it is seen particularly in the ants, bees and wasps (order Hymenoptera), and in the vertebrates in most birds and mammals. Some fishes, such as Fighting fish *Betta* and sticklebacks *Gasterosteus* build nests for the protection of their eggs. In all cases, nest-building is governed by a complex of hormonal and innate psychological factors, but the most complicated example is that seen in man where cultural influences are added.

In birds, where nest-building has been most studied, every degree of complexity of nest-building may be seen from virtually no nest at all, as in auks (Alcidae) which lay their eggs on bare rock, to the complex nests of weavers (Ploceidae) which build elaborate, enclosed, woven nests, anchored to branch supports by half-hitch ties. A great variety of sites are used for the building of nests by birds, including the surface of the ground or in burrows, cliff faces (or ledges of buildings, which make excellent substitutes) and the surface of the water at the edges of ponds or lakes. Some birds, for example certain penguins and grouse, even nest amongst snow and ice. No bird, however, deposits its eggs

directly on ice. The Emperor penguin *Aptenodytes forsteri*, obliged to incubate on ice during the antarctic winter, supports the egg on its feet.

Many birds build their nests in vegetation;

some amongst the ground cover, some at the tops of tall tress, still more at some point in the great range of possible sites in between these two extremes. In temperate climates the typical nest is cup-shaped, with the bulk of the nest built of a variety of plant materials with a lining of hair, feathers or soft fibre. Sometimes, as in certain finches (Fringillidae) and the Long-tailed tit *Aegithalos caudatus*, moss and lichen is woven into the fabric and helps to camouflage the nest. Occasionally, bizarre materials such as plastic bags or discarded pieces of wire may be used in nest construction. In tropical climates where snakes are common, nests are more often domed, or even with funnel or tunnel entrances for extra protection. Birds of a number of groups, particularly the woodpeckers, build simple nests in tree holes.

All types of nest are built – commonly by the female only – in a set sequence of behaviour, the programming of which is inherited in the brain. Given the appropriate environmental stimuli and the correct hormonal state the bird will begin to perform the correct sequence of nest-building behaviour, each component triggering the next, until the nest is complete. The sequence is improved by the bird learning the location of nest-building materials and by experience of their manipulation, but basically the ability to perform

A Penduline tit *Remiz pendulinus*, of the Palearctic region, at its nest.

Smooth newts courting. The male (left) develops a crest during the breeding season. Positioning himself in front of the female he vibrates his tail to drive a stream of water at her.

during the elaborate courtship displays by the male prior to breeding. The male's sperm are deposited in the water in a structure called a spermatophore produced by special glands in the wall of the cloaca. This is picked up by the female with her cloaca and the sperm then leave the spermatophore and swim to a specialized portion of the female reproductive system, the spermatheca or receptaculum seminis, and are stored there. The female generally lays 200–450 eggs which are fertilized inside her by the sperm. Laying usually starts three to ten days after the spermatophore is picked up and the female will not accept further spermatophores until the eggs are laid. These may be deposited singly or in small clusters and they are usually attached to the stem or leaf of a water plant or to a small rock. Laying usually takes place in the spring and metamorphosis is usually complete by the end of the summer when the young adults leave the water. They then remain on land until they become sexually mature three or four years later when they return to water to breed for the first time. Hibernation during the cold months of the year also takes place on land.

The Fire salamander, or Spotted salamander also extends into North Africa and was the first caudate amphibian to be described as such by Linnaeus in 1758. In ancient times it was thought this salamander was able to live in fire. The myth probably

nest-building activities is inherited. Birds of some species, deprived of nest-building materials for three generations, will nevertheless build sound nests given the proper facilities.   P.M.D.

NESTLING, a young bird while it is still in the nest. The term is usually restricted to those birds in which the young are hatched blind, naked, helpless and stay in the nest for some time, as in the perching birds, Passeriformes. Where the young are active within a few hours of hatching, as in the pheasants and grouse, the young bird is known as a chick. True nestlings are fully dependent on their parents until they leave the nest.

NEWTS. Considerable confusion exists about the use of the terms, salamander and newt. *Salamandra* means 'lizard-like animal' and is the generic name for the terrestrial salamanders of Europe. The noun 'salamander', however, is frequently applied to all caudate amphibians and more especially to the more terrestrial forms. The term newt originated in the Old World, and in Europe has a precise meaning. It refers only to the European newts of the genus *Triturus*. In the New World the use of the name newt is less specific and it includes other genera such as *Salamandra, Pleurodeles, Diemictylus* and *Taricha* as well as *Triturus*. It seems advisable to use the term 'newt' for those forms which constitute the family Salamandridae, and the term salamander for those tailed amphibians not in this family. The major objection to this is that the Fire salamander *Salamandra salamandra,* the species for which the name 'salamander' was first used belongs to the family Salamandridae and should logically be called the 'Fire newt'. However, in view of the largely terrestrial habits of this form, the antiquity and familiar-

ity of the name, the term Fire salamander is usually retained.

Newts such as the Smooth newt *Triturus vulgaris* and the Warty newt, *T. cristatus* are terrestrial during the greater part of the year and become aquatic during the breeding season when the male develops a prominent crest on back and tail. The crest is nonmuscular, sensory and is usually brightly coloured. It is used to attract the female

Alpine newts often develop neotonously in the cold waters of high level lakes.

Two male Warty newts leaving their breeding pond in the autumn at the end of the breeding season.

arose from people seeing the animal emerging from a log, in which it had sheltered, when this was put on the fire. The Fire salamander mates on land usually in July and about ten months later the female enters the water to bear live young. Each litter contains 10–15 young about 1 in (2·5 cm) long and possessing external gills which are lost during metamorphosis when the animals become terrestrial and acquire the orange-yellow patches characteristic of this species. The skin of the adult is kept moist by secretions of the dermal glands which also produce poisonous substances which afford some protection from predators. In laboratories the Fire salamander has been known to survive for at least 12 years.

Newts of the genus *Pleurodeles* occur in Spain, Portugal and northern Africa and have long pointed ribs which may even pierce the skin. The Waltl newt *Pleurodeles waltl* is said to live for 20 years in captivity.

The Red spotted newt *Diemictylus viridescens* of the eastern United States has a terrestrial stage the 'red eft' which lasts two to three years. After this individuals re-enter the water and become permanantly aquatic. They lose their bright red colour and assume a dull green appearance.

The California newt *Taricha torosa* lives in the coastal mountain ranges of California, is usually aquatic and develops a crest during the breeding season. Newts also occur in China and Japan and the Japanese newt *Cynops pyrrhogaster* is commonly kept as a pet.

Development in newts often involves *neoteny. This is especially well documented in the Alpine newt *Triturus alpestris*. Members of those species which inhabit freshwater areas in the low-lying plains of France and Italy metamorphose in the normal way and are not neotenous. In the cold lakes at higher altitudes development is retarded and neoteny is common.

Neoteny should not be confused with overwintering which also occurs in newts, when there is an early winter or a late spawning and the larvae, unable to metamorphose in time, are forced to hibernate as larvae. These tend to grow unduly large, so resembling the partially neotenic forms, but will metamorphose in the normal way the following spring or summer.

Newts are voracious feeders and will eat worms, slugs, snails and insects when on land, and aquatic larvae, small crustaceans, mollusca and even frog's spawn when in the water. Food is detected by sight and smell, and swimming is achieved by the use of the tail with the limbs being usually held alongside the body.

Newts like most tailed amphibians can regenerate amputated parts such as the tail, limbs and even some parts of the head. The power of regeneration decreases with age.
FAMILY: Salamandridae, ORDER: Caudata, CLASS: Amphibia.   R.L.

NEWT POISON. Several newts are poisonous, the venom being produced from the dermal glands as in the Fire salamander. The Warty or Crested newt exudes poison when squeezed. It has an unpleasant, burning taste and it is known to dissuade Grass snakes from eating the newts. The California newt is extremely poisonous, having the same venom, tetrodotoxin, as the pufferfish. The venom is found in the muscles, blood and even in the eggs.

NEWTS FIREPROOF. The Fire salamander was not only supposed by the ancients to be able to live in fire but to put fire out. The myth was popularized by Pliny although he himself used their burnt ashes as medicine. When asbestos was first discovered it was thought to be the hair of the Fire salamander and clothes made of 'salamander skins' were highly valued. Asbestos is now known to be a mixture of minerals that forms soft, silky fibres.

NEW WORLD MONKEYS, a highly successful and diversified group of monkeys of South and Central America established since the Oligocene. The term 'New World monkeys' corresponds to the primate infraorder Platyrrhini, but one family, the Callitrichidae or marmosets, are less obvious 'monkeys', and are therefore treated in a separate article.

The Platyrrhini differ from the Old World monkeys and apes (infraorder Catarrhini) in several respects which, though they may appear trivial, are fundamental for the distinction. Most important is a difference in the form of the nose, which gives the two groups their names. In the 'flat-nosed' Platyrrhini, the nasal septum is very wide, often grooved down the middle and the nostrils are consequently broadly separated and face sideways. In the 'downward-nosed' Catarrhini, however, the nostrils are close together, the septum being narrow, and face forward and downward, the nose being raised somewhat above the muzzle. There are some intermediate forms to be found, especially among the platyrrhines (such as *Aotus*), but on the whole the difference is characteristic and sharp.

The platyrrhines retain the second premolar teeth which, in catarrhines, has been lost as has the first premolar. Thus the dental formula is $\frac{2.1.3.3}{2.1.3.3}$ in platyrrhines as opposed to $\frac{2.1.2.3}{2.1.2.3}$ in catarrhines (marmosets, however, have lost the third molar). This difference permits immediate recognition of the two groups. The molars of platyrrhines are simpler than those of catarrhines, while the incisors are generally unspecialized, except that the lower ones may be somewhat procumbent. The canines are never as large as in male catarrhines and lack the sexual dimorphism seen in all catarrhines except for man and the gibbons.

In the auditory region of the skull there is a rounded, rather inflated bulla—a paper-thin, air-filled sac of bone surrounding the middle ear. Attached to the mouth of the bulla is a ring of bone, the tympanic bone, which may be slightly drawn out into a tube. The tympanic membrane, or ear-drum, is stretched across this. In contrast, catarrhines have no bulla and the tympanic bone is always extended into a long tube.

The hand tends to differ in the two groups. In platyrrhines the thumb is hardly, or not at all, opposable to the fingers, but works together with them: objects are grasped between fingers and palm as readily as between thumb and forefinger; and often they are held with the second and third fingers between which there is as much divergence as between the thumb and the second finger. The great toe, however, is widely divergent in platyrrhines as it is in all catarrhines except man. The nails on the hands and feet of platyrrhines are more rounded, convex and clawlike than are those of catarrhines. Indeed in the marmosets they have become true curved, pointed claws, except on the great toe.

The skulls of New World monkeys are all short and rounded, with a small face and large braincase. Only the Howler monkey deviates somewhat from this pattern. The platyrrhines never have the protruding muzzles or heavy jaws found in Old World monkeys or apes. The brain can reach a state of complexity rivalling that of the apes: the Capuchin monkey tends to do much better in psychological tests than the Rhesus monkey of the Old World and approaches the chimpanzee.

It is among the platyrrhines that the tail reaches its highest specializations among Primates. In *Cebus*, *Lagothrix*, *Ateles* and *Alouatta* it is prehensile. It can grasp objects at its tip and can curl round a branch and support the whole weight of the animal by itself. In the latter three genera, indeed, the undersurface of the tail is strikingly modified, being naked and having a pattern of dermatoglyphics, like 'finger-prints', on the underside of the tip, thereby increasing friction. In *Ateles* the tail is used as a fifth limb and is, indeed, often used in preference to the feet. The tail is even used for holding food in many species. In *Alouatta*, a less active and agile animal, the tail is used mainly as a stabilizing anchor while the animal reaches out for food or for a new handhold. Even in *Cebus*, which lacks the dermatoglyphic modifications, the tail is very powerful although not dexterous, and the monkey can hang by it but can not use it for food carrying. In all New World monkeys, with the sole exception of *Cacajao*, the tail is at least as long as the head and body and acts as a balancing organ, often being held coiled. It is never as reduced as it is in many catarrhines.

Finally, in line with the structure of the nose, New World monkeys have a more highly developed olfactory apparatus than Old World monkeys. Males of many species have a glandular patch on the sternum which they rub against branches to act as scent-markers and marking by means of urine or faeces is also common. This contrasts with catarrhines which communicate almost entirely by sight and sound.

Both Catarrhini and Platyrrhini evolved from a prosimian family, Omomyidae, in the Eocene or Oligocene, but from different branches of this family, in the Old and New worlds respectively. In the New World, about 30–40 million years ago, a branch of the omomyids entered South America where there were no Primates previously. Immediately a radiation into unoccupied niches began, the group diversifying into a number of types which broadly paralleled the Primates of the Old World. Whereas, however, the Old World primate faunal niches were, and are, split between several different groups—superfamilies Lorisoidea, Tarsioidea, Cercopithecoidea and Hominoidea, drawn from both Prosimii and Anthropoidea—the South and Central American niches were all filled from a single group, the Platyrrhini (Ceboidea). The New World situation is thus comparable to that on Madagascar, where a single group of Primates, the lemuriform lemurs, have radiated out and occupied all the niches which it has taken four superfamilies to fill in the Afro-Eurasian land fauna.

Among the platyrrhines there are the following parallel developments to the catarrhines and prosimians: 1 In a nocturnal niche are the Night monkeys *Aotus*. A niche filled by the prosimians in the Old World. 2 In the small, agile niche—fast-breeding, nesting, part insectivore—are the marmosets, corresponding again to some prosimians. 3 In the 'generalized monkey' type of niche—feeding indifferently on fruit and leaves, active, medium-sized—is *Cebus*, the Capuchin monkey, paralleling *Cercopithecus* in the Old World. 4 Among rather slower-moving, leaf-eating monkeys, *Alouatta* in the New World occupies a similar niche to the Colobinae in the Old World. It may be coincidence that both *Alouatta* and *Colobus* have loud territorial vocalizations. 5 *Callicebus* in South America is a strictly territorial monkey, eating fruit and small animals (insects, eggs, young birds), like the gibbon. Both live in mated pairs and have vocal territorial defence. 6 Finally, there is a larger fruit-eater, living in large groups, not territorial but with a highly plastic social structure—the Spider monkey (*Ateles*) which parallels the chimpanzee and, to a lesser extent, the orang-utan.

In each case, the morphological specializations are remarkably similar: specialized digestive tract for the leaf-eaters, big orbits and sophisticated vocal repertoire for the nocturnal forms, long hindlegs and jumping features for the small active forms, and so on. Of course the parallelism must not be carried too far. There are niche overlaps from one fauna to another and some niches are quite unrepresented, notably the savannah-living niche in the New World, which is probably already filled from outside the Primates.

J. Anthony, after a detailed study of the brain, divided the family Cebidae into two full families, Cebidae and Atelidae. The first of these families contained the genera *Callicebus*, *Pithecia*, *Cacajao* and *Cebus*; the second, *Aotus*, *Saimiri*, *Lagothrix*, *Ateles* and *Alouatta*. (Certain genera not generally regarded as valid today have been omitted from these lists.) The difference between the two resides in the opercularization of the insula of the brain. The processes are too complicated to explain in detail, but result in the restriction in the Cebidae of the Sylvian sulcus, separating frontal and temporal lobes of the brain, and its expansion in the Atelidae to fuse with the intraparietal sulcus. Most authorities today would accept the naturalness of Anthony's two groups, while not giving them family rank. Probably also it would be preferable to separate out the three genera with prehensile tails from the two without in the 'Atelidae', and thus make three subfamilies of a single family Cebidae.

Common Spider monkey eating shoots at the summit of a Royal palm. Spider monkeys eat insects, spiders and young birds as well as plants.

One White-throated capuchin grooming another. The name is derived from the similarity of hair on the head to the cowl or capuche of monks.

1 Subfamily Cebinae. Primitive method of opercularization of the insula; tail not modified prehensile. Quadrupedal locomotion.

    Genera: *Callicebus* Titi monkeys
           Pithecia sakis
           Cacajao uakaris
           Cebus capuchins

2 Subfamily Aotinae. 'Advanced' method of opercularization; tail not prehensile; elongate hindlegs, 'springer' mode of locomotion.

    Genera: *Aotus* Night monkey
           Saimiri Squirrel monkey

3 Subfamily Atelinae. 'Advanced' opercularization; tail prehensile, modified; locomotion semibrachiatorial or brachiatorial.

    Genera: *Lagothrix* Woolly monkey
           Ateles Spider monkey
           Alouatta Howler monkey

The mode of locomotion varies from group to group. Erikson has recognized two polar types, which he calls 'springers' and 'swingers and hangers'. Napier and Napier, in their *Handbook of living Primates,* call them simply 'quadrupeds' and 'semibrachiators'. The two classifications overlap somewhat and in reality no hard and fast lines should be drawn. The small, lightly springing Aotinae, however, are markedly 'springers', with short necks; a short thorax (11–12 vertebrae) and long lumbar spine (six to nine vertebrae); the thorax is narrow and deep; the clavicle short; the hindlimbs long (intermembral index—forelimb as a percentage of hindlimb—is 74–78); and the calcaneus or heel-bone is long to provide a long fulcrum for jumping. In these characters they recall the marmosets. At the other end of the scale are the Atelinae, with relatively longer necks; long thorax (13–15 vertebrae); short lumbar spine (four to six vertebrae); broad thorax with a long clavicle; long forelimbs (intermembral index 96–104); and short calcaneum. The two types simply reflect what we may call 'hindlimb' and 'forelimb dominance' respectively. The Cebinae fall neatly in between.

It is interesting to note that the three subfamilies first appear as fossils in the early Miocene: *Cebupithecia* among the Cebinae, *Neosaimiri* as the earliest aotine, and *Homunculus* as a possible (but not confirmed) early ateline. The marmosets first appeared a little earlier, in the late Oligocene, with *Dolichocebus.* The fact that at least two of the three Miocene cebids can be unhesitatingly referred to their subfamilies, and can even be related to one or other of the genera within the respective subfamily, testifies to the very early radiation of the platyrrhines as a whole.

Probably *Callicebus* is the most primitive living genus of the Cebidae, many of its characters recalling the marmosets. Its behaviour is also quite peculiar. The genitalia, as in marmosets, are so clearly homologous between male and female that it is difficult to tell the sex of some individuals. The penis is small and projects from the anterior wall of the scrotum like the clitoris from between the labia. The teeth are primitive. The canines are short and do not project. The auditory bullae are strongly inflated and the mandibular angle projects backwards. On the hands and feet the tactile pads are very distinct. The members of the genus, known as Titi monkeys, are quite small, 11–15 in (28–38 cm) long with a tail 14½–18 in (37–46 cm) in length and they are not very 'monkeylike' in appearance owing to their short limbs, short neck and the rather long rough fur. The mode of locomotion is more

The Squirrel monkey varies greatly in colour. The face is always white and the 'arches' may be rounded 'Roman type' or pointed 'Gothic type'.

like the scurrying of a large squirrel than that of a more typical monkey, but the face is short and monkey-like.

There are two species of titi, which are normally easy to distinguish, but sometimes come to resemble one another. The Dusky titi *Callicebus moloch* is grey, reddish or brown, while the tail is grey or blackish with a tip of grey or grey-black. The throat and chest are similar to the back or are orange in tone. The forearms are grey, red, dark brown or black. The Collared titi or Widow monkey *C. torquatus* is reddish to black. The tail is blackish with a tip of the same colour. The throat has an orange patch or ruff, sharply defined from the chest and the forearms are black and, except in one race, the hands are white. The Widow monkey has a restricted range mainly north of the Amazon, in tropical forest, but the Dusky titi is widespread, from the tropical forests south of the Amazon (and a little to the north of it, overlapping with the Widow monkey) to the dry forests of southeastern Brazil.

Titis live in mated pairs. Characteristically, they rest side by side on a branch with their tails hanging down behind, and intertwined. The body is hunched with the hands and feet brought together on the branch, the great toe grasping the branch, the thumb not. The most recent offspring of each pair inhabit the same territory, thus a group numbers from two to four animals. The pairs appear to be permanent, or at least

long-lasting. At daybreak all the members of the group, both adult and subadult, begin to call, in a series of rapidly increasing moans, with a sharp clicking noise at the end of each. These calls continue for a minute or more and may end in a series of slowing, intense 'o-o-o' sounds. The animals begin to feed, moving out towards their territorial boundaries where daily conflicts occur. The members of each pair sit side by side, the opposing pair opposite, one of the pair calling and the other member ultimately joining in. Mason, who studied the titi in its natural habitat, could not determine whether the male or the female was wont to begin the calling. While calling the titis arch their backs and lash their tails and there may be a chase with a quick withdrawal, but one male may chase the other deep into its territory, where the stronger animal mates with its rival's female consort. After these 'battles', they continue feeding within their own territories.

Mason also describes a gobbling call, like a turkey's, which is given simultaneously by all the groups in an area. It lasts for 10 sec and is repeated at 5–10 min intervals, with a series of short whistles before and after it. The cause of these calls has not been ascertained. The calls of the two species of titi monkey are reported to differ slightly.

Titis have a single young at a birth, but this, as in marmosets, is carried around mainly by the father, being given to the female only for suckling. The breeding

season, at least in Colombia, is restricted to the winter, from December to March.

Sakis and uakaris are quite closely related, although they undoubtedly form two separate genera and there are a number of things in common. The lower incisors in both groups are elongated, compressed and slightly procumbent, recalling those of lemurs; the canines are long, tusk-like and divergent—more so than in other New World monkeys. The nasal septum is exceptionally wide. The shafts of the ribs are expanded, making the thorax a tough, well-protected barrel. The curious hand-posture, with the first two digits opposed to the rest, is very common in this group.

The Saki monkeys, genus *Pithecia*, have long tails of 26–30 vertebrae. The skull is rather extended and low and the coat is long and lank, more woolly underneath. The face too is hairy and there is a whorl on the crown from which a hood of hair may arise. There is a beard on the chin. They are larger than titis, with a head and body length of 12–16 in (30–40 cm) and a tail of up to 20 in (50 cm). Within the genus there are two subgenera: the nominate subgenus *Pithecia* has a whorl on the back of the head and a short beard; the subgenus *Chiropotes* has the whorl on the top of the head, a very long beard, the elongation of the incisors is more marked and there are usually 14 ribs instead of 12 or 13.

In *Pithecia* there are two species. The extraordinary White-faced saki *Pithecia (P.) pithecia* has a short coat and short hairs on the front of the crown so that the forehead is not covered by them. The sexual dimorphism is quite remarkable, the male being black with a white face, the female brown with a blackish face and a white stripe on either side of the nose, extending down to the chin. It is hardly surprising that the two sexes were for a long time thought to be two different species. This species is found north of the Amazon, as far as the Guianas. The second species is the Monk saki *P. (P.) monachus* which has a longer, coarser pelage and hairs that partly cover the face. There is no sexual dimorphism, both sexes being greyish to black and closely resembling the female of the White-faced saki except that the two white streaks do not extend down to the chin. Also the underside is yellow or red, not black. The Monk saki is found north of the Amazon, but extends west of the White-

New World monkeys

faced saki's range to Colombia and just into the Guianas.

In the second subgenus there are also two species. The Black or Humboldt's saki *P. (Chiropotes) satanas* has a long bushy beard and twin bouffant tufts on the crown. The face is nearly bare. Different races are black or golden brown with only the head black. This species is found in the same territory as the two previous ones. The White-nosed saki *P. (C.) albinasa* is not very closely related. Its beard is shorter, there is a whorl on the head and the face is hairy. The colour is generally black, but the nose and upper lip are bright red with short white hairs. This is the only species of saki with a range south of the Amazon.

Sakis are said to live in the shrub layers of the forest and to be especially common on the savannah borders, but this description has not been substantiated by a detailed study. Humboldt described how the species named after him drinks daintily with cupped hands, being careful not to spill any water on its beard.

The related uakaris, genus *Cacajao,* have short tails with only 15–18 vertebrae. The skull is higher and rounder and the orbits are round instead of high and narrow. The pelage is long and loose and sparser on the underside. Hair is almost completely absent from the face and the face also lacks subcutaneous fat, looking bony and starved even when the animal is in the best of health. There are no whorls or partings on the head and uakaris are on average larger than sakis, with a head and body length of $12\frac{1}{2}$–$18\frac{1}{2}$ in (32–47 cm) but with a tail of only 4–7 in (10–18 cm). The more familiar of the two species is the Bald uakari *Cacajao calvus* from the upper Amazon region in Brazil and Peru, in which the head is nearly bare, becoming completely so with age, and the face is bright red in sunlight (fading, if denied access to sunlight, to a pale pink). Different races of this species have red or whitish coats. The adult male develops enormous jaw muscles which attach in the midline of the skull behind the forehead, creating very noticeable twin bulges.

The Black-headed uakari *C. melanocephalus* is much less frequent in captivity than the Bald species. It is black, with a black face and the forepart of the crown is hairy. The lower part of the back is chestnut brown, as are the hindlimbs, and the coat is coarser than in the Bald uakari. This rare form inhabits the extreme southwest of Venezuela and adjoining regions in the north of Brazil.

Although they look bulky and thickset, uakaris are very lean and spidery under their long shaggy hair. They are agile and versatile, running, leaping horizontally or swinging by their arms.

The Capuchin monkeys, genus *Cebus,* are

perhaps the best-known of all the New World monkeys. They are medium-sized, brownish short-haired monkeys, 15–21 in (38–53 cm) long, with tails somewhat longer than this. The tail is hairy throughout but none the less prehensile. Although they are probably the most 'highly evolved' of the Cebinae, certainly the most intelligent, Capuchin monkeys retain some surprisingly primitive features. For example, they have mystacial vibrissae (tactile hairs on the upper lip) and a single supraorbital vibrissa on each side. The baculum (penis bone) is rather longer than in other platyrrhines. The labia majora are swollen and closely resemble a scrotum, as in the marmosets and Titi monkeys. The braincase, however, is rounded and the face reduced. The molars are quadritubercular with slightly developed cross-crests, which are advanced features.

White-throated capuchin searching for insects in the trunk of a palm tree. They also eat leaves, shoots and small birds and mammals.

Opposite. Male Mantled howler monkey resting on a branch. Howlers are the largest of the New World monkeys. Their calls can be heard for several miles.

The most distinctive species of the genus is the Tufted capuchin *Cebus apella*. In this species, there are tufts of hair on the forehead, usually a pair but sometimes a single ridge of hair. There is a dark brown cap on the head with a rounded border. The skull is high and vaulted, the brow-ridges weak and in old males the jaw muscles tend to meet over the top of the skull and form a sagittal crest between them. This species, with its rather cross-looking, scowling face, is common throughout the forests of South America.

The untufted group of capuchins are more restricted, not found south of the River Amazon. They have no frontal tufts but females may have an eyebrow brush of hairs, or long stiff hairs radiating from the middle of the forehead. The face, throat, sides of the neck, shoulders, chest and inner surfaces of the arms are pale, while on the crown is a dark cap which is often pointed in front. The skulls of the untufted forms are lower and flatter with stronger brow ridges and never develop sagittal crests. These are more active animals, with longer spines (19–20 thoraco-lumbar vertebrae instead of 18). There are three species: the White-throated capuchin *Cebus capucinus* from Central America, western Colombia and the Pacific coast of Ecuador, which is black with the pale areas white; the White-fronted capuchin *C. albifrons* from northeastern South America, as far south as the Amazon, which has the black replaced by yellowish to dark brown; and the Weeper capuchin *C. nigrivittatus* which replaces the last in the Guianas and extends into Venezuela, Colombia and Brazil, and has a much smaller, wedge-shaped cap and a less contrasting, more restricted white area, with a coarser brownish coat.

Strangely, little is known about these common and conspicuous monkeys in the wild. They are said to live in fairly large troops and to feed mainly on fruit with some leaves, although this is disputed.

The second subfamily, the Aotinae, contains a pair of primitive and widespread, but monotypic, genera with long, low skulls, tritubercular cheek teeth and large orbits which are close together. Both are very common and used in medical laboratories as experimental animals, as well as being kept as pets.

The genus *Aotus* contains a single species,

the Night monkey or douroucouli *Aotus trivirgatus*. It is the only nocturnal species of higher Primate and thus occupies a position in the South American ecology similar to the lorises and tarsiers in the Old World. The face is very small and orthognathous, and the orbits are very large—their combined width is greater than the length of the skull.

The external eyes of Night monkeys are also very large. The retina consists of rods only, suitable for nocturnal discrimination, and has no cones (for colour vision). The ears are small and hidden in the fur, but hearing is extremely acute. The nails are compressed and claw-like and the hands and feet have well-defined, coarsely ridged pads for friction. The nasal septum is narrower than in other platyrrhines. The fur is very thick and soft, grey-brown with bands on the body. There are prominent white rings round the eyes, which are larger above the eyes, and three stripes from the forehead to the crown. The animal is smaller than any other platyrrhine, except perhaps the titi, with a head and body length of 9½–19 in (24–48 cm) and a tail length of 9½–17 in (24–44 cm), but the giant forms are relatively rare.

The douroucouli occupies approximately the same position along the aotine-ateline line of descent as the Titi monkey does along the cebine. It is primitive in its general morphology and recalls marmosets in many features. Thus it has a 'springer' type of build and locomotion, with a very short neck, long strong lumbar region and very elongated hindfeet. The scrotum, however, is pendulous, as it is in most platyrrhines, and there is no baculum. The incisor teeth are specialized, broad and concave, while the molars have a well-marked cingulum. These are advanced characters. The visual cortex of the brain is very large, causing the braincase to project well backward.

Douroucoulis become active a little before dusk and again around dawn. When it becomes really dark they are as inactive as during the day. They sleep by day in a hole in a tree, and at night never venture to the ground, living at 20–100 ft (6–30 m) in the trees. They live, like titis and marmosets, in mated pairs with one or two young, but the pair is less cohesive than in Titi monkeys, often straying some distance apart. There is also less mutual grooming (except in courtship) and considerable urine-marking occurs, implying relative lack of direct contact during waking hours. Since visual communication is of little use in darkness, there are few facial gestures, but, as Moynihan has emphasized, the vocalizations are very elaborate: according to him, each portion of a given call has a distinct significance instead of a single, less well-defined call carrying the whole message. This quasi-linguistic situation is an adaptation to night-living, since vocalizations cannot be reinforced by visual signals as they are in diurnal Primates.

Again like Titi monkeys, douroucoulis are territorial. In contrast, however, the territorial displays are largely silent, with arching of the back followed by actual attack, not redirected aggression onto branches or in the form of jumping about noisily. The opponents sit opposite one another, jabbing with their hands. The apparent victor often gives what has been described as a 'triumph call', a loud resonant grunt ending in a roar. Territory is marked mainly by means of urinating on the hands and feet and rubbing them on the branches. As in titis, there is a single infant which is at first carried by the mother. After about nine days the father does most of the carrying. Also like Titi monkeys and marmosets, douroucoulis are 'springers', that is they have an almost tarsier-like 'vertical clinging' type of locomotion. Often from vertical supports, they make considerable leaps, pushing off with the hindfeet. The diet is herbivorous and partly insectivorous.

The Squirrel monkey *Saimiri sciurea* is small like the Night monkey but less thickly furred and stockily built. The head and body length varies from 8½–15½ in (22–40 cm), with a tail of 14–18 in (36–46 cm). The build is lanky and long-legged, the back often carried arched, and the tail curves down, forwards and upwards again and is often held in a coil. This enables it to obtain a partially prehensile grip at times. The general colour is greenish with a white face and black cap, but the muzzle is black, including the nostrils. Different races vary considerably from this, but all have more or less similar patterns: some are more reddish than green, and others lack the black cap. On the face, the white arches above the brows may be either rounded ('Roman' type)

or pointed above ('Gothic' type). These two types reportedly differ somewhat in their behaviour-patterns, according to MacLean who states that the Gothic type commonly exhibits a penile erection, the common threat/dominance gesture, on encountering its image in a mirror, which the Roman type does not. The two represent clearly defined geographic races from Peru and north-western Brazil respectively. Squirrel monkeys are found all over the South American forests as far as 11°S and also occur in Central America. In the Llanos de Guarayos they reach 17°S.

The Squirrel monkey has an exceptionally long skull with a low narrow braincase bulging backwards. The orbits meet in the mid-line and the septum between them is perforated. It has longer canines than most platyrrhines and the upper molars are tritubercular. Supraorbital and mystacial vibrissae are present.

This species, one of the most abundant of all platyrrhines, is most common in gallery forest and on the forest edge. It lives at all levels, in the closed canopy as well as the emergent crowns, and in the shrub layer, descending even to the ground. Its diet consists mainly of fruit, but many insects are eaten also. The troops are large, with a marked rank order in both sexes. Aggression between individuals in common in the form of threat or penile display in males, but overt fighting rarely occurs. At rest a Squirrel monkey wraps its tail around its body. When sleeping, individuals huddle together with their heads between their knees. Breeding is non-seasonal and a single young is born, which is carried by either parent, clinging unaided even when asleep. Sometimes a parent is observed walking bipedally while carrying an infant.

The group containing the Woolly monkey, Spider monkey and Howler monkey is distinguished by the very distinctive feature of the naked, specialized tail-tip. There are also skull features common to all three, and all have a tendency towards brachiation as a dominant way of life. In all the arms are long (the intermembral index being 98–99 in the Woolly and Howler monkeys and 103 in the Spider monkey). The hand is elongated in comparison with the foot, and the thumb is short compared with the palm and the other fingers, and does not work in opposition to them. The hand is thus strongly specialized as a hook, as is common in brachiators, and indeed in the Spider monkey—the only one of the three whose normal mode of locomotion is brachiation—the thumb is completely absent, or at the very most represented by a mere nubbin.

Pigmy marmosets *Cebuella pygmaea*. Although New World monkeys of the infraorder Platyrrhini, marmosets are less 'monkeylike' than the others.

The Woolly monkeys, genus *Lagothrix,* are the least specialized of the three genera. The thumb is not very reduced and the arms are not so elongated as in the Spider monkey. There is no elaboration of the vocal apparatus as in the Howler. The build is robust and the belly is rounded and prominent. The skin is jet black. The coat is soft and woolly, forming a dense mat. The penis is short and the clitoris of the female is at least as large, with prominent labia majora. The third molar is very reduced, even more so than in most platyrrhines, and has only two cusps, on both upper and lower jaws. There are two species: Humboldt's woolly monkey *L. lagotricha* from the lowland forests of the middle and upper Amazon, and Hendee's woolly monkey *L. flavicauda* from the slopes of the Peruvian Andes. The latter is very rare and only three or four specimens of it are known.

Humboldt's woolly monkey varies in colour from pale brown or pale grey to blackish, the head often being darker than the body. Hendee's woolly monkey is deep mahogany in colour with a buff patch on the nose. The hair on the scrotum and the underside of the distal half of the tail is yellow. The skull is rather different, being narrower but with wide zygomatic arches and very strong supraorbital ridges. This monkey is also larger with a shorter tail, the head and body length being 20–21 in (51–54 cm) with a tail of 22–24 in (56–61 cm). Humboldt's woolly monkey has a head and body length of 16½–21 in (42–54 cm) with a tail of 22½–29 in (57–73 cm).

Humboldt's woolly monkey prefers for-ests in somewhat swampy country, living mostly in the high canopy, but descending to the shrub layer sometimes to feed. The food is mainly fruit and leaves. Much hard-shelled fruit is eaten which is peeled with the sharp canines and caniniform anterior lower premolar. The troops are up to 50 in size, although their structure is not known. Solitary males have been seen and probably the social system will prove to be similar to that of the Spider monkey. Woolly monkeys move rather slowly as a rule, both brachiating and quadrupedally. When frightened the troop moves fast, swinging along and often dropping through the branches to cross gaps in the canopy—no horizontal leaps have been recorded. On the ground they walk on all fours with their fingers flexed. Young, one per birth, are born after a gestation of 225 days. They suckle for twelve months or more and are not sexually mature for four years.

The Spider monkeys, genus *Ateles,* are more slenderly built than the Woolly monkeys, with long limbs especially the arms, but they too are pot-bellied. The fur is rather wiry (at least it is never as woolly as in the Woolly monkeys) and is sparser below, The face is often only patchily or lightly pigmented. The penis is short and the clitoris is very long. This apparently parodoxical state of affairs provides the best means of sexing the Spider monkey. The third molar is even more reduced than in the Woolly monkey and is actually absent in about 15% of cases.

There are two species of Spider monkey. The Common spider monkey *Ateles paniscus* has wiry hair and is very slenderly built. The incisors are large, especially the central

Bald uakari showing short tail. Its face is pale away from sunlight, but crimson in the sun.

upper ones. It is usually black to buff, sometimes particoloured or pale below, but one race is black with a red face. This species is found in South America from the upper Amazon tributaries into Central America and Mexico as far as 23°N. The so-called Woolly spider monkey *A. arachnoides* of southeast Brazil has sometimes been placed in a separate genus, *Brachyteles*. It is more thickset than the common species with more woolly hair, although nothing like the Woolly monkey. The incisors are rather small and the colour is yellow-brown to ashy-brown, often darker on the head and neck. Both species are about 15–25 in (38–63 cm) in length, with tails of 23–35 in (58–90 cm), but the Woolly spider monkey weighs about 21 lb (9·5 kg) as compared with the 12–15 lb (5·5–6·9 kg) of the Common, being more robustly built.

Spider monkeys also live in the high canopy, feeding entirely on fruit. They are very selective feeders, sniffing fruit to see if it is ripe and sometimes biting into it and then dropping it without eating much. They sleep in big groups of up to 100, at least in some areas. These break up during the day into smaller groups. The most cohesive are the groups of females with young, which may or may not be accompanied by an adult male. Under most conditions, males are antagonistic to one another in the presence of females. There is a weakly marked rank order among the females. Males are dominant to females and when present they threaten intruders with barks, breaking branches and dropping them onto the foe, often also defaecating onto them. Males often wander by themselves. Their home range varies with the food supply and there can be as many as 200 per sq mile (per 2·7 km²). They walk either quadrupedally or bipedally, or brachiate or leap (usually

simply dropping) as much as 25 ft (7·5 m). At night they sleep curled up, in a sitting position (often two or three together), with the tail curled round a support.

Eisenberg and Kuehn have described the 'grappling' of Spider monkeys, which is probably a type of courtship. The pair push each other away and pull back together again, with much biting, slapping and chasing, sometimes roaring loudly. They then settle down, often with the female sitting on the male's lap facing him, and begin to manipulate each other's genitalia with their hands, feet and mouths. Mating probably takes place from behind, and certainly happens at night.

Grooming is an activity performed mainly by high-ranking animals, but mothers and infants are a focus for grooming as well. Gestation lasts 139 days. The young, one at a birth, weighs 7% of its mother's weight. At first the young is carried on the abdomen, then on the mother's back, with its tail curled round that of its mother. The offspring play a great deal among themselves. Spider monkeys are gentle, unaggressive animals and there are few fights within their groups.

The genus *Alouatta* contains the Howler monkeys. Less closely related to the Woolly and Spider monkeys than they are to each other, they are so highly modified in the vocal apparatus and surrounding structures that it is difficult to tell exactly how close they are to any other forms. The skull is robust and long, with a small, low braincase with strong sagittal and nuchal crests. The foramen magnum faces backwards, indicating the animal's basically quadrupedal posture. The hyoid bone, in the throat, is enlarged and hollow, making a resonating chamber for the voice in both sexes, but much more markedly so in the male. Be-

cause of the form of the hyoid the whole skull is grossly modified as described, and the partially leaf-eating diet accounts for parallel specializations, such as the expanded jaw angle both for muscle insertion and for protection of the hyoid. Externally, there is a thick beard at the throat and jaw angles. The canines are rather large and the third molars are very large, being quite different to those of the other Atelinae. The body is thickset and robust. The Howler is the largest of the Ceboidea, with a head and body length of 19½–28 in (50–71 cm) and a tail of 19–28 in (48–71 cm), just slightly less than the head and body. The fingernails, like those of the Woolly spider monkey, are rather convex. The genitalia are modified as social signals and the scrotum is very large, pendulous and brilliant white. Correspondingly the labia majora are elongated and white, with black borders which make them even more conspicuous. The penis is peculiar as its glans is very little differentiated and entirely covered by the prepuce. According to Anthony, the brain is much less advanced than that of the other Atelinae and only a little more complex than that of *Aotus*. Indeed it is possible to suppose from skull structure that *Aotus* and *Alouatta* are perhaps not too distantly related, and that the relation between the Aotinae and Atelinae, already discernible through similarity of brain structure, may be quite close.

There are five species of Howlers. In the four northern ones the sexes are similar in colour. The Red howler monkey *Alouatta seniculus* (South America, north of the Amazon and Madeira rivers) is red, while the Brown howler *A. fusca* (Brazil coast from Bahia to Santa Catarina) is brownish and the Red-handed howler *A. belzebul* (South of the Amazon in the interior of Brazil) is black or brownish with red hands, feet and end of tail. The Mantled howler *A. villosa* (Central America and western Colombia) is black and long-haired, usually with a long yellowish flank-fringe. In the southernmost species, the Black howler *A. caraya*, from the interior of southern Brazil, Paraguay and northern Argentina, the male is black with light brown tones, and the female is yellowish. These five species differ in the form of the hyoid, that of the Mantled howler being smallest and least specialized, and that of the Red howler by far the largest, most inflated and most evolved, measuring 1½–2 in (3·8–5·5 cm) in width and 2–3 in (5·5–8 cm) in depth in the male. In the female the volume is only ¼ that of the male's. The voice of the Red howler carries for 3 miles (4·8 km).

Howlers live in groups of 15–20, at least in the Mantled species, with a proportion of three and a half females to one male, but nearly always more than a single male in the group. They are entirely arboreal. They move slowly, both quadrupedally and by brachiation, occasionally leaping but usually making sure to have a firm handhold on one branch before leaving go with the feet and tail from the other. When crossing gaps in the foliage, large Howler monkeys will allow themselves to be used as a bridge by juveniles, who walk across them as they cling with hands and tail. When walking through the trees, the adult male goes in front and the whole troop follows in the same path, conga-style. They feed in the high canopy and are even more highly selective of their food than Spider monkeys, up to $\frac{1}{3}$ of the food plucked being dropped, half-eaten. Food is held between the fingers and palm, or between the second and third fingers.

Howler groups are territorial, and distance between them is maintained by howling. The smaller-hyoid northern species, living in lush tropical rain-forest, finds sufficient food within a relatively small area, but the Red howler, with its immensely powerful voice, has a much wider range and territory in the drier hardwood forest. Howling precedes early morning movement, being initiated by the leading male and taken up by other troop members. As the animal howls the jaws are opened and thrust forward with lips protruded, saliva flowing copiously. When two troops meet at the territorial boundary a vocal 'battle' ensues, both troops howling, breaking off some branches and shaking others violently, but very rarely is there any fighting. Although territorial boundaries are stable over short periods, in the long term the larger troops, the leading males of which are stronger and can keep a larger number of animals together, manage to shift boundaries in their favour so as to include not merely a larger area but more particularly an area with more abundant food for the particular season of the year.

Intruders on the ground, such as man, are met with showers of branches, urine and faeces. Defaecation seems to be, at least in part, ritualized, so that when one individual does it the rest are encouraged to follow suit. Greeting behaviour consists of rhythmic tongue movements, which between male and female are invitations to mate. Between males of the same troop, cohesion is maintained by gurgling noises. Females in oestrus are promiscuous, mating with several males in turn, with tongue clicks before each act. When giving birth the female sits flexed and seems to assist with her hands. The infant clings to its mother's belly and later, after a month or so, moves onto her back. Lactation lasts for a year. The young play very little, for they are as ponderous as their elders, but the whole troop is very solicitous of them, not only providing a 'bridge' for them but even going down to retrieve them when they fall.

The Monk saki moves on all fours but sometimes runs along branches erect, arms extended.

Howlers are surprisingly delicate animals for such a robust species, but like the colobus and langurs, the leaf-eaters of the Old World, they do not do well in captivity and soon die. They rarely live more than a few years outside the tropics. INFRAORDER : Platyrrhini, ORDER : Primates, CLASS : Mammalia.   C.P.G.

NEW ZEALAND FAUNA. New Zealand, consisting of two major and numerous smaller islands, lies in the South Pacific Ocean 1,000 ml (1,600 km) to the southeast of Australia. Although only 103,416 sq ml (268,882 sq km) in total area the main islands of New Zealand extend over a distance of 1,000 ml (1,600 km) from latitude 34° 24′ S. to 47° 17′ S. The topography of the country is mountainous, hilly or rolling; only 7% is flat. The climate is essentially maritime, characterized by rapid weather changes, an abundance of sunshine, frequent though not excessive rainfall and a small range in seasonal temperatures. Vegetation prior to European settlement in 1840 consisted of subalpine scrub or fellfield high on the mountains, dense rain-forest or scrub in the humid areas, and tussock grassland on the drier areas. Introduced pasture has today largely replaced the native vegetation.

Since the Cretaceous Period, over 60 million years ago, New Zealand has been isolated from neighbouring land masses. Terrestrial animals which evolved since the Cretaceous have therefore been impeded in colonizing New Zealand. The native land fauna therefore contains relatively few species, with groups such as the amphibia, reptiles and mammals being poorly represented. Nevertheless, many of the native animals are among the strangest and oldest of the world's living fauna.

Indigenous land mammals consist only of two species of bat, the Long-tailed bat *Chalinolobus morio* and the now rare Short-tailed bat *Mystacops tuberculatus*. The latter is a remnant of an ancient more widespread fauna which is today found only in New Zealand. Although the large expanse of ocean surrounding it has formed an impenetrable barrier against the colonization of New Zealand by land mammals it has itself provided a suitable habitat for aquatic mammals. Thus the coastal waters have a considerable fauna of whales and seals. These mammals once formed the basis for a prosperous oil and fur industry. With the European settlement many exotic mammals, which are today free ranging and widespread throughout the country, were introduced, either for game or sentiment. These include the Australian wallaby and opossum, numerous species of deer from Europe, America and Asia, together with the stoat, ferret, weasel, rabbit, hare, hedgehog, pig, goat, cattle, sheep and horse: the rabbit, Red deer and opossum became serious pests in New Zealand until controlled by myxomatosis (in the rabbit), shooting and trapping.

The native bird fauna has descended from an Australian–Melanesian stock. Many New Zealand birds are only slightly different from those in Australia. Therefore it seems probable that during recent geological times Australian species assisted by a prevailing wind, have crossed the dividing seas to colonize New Zealand. Amongst its most remarkable land birds are the flightless kiwi *Apteryx* spp, kakapo *Strigops habroptilus*, weka *Gallirallus greyi* and takahe *Notornis mantelli*. The kiwi excepted, loss of flight has occurred only after the species' arrival in New Zealand, possibly as a consequence of the absence of land mammals. Categorizing the native fauna according to habitat, four groups are realized. Forest birds: the 'wattle birds' (tui *Prosthemadera novaeseelandiae*, kokako *Callaeas* spp, saddleback *Creadion carunculatus*), wrens and thrushes, which have no close relatives elsewhere in the world today; kaka *Nestor* spp, stitchbird *Notiomystis cincta* and bellbird *Anthornis melanura*. The essentially open country birds: harrier *Circus approximans*, pipit *Anthus novaeseelandiae*, quail *Coturnix novaezelandiae* and kea *Nestor notabilis*. The waterfowl: Brown and Grey duck *Elasmonetta chlorotis*, *Anas superciliosa*, scaup *Fuligula novaeseelandiae*, pukeko *Porphyrio melanotus* and rare White heron *Casmerodius albus*. The sea birds: essentially coastal gulls, terns, shags, penguins and petrels. In association with certain of the originally forest inhabiting native birds, many species of European and North American birds of parks, orchards and pastoral lands, including thrush, blackbird, chaffinch, House sparrow, starling, pheasant and Californian quail, are a familiar and well established element in the present-day landscape.

Reptiles are represented by some few species of skink, gecko and the tuatara *Sphenodon punctatus*. New Zealand geckos and tuatara are unique as the former are the only viviparous members of the world-wide family, Gekkonidae, while the tuatara is the sole surviving member of the order Rhynchocephalia, other members of which became extinct during the Mesozoic Period.

The amphibian fauna is limited to three species of the indigenous genus *Leiopelma* and three introduced species of Tree frogs *Hyla. Leiopelma*, restricted to New Zealand, exhibits some of the most primitive skeletal and anatomical features of any known frog or toad.

Thirty of the forty species of freshwater fish are indigenous. Most numerous are species of the families Galaxidae and Gobeomorphidae. Game fish, such as Brown trout, Rainbow trout, Quinnat salmon, Atlantic salmon, perch and carp have been introduced, for the pursuit of sport, and today abound in the many lakes and rivers throughout most of New Zealand.

The terrestrial invertebrate fauna is basically a peripheral one of the Australian region. The most important elements because of their archaism are *Peripatus novaezelandiae* and two genera of snails *Paryphanta*, exclusive to New Zealand, and *Placostylus*.

The prolongation of New Zealand over thirteen degrees of latitude, together with it straddling two large and distinctive water masses, subtropical and subantarctic, gives New Zealand a rich and varied marine fauna. Almost 25% of the species of fish are endemic to New Zealand, a slightly larger proportion are Australasian, while the remainder are

more cosmopolitan occurring in all but the coldest seas. Shellfish, similarly exhibit a high degree of endemism, together with species from subtropical and subantarctic regions.
J.H.M.

NIBBLERS, small perch-like marine fishes, the common name of which derives from their constant nibbling behaviour. Widespread over the Indo-Pacific region, they rarely grow to more than 20 in (51 cm) in length and are most commonly found in shallow, rocky areas where they nibble at small organisms and plants on rocks and on the seabed. The blackfish *Girella tricuspidata* is almost entirely herbivorous and lives in huge shoals in weedy areas. It is common around the Australian coasts, even entering rivers, and it is an important food fish. It has an oval body with one long dorsal fin (the first part having spiny rays) and a short anal fin. The oval body is brownish-grey above, lighter below, with about six dark vertical bars on the flanks. The lips, as in all nibblers, can be drawn back to expose the teeth. This species can attain 28 in (71 cm) but most specimens are about half that length. FAMILY: Girellidae, ORDER: Perciformes, CLASS: Pisces.

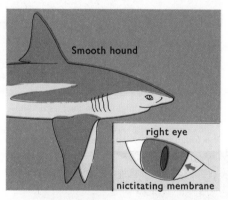

A nictitating membrane is present in many sharks, including the Smooth hound *Mustelus* and the Blue sharks *Carcharhinus*. Red arrow shows direction in which the membrane is drawn across the eye (fish facing to the left).

NICTITATING MEMBRANE, or third eyelid, a membrane found in many vertebrates that can be drawn horizontally over the eyeball. It is found in some mammals such as the platypus, the marsupials and the horse, and in carnivores where it cannot be drawn completely over the eye. In man, it is probably represented by the *plica semilunaris*, the pink triangle of flesh in the corner of the eye. The nictitating membrane is found in reptiles and is well-developed in birds. In birds the nictitating membrane lubricates and cleans the eyeball without the necessity of blinking and it is thought that it is drawn over the eye during flight to prevent drying up. Some diving birds, such as auks

and divers, have a clear window in the nictitating membrane which acts as a lens making up for the loss of focussing at the cornea when underwater.

NIDICOLOUS, the term given to those birds in which the young are hatched blind and helpless and remain in the nest for some time as nestlings in the complete care of their parents. All the perching birds, Passeriformes, including the sparrows, songbirds and crows, have nidicolous young.

NIDIFUGOUS, the term given to those birds which can leave the nest almost as soon as they have dried after hatching, e.g. ducklings and the chicks of pheasants. Nidifugous young have well-developed legs and sense organs and are covered in down. Their parents act largely as mobile brooders and protectors.

NIGHT ADDERS, a dozen species of *vipers of the genus *Causus* ranging from the Sahara to South Africa, with one species in Israel and Sinai. They are usually regarded as the most primitive of the vipers, their fangs being shorter and cruder than in typical vipers. FAMILY: Viperidae, ORDER: Squamata, CLASS: Reptilia.

NIGHT HERONS, wading birds closely related to, but smaller than, other herons. They are mainly active at night. The typical race of Night heron, the Black-crowned night heron *Nycticorax nycticorax*, has a range extending across southern Europe, Asia and Africa, with small colonies farther north. *Birds of the Soviet Union* mentions colonies exceeding 2,500 and states that there it is the most commonly seen heron. First recorded in Britain in 1782, the Black-crowned night heron is now an irregular visitor. It is replaced in the Americas by geographical races making it one of the most cosmopolitan of birds. Three other species are American and a fourth, the Nankeen night heron *N. caledonius*, is found in Australia, the Philippines and Polynesia. Another Old World genus includes species which boom like bitterns. The boatbill also belongs to the same subfamily.

The Black-crowned night heron is about 24 in (60 cm) long. Juvenile plumage, present for two years, is entirely different from that of the adult, having upper surfaces chocolate-brown streaked with buffish-white and longitudinally streaked grey underparts. It is easily distinguished from a bittern, however, as it habitually perches in trees. The crown and back of adults are black with a greenish gloss, the forehead and throat are pure white and the rest of the plumage is dove-grey or white tinged with grey. The sexes are similar in appearance. On assuming adult plumage they acquire pale cream plumes, usually three, which fall from the nape and may measure 8 in (20 cm). Except when wind-blown, or at a nest, these are held together and resemble a single plume. The large eyes have crimson irises. The bill is black and shorter than that of a typical heron while the yellow legs, which may redden at nesting time, are comparatively short giving the bird a characteristically hunched appearance when perching.

Throughout the daylight hours the birds perch gregariously in trees, becoming active soon after sundown, when they fly to the marshes looking, with their rounded wings, very owl-like. They feed on small fishes, amphibians and a variety of other animals, including small mammals.

They breed in large colonies, sometimes consisting of several heron species. Said to be very tame, those nesting with Little egrets in stone-pines in the Rhône delta remained on the nests until approached very closely by the author. The nests of sticks are small compared with the size of the bird and are sometimes so flimsy that the contents are visible from below. Many colonies are in low bushes—alders, tamarisks and sometimes even in reed-beds. Pair-formation follows the general pattern of the Grey heron, the male taking up a position in a potential site and advertising for a mate. According to Konrad Lorenz it is at this stage that the purpose of the plumes becomes apparent. They are raised in an 'appeasement ceremony' admitting the female to the immediate nesting-site. Four eggs are an average clutch, incubated by both parents for three weeks. Feeding the young by regurgitation is also shared. In the northern part of its range the species is migratory. FAMILY: Ardeidae, ORDER: Ciconiiformes, CLASS: Aves. F.A.L.

When singing, the nightingale flutters its wings and tail.

Night heron, easily distinguishable from Grey herons by its black plumage and short neck and legs. It is found over Europe, Asia and Africa and occasionally visits the British Isles.

NIGHTINGALE *Luscinia megarhynchos,* bird of the thrush subfamily Turdinae, renowned for its outstandingly beautiful song. The nightingale is a rather ordinary-looking bird, some 6½ in (16·5 cm) long, warm brown in colour, lighter beneath, and with a chestnut-brown tail. It has a southwestern palearctic distribution, including much of Europe, and its preferred habitat is deciduous woodland with dense undergrowth and a rich humus layer on the ground in which it searches for insects and other invertebrate food. It is frequently found in damp places. It nests near the ground, usually laying four or five eggs which are incubated for 13–14 days.

Some other closely-related species are also known as nightingales, particularly the Thrush nightingale *L. luscinia,* which overlaps with the nightingale in western Asia and which also has an outstanding song. FAMILY: Muscicapidae, ORDER: Passeriformes, CLASS: Aves.

NIGHTINGALES BANNED. The poets are full of praise for the sweetness of the nightingale's song:

> I grant the linnet, lark, and bullfinch sing,
>
> But best the dear good angel of the spring,
>
> The nightingale
>
>   Ben Jonson

This praise is probably due more to imagination than the reality of living in nightingale country, for there are many accounts of people being driven to despair by the continual chorus, that makes sleep or study impossible. That peace-loving, meek saint, Edward the Confessor, prayed that nightingales might disturb his vigils no more and even the poets say that the nightingale sings with a thorn pressed against its breast to keep it awake.

> But leaning on a thorn her dainty chest
> For fear soft sleep should steal into her breast
>
>   Giles Fletcher

NIGHTJARS, birds of the family Caprimulgidae, otherwise known as goatsuckers, a term favoured in the Americas and derived from a myth that these birds drank milk from nanny goats. There are some 67 species, usually nocturnal, insectivorous and well-camouflaged, covering most parts of the world excepting high latitudes, New Zealand and some oceanic islands.

In the Old World the term nightjar is generally restricted to the Old World species, all of which belong to the subfamily Caprimulginae. Other species of this subfamily live in America and several of them have some general name which is derived from the bird's call, for example the whip-poor-will *Caprimulgus vociferus* of North and Central America, chuck-will's-widow *C. carolinensis* of the eastern United States and the poorwill *Phalaenoptilus nuttallii* of the west.

The word 'nightjar' is derived from the churring or jarring song of several species, particularly the European nightjar *C. europaeus*. This species is some $10\frac{1}{2}$ in (26 cm) long with a grey-brown plumage which is mottled and barred to provide extremely good camouflage. Nightjars nest on the ground and rest on the ground or on branches, typically along the branch rather than across it. The rapid churring of the European nightjar may continue for several minutes, rising and falling, and is normally heard only at night.

The subfamily Chordeilinae contains the various species of nighthawk and is restricted to the New World. The Common nighthawk *Chordeiles minor,* 9 in (23 cm) long, is

Male European nightjar hovering. The farther wing is twisted round, in the act of hovering, so that the primaries point forwards.

widespread in North America and is one of the relatively few species in the family which habitually flies by day. It may be seen over cities as well as in the open country.

The nightjars as a family are almost entirely insectivorous, although some will eat other small invertebrates. Most of them have large eyes, being nocturnal or crepuscular, 'hawking' for insects on the wing. As an adaptation for their mode of feeding the mouth has a very broad gape and most species have a fringe of stiff, bristle-like feathers around the mouth to increase the catchment area. As in the European nightjar, the plumage normally matches the ground on which they nest. The eggs also are highly cryptic, marbled and blotched with shades of brown, grey, purple, on a pale background. Eggs and young are cared for by both sexes.

Birds of this family vary in length from $7\frac{1}{2}$–$11\frac{1}{2}$ in (19–29 cm), excluding the much elongated tail or wing feathers seen in some species. An extreme example of this kind of modification is seen in the Standard-winged nightjar *Macrodipteryx longipennis,* which lives in the woodland savannah north of the African equatorial forest. In breeding plumage, the males of this species have the second primary of each wing enormously elongated to form a flag or standard-like plume up to 18 in (45 cm) long, with the midrib bare for its lower two-thirds but having a very large vane on its outer third. The general impression of this bird in flight at dusk is that it is being

followed by two small bats or other birds. The standards are moved by muscular or aerodynamic forces during the display flights.

The *poorwill is apparently unique in the depth of dormancy shown, at least in the winter. It may retire amongst rocks and become so torpid, with a temperature drop from 106°F (41°C) to 66°F (19°C), that it must be regarded as being in hibernation. Its loss of weight during the winter period, while it is in this state, is minimal. In this way it survives the winter when flying insects are scarce. FAMILY: Caprimulgidae, ORDER: Caprimulgiformes, CLASS: Aves.   P.M.D.

NIGHT LIZARDS, a small family of lizards exclusively American. They become active at twilight and during the day hide in rock crevices and under stones. There are 12 species and four genera distributed over the southwestern states of the USA, a few Californian islands, Mexico and Central America as far as Panama. One species is confined to the Oriente province in Cuba. They are similar to *geckos and like them have immovable eyelids with a transparent window in the lower eyelid. The skull characters and those of the rest of the skeleton show that they are not related to geckos but to skinks, the development of the spectacle in the eyelid is due to parallel evolution.

They are inhabitants of arid areas and some species have a very restricted distribution. For example, *Cricosaura typica* of eastern Cuba is found only among limestone boulders. *Klauberina riversiana* is found on only a few islands along the coast of California. *Xantusia vigilis,* the best known of the Night lizards, lives in the semi-deserts of the southwest of North America where the yucca grows, the Night lizard living among the rotting logs and branches of this shrub.

Night lizards feed on small insects and their larvae which they catch by short jumps when foraging at night. The female gives birth to living young, so far as we know, and each bears only a few, sometimes only one, young at a time. FAMILY: Xantusiidae, ORDER: Squamata, CLASS: Reptilia.   K.K.

NILEFISH *Gymnarchus niloticus,* a 6 in (15 cm) fish flattened from side to side, its body tapering to a 'rat's tail', and with a long ribbon-like dorsal fin. It lives in the Nile and other African rivers westwards to the Niger river. Muscles in its tail generate electricity, surrounding the fish with a magnetic field which, when this is disturbed, alerts it to obstacles, enemies and food. See electric organs and electric fishes. FAMILY: Gymnarchidae, ORDER: Mormyriformes, CLASS: Pisces.

NILE PERCH *Lates niloticus,* the largest of the freshwater fishes in Africa. It is found in the Nile, in some of the African lakes and in

Nilgai

the larger West African rivers such as the Congo and the Niger. Its distribution reflects an ancient drainage system that linked some of the present rivers of West and Central Africa with the Nile system. Most specimens of the Nile perch are 4–5 ft (1·2–1·5 m) in length, but giants of 6 ft (1·8 m) and weighing more than 250 lb (113 kg) are by no means rare. These powerful fish make a splendid adversary for the angler and have been introduced into other parts of Africa both as a food fish and for sport. Nile perch have now been introduced into Lake Victoria, where they have some effect on the important fisheries for *Tilapia*.

The Nile perch was well known to the ancient Egyptians, who drew accurate pictures of it on the walls of their tombs. These fishes were not infrequently embalmed and placed in tombs. At Esneh on the Nile in Upper Egypt, the Nile perch seems to have been worshipped as an important god and this town was later renamed Latopolis, the City of Lates. Some of the fishes were so well preserved that even the fin membranes are intact.

Investigation into their biology has shown that they spawn in relatively sheltered conditions in water of about 10 ft (3 m). The eggs are pelagic and contain a large oil globule which gives them buoyancy. The adults are fish-eaters and are sometimes cannibalistic. In certain parts of Africa the Nile perch is an important element in local fisheries. FAMILY: Centropomidae. ORDER: Perciformes, CLASS: Pisces.

NILGAI *Boselaphus tragocamelus,* a large antelope of the hilly grasslands of peninsular India. Its closest living relative is the Fourhorned antelope, but the abundant fossil remains from the Siwalik Hills (India and Pakistan) show that it is a living relic of the group which gave rise to the cattle and buffaloes. Bull nilgai reach 52–56 in (130–140 cm) at the shoulder and may weigh 600 lb (270 kg); females are much smaller. The horns are short, smooth and keeled, averaging 8 in (20 cm) in length; they are found only in males. The build is fairly robust, though less so than in cattle, and the withers are higher than the rump. Males are irongrey, looking blue in some lights (hence the alternative name of 'Blue bull'), but females and young are tawny. Both sexes have a white ring above each hoof, two white spots on each cheek, and white lips, chin, inner surfaces of ears, and underside of the tail. There is a dark mane on the neck and the male has a tuft of stiff black hair on the throat.

Nilgai are found from the base of the Himalayas to Mysore, but on the peninsula only, not in East Bengal, Assam or West Pakistan nor on the Malabar coast. Small groups of four to ten are seen together (sometimes more) consisting of cows, calves

Nilgai or blue bulls, showing the white ring above the hoof.

and young bulls. Adult bulls live alone or associate together in bachelor groups. In the rutting season, which varies from place to place but in northern India is usually March to April, the bulls fight, dropping to their knees and locking their foreheads, pressing down with their necks. The gestation period is between eight and nine months. The herds have no territories, but have much-used core areas in their home ranges, with habitual places for resting, defaecation, drinking and so on. The herds may mingle while grazing, which they do in the morning and evening. They sometimes enter cultivated areas and damage crops. When walking, the tufted tail is carried tucked between the legs; when running it is whisked up to show the white underside as a warning to others. A low grunting alarm call sends the herd galloping off in what has been described as a 'slouch', with the heads held high as if stargazing. The ungainly effect is misleading, as the speed rivals a good horse, even over broken ground. The senses of sight and smell are very good. FAMILY: Bovidae, ORDER: Artiodactyla, CLASS: Mammalia. C.P.G.

NOCTILUCA, a marine protozoan of relatively large size (up to 2 mm), remarkable for being highly luminescent. It often occurs in enormous numbers in surface waters and is responsible for the 'phosphorescence' of the sea at night and its reddish tint by day. See dinoflagellates. FAMILY: Noctilucidae, ORDER: Dinoflagellata, CLASS: Mastigophora, PHYLUM: Protozoa.

NOCTURNAL BEHAVIOUR. Most animals are active by day (diurnal) and of those active by night a fair proportion are crepuscular (active at twilight and dawn) rather than wholly nocturnal. Our main interest in nocturnal animals is how they find their way in the dark, both for moving about and for catching prey. *Bats use echolocation, so do some birds, including the *oilbirds of South America and the swiftlets of Southeast Asia. Other nocturnal animals tend to rely more on hearing and smell, and nocturnal animals generally have either very large or very small eyes, and usually have contractile pupils (see vision). Nocturnal mammals usually have well-developed vibrissae (whiskers).

There is evidence that whether the animal uses hearing or smell, or even echolocation, it tends to follow the same trails when hunting or foraging, and is guided to a large extent by a detailed memory of its surroundings. See rhythmic behaviour.

NODDIES, five species of birds of the subfamily Sterninae. They are small terns restricted to tropical seas. Two species are dark coloured, two are intermediate and one, the Fairy tern *Gygis alba,* is pure white. Some species lay their single egg in an untidy nest in bushes or on the smallest of rock protuberances. The Fairy tern has the most unstable of any birds' nest-site—the egg is commonly laid in a crevice or depression on a bare tree branch. In some areas the Common noddy *Anous stolidus* nests at less than annual intervals and is one of the few sea birds to breed and moult at the same time. FAMILY: Laridae, ORDER: Charadriiformes, CLASS: Aves.

NORWAY HADDOCK *Sebastes marinus* or redfish, a marine fish from the North Atlantic and a member of the order of Mailcheeked fishes. This is a fairly deep-bodied fish with a perch-like appearance. The head is spiny and scaled as far forward as the eyes, there is a single dorsal fin which is notched between the spiny and soft portions, and the general body colour is a bright red. The Norway haddock is found in the northern parts of the North Atlantic, both along American and European coasts, and it lives at depths of 300–700 ft (90–200 m). It is of some commercial importance, particularly to the Norwegians but also along American coasts, where it is known as the rosefish. The Norway haddock is a viviparous species and a female of about 13 in (32 cm) has been known to bear as many as 20,000 young, the eggs being extremely small. When released from the female, the young are only 6 mm long. This fish reaches 3 ft (90 cm) and specimens weighing up to 20 lb (9 kg) have been recorded, although commercial catches are usually half this size.

A closely related species, *S. viviparus*, is also found in the North Atlantic. It is a smaller fish, only growing to 2 ft (60 cm) in length and is of no commercial value. A third and rather similar fish is *Helicolenus dactylopterus*, another deep-water fish which differs from the other two in having a slate-blue mouth and throat. It is a well-flavoured fish but attains only 18 in (45 cm). FAMILY: Scorpaenidae, ORDER: Scorpaeniformes, CLASS: Pisces.

NORWAY LOBSTER *Nephrops norvegicus*, also known as the Dublin Bay prawn, is lobster-like, 3 in (7·5 cm) long in the body with claws of nearly equal length, and is a beautiful orange-red. It lives in depths of 60–300 ft (20–100 m) on a soft mud bottom. It used to be fished in the Irish Sea but is now more commonly taken in the North Sea and exported to Italy where it is eaten as *scampi. It is also fished in the Mediterranean. ORDER: Decapoda, CLASS: Crustacea, PHYLUM: Arthropoda.

NOTOCHORD, the primitive longitudinal skeletal element of chordates, which prevents telescoping of the body during the muscular contractions of locomotion. The cells of the notochord are thick-walled and highly vacuolated. The pressure produced by these cells keeps the outer, fibrous, cylindrical sheath rigid, just as does the air pressure within a balloon.

A notochord is present in the larvae of tunicates (where its presence is an important piece of evidence relating the group to the other chordates) and in the Amphioxus *Branchiostoma*. It is well developed in all vertebrate embryos, lying below the brain and spinal cord and extending from the pituitary region of the brain to the end of the tail. In the adult vertebrate it is usually replaced by the cartilage or bone that forms the vertebral column.

NOTOUNGULATA, fossil mammals described under South American Ungulates.

NUCLEUS, a Latin word for kernel and one used widely to signify the centre around which materials, even ideas, aggregate or are wrapped. In a biological sense it seems to have been first used in 1829, for the dark spherical body seen, under the microscope, at the centre of the living cell. Further study revealed the immense importance of the nucleus, as compared with the cytoplasm, the rest of the cell-protoplasm surrounding the nucleus. Beginning with the realization that the nucleus controls very largely the activities of the cell—acting as a sort of 'brain centre'—there came the discovery that the nucleus contained the chromosomes responsible for passing hereditary factors from one generation to another. It is, however, only since the invention of the electron microscope that a clear picture has emerged of the complex structure of the nucleus and of its importance as a carrier of the 'genetic blue-print'. The complexity of the subject is emphasized by the presence in some Protozoa of two kinds of nucleus, a micronucleus and a macronucleus, which are dealt with in detail below. See also cell, mitosis and meiosis.

Micronucleus. A ciliate protozoan has two kinds of nucleus, the macronucleus which fulfils the vegetative functions of the nucleus in other cells, and a micronucleus. The function of the micronucleus is that of a 'genetic blue-print'. It enables the ciliate to replace the old macronucleus with a new one during sexual reproduction. During asexual reproduction (binary fission) of the ciliate, both micronucleus and macronucleus divide, but repeated binary fission over long periods leads to loss of vitality (senescence) and death of the population owing to irreversible deleterious changes in the macronucleus. Sexual

reproduction results in replacement of the macronucleus and so this senescence is averted.

There are two basic types of sexual reproduction in ciliates, called conjugation and autogamy. In conjugation the ciliates come together in pairs (conjugants) and each micronucleus undergoes meiosis followed by mitosis to produce four haploid daughter nuclei. In each conjugant all except one of these daughter nuclei disintegrate, and this remaining one undergoes mitosis once more to produce two gamete nuclei. The conjugants then exchange one of their gamete nuclei, the migratory nucleus of one conjugant fusing with the sedentary nucleus of its partner to give a diploid zygote nucleus. Meanwhile the old macronucleus has broken down completely and is no longer functional. The conjugants separate and each zygote nucleus divides mitotically twice to give four nuclei. Two of these develop into macronuclei, the other two become micronuclei. The ex-conjugant then undergoes fission to distribute a macronucleus and a micronucleus to each daughter ciliate.

In autogamy the ciliates do not pair but meiosis and the formation of gamete nuclei occur in solitary individuals. The two haploid gamete nuclei in each ciliate then fuse to form a diploid zygote nucleus which gives rise to new macro- and micronuclei by similar division and differentiation processes to those that occur after conjugation.

So, both conjugation and autogamy result in renewal of the macronucleus from the micronucleus, but the genetical consequences of the two processes are different. As a result of conjugation two genetically different individuals will produce offspring with identical genetical constitutions. For example, if two

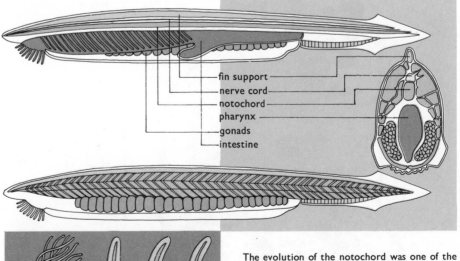

fin support
nerve cord
notochord
pharynx
gonads
intestine

The evolution of the notochord was one of the great advances towards the higher animals, leading eventually to the development of a flexible internal skeleton against which antagonistic muscles could act to produce movement. Contraction in a soft-bodied animal like a hydra leads to bending or total deformation.

conjugants are homozygous for different allelic genes, the genetic constitutions of their micronuclei may be written as AA and aa respectively. Following conjugation the zygote nuclei and the micronuclei of all descendant individuals will have the constitution Aa, so that conjugation has resulted in heterozygosity from homozygosity. Autogamy, however, always results in homozygosity. Thus autogamy of heterozygous individual of constitution Aa will give progeny of constitution AA or aa depending upon which product of meiosis disintegrates during the formation of gamete nuclei.

Macronucleus. The ciliate Protozoa are characterized by segregation of the genetic and transcriptive (vegetative) functions of the nucleus into two separate structures termed respectively the micronucleus and macronucleus (meganucleus). Genes in the macronucleus determine the phenotype of the organism. Both macro- and micronucleus divide when the ciliate undergoes fission. Some sand-dwelling forms have several macronuclei and several micronuclei but most ciliates have one macronucleus and one to several micronuclei. In this majority group the macronucleus is highly polyploidy and may be of bizarre shape; in *Paramecium,* for example, the macronucleus contains 450 times as much DNA as the diploid micronucleus. The macronucleus disintegrates when the ciliate undergoes conjugation or autogamy (sexual processes); a new macronucleus is then produced from the zygote nucleus which is formed when the micronucleus-derived gamete nuclei fuse together. The nuclei formed as a result of division of the zygote nucleus develop into macronuclei or micronuclei according to the location in which they find themselves in the cytoplasm.

Ciliates can survive for several fissions without the micronucleus but not for more than one or two without the macronucleus.

Division of the macronucleus is often described as 'amitotic' as no segregation of chromosomes on a spindle is discernible though the bipartition of genetic material appears to be precise. There is genetic and cytological evidence that the macronucleus is composed of composite chromosomes (sub-nuclei), each representing a complete genome (or diploid genomes), and it is segregation of such entire genomes that prevents the unequal distribution of chromosomes which might be expected to result from true amitosis. It is postulated that these composite chromosomes replicate by endomitotic longitudinal splitting in order to give rise to the polyploid condition during the macronuclear differentiation which follows a sexual process or in order to restore the proper degree of ploidy after each fission. A small fragment of macronucleus can generate a new whole as shown naturally in the life-cycles of some ciliates (for example, the budding of suctorians) as well as by experimental surgery. In some ciliates an extrusion of macronuclear chromatin into the cytoplasm (hemimixis) is known and this most often occurs at macronuclear division. Why the macronucleus should need to eliminate chromosomal material is explained. The species in which such elimination occurs do not appear to be subject to clonal ageing through prolonged vegetative reproduction and it is possible that such elimination serves to restore normal nucleo-cytoplasmic relations by destroying excess macronuclear genomes.

Cytochemistry and electron microscopy show that the polyploid macronucleus is limited by a typical 2–membrane envelope (which persists throughout division), and contains small (less than 1μ) DNA-containing (Feulgen positive) chromatin bodies, also larger RNA-rich (Feulgen negative) nucleoli. The ultrastructure of the macronuclear chromatin bodies is similar to that of chromosomes from other eukaryote cells, that is, they are composed of 10nm-thick fibrils of DNA plus histone: the chromatin bodies are therefore probably macronuclear chromosomes. The period of DNA synthesis in the macronucleus need not coincide with that in the micronucleus, and is usually longer in duration. K.V.

NUCULA, the scientific name, sometimes used as a common name, for the marine Nut clams, or Nut shells which are commonly found offshore throughout the world. See clams.

NUMBAT, aboriginal Australian name for the *Banded ant-eater.

NUMMULITES, an extinct genus of bottom-living *Foraminifera (Protozoa) some species of which grew to considerable size. They secreted a complicated, disc-shaped, calcareous test up to an inch (25 mm) in diameter. The geological range is from Lower Paleocene to Upper Oligocene. During the Eocene they became so abundant in the seas of certain parts of the world that their remains formed the major part of thick limestone deposits, for example, the Atlas Mountains. The great pyramids of Gizeh in Egypt were built of this nummulitic limestone.

NURSE SHARK, a shark closely related to the Carpet sharks and dealt with under that heading.

NUTCRACKER, name for two species of smallish crow-like birds, the Old World nutcracker *Nucifraga caryocatactes,* found at high altitudes and latitudes in coniferous forest throughout the Palearctic region (with eastern thin-billed and western thick-billed forms) and Clarke's nutcracker *N. columbiana,* which occupies similar habitats in western North America.

The Old World nutcracker is some $12\frac{1}{2}$ in (32 cm) long, dark brown with noticeable white spots, white under-tail coverts, a white tail tip and white beneath the tail at the

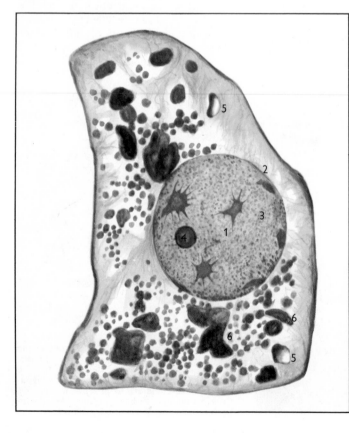

Cell from the liver of an axolotl: 1. nucleus, 2. nuclear membrane, 3. chromatin, 4. nucleolus, 5. vacuole, 6. albumen capsules.

Generalized cell to show the relationship of the nucleus to the cytoplasm and also some of the organelles included in them.

Old World nutcracker. The strong bill is used for opening nuts and digging for seeds and insects.

edges. The tail is otherwise very dark, as are the wings. The flight is rather heavy and undulating. On the ground progress is by strong bounding hops. The bill is black, long and strong and is used for digging in the ground for a variety of food—particularly fruits, seeds and invertebrate animals—and for hacking open nuts or pine cones.

Clarke's nutcracker is very similar in general form and habits but its plumage is light grey and it has conspicuous white patches in the wings and tail. It is occasionally found as far east as the Great Lakes or beyond.

The nutcrackers are outstanding examples of birds which store food. Many other members of the crow family spend a certain amount of time carrying and storing food, but in the nutcrackers this has become a fundamental part of their annual cycle of activities. Much of our knowledge of this comes from the studies of P. O. Swanberg on the Thick-billed nutcracker in Sweden. Birds of this population have become almost dependent on the nuts of hazel and the fruits of the arolla or cembran pine. During the two or three months of autumn almost all the daylight hours are spent in finding, carrying

and storing the nuts. Journeys of up to 4 miles (6·5 km) are made from the spruce forests where the birds have their territories and their stores to the hazel coppices where they forage. Nuts are carried as long as they are available, the maximum storing activity being when the nuts are ready to drop. Some nuts are still present in the stores, which are usually in the ground, in the spring and are fed to the young in the nest. The exact position of the stores is remembered and the birds will dig down to them with accuracy even through snow. Relatively few stores are mislaid and the birds seldom dig down to an already emptied store. How nutcrackers locate and use their stores so efficiently is not known.

Nutcrackers nest in conifers, the nest being made of twigs, moss, lichens and earth, lined with grass and hairy lichen, and typically placed near the main trunk, 15–30 ft (4·5–9 m) from the ground. Three or four eggs are laid and incubated by the female who is fed on the nest by the male from his throat pouch. The young are fed by both parents, largely from this pouch. FAMILY: Corvidae, ORDER: Passeriformes, CLASS: Aves.   P.M.D.

NUTHATCHES, a family of typically small, dumpy birds, usually to be found foraging on tree trunks for insects and spiders. Like their closest relatives the tits, they are found almost throughout the forested regions of Asia, Europe and North America. The true nuthatches are all placed in the genus *Sitta* (subfamily Sittinae) and number about 18 species. The wallcreeper *Tichodroma muraria,* which is found in mountain areas from southeastern Europe to the Himalayas, is placed alone in the subfamily Tichodromadinae. The Australian and New Guinea treerunners, often placed together in the subfamily Daphoenosittinae, are probably an unrelated group which shows convergence with the true nuthatches.

Most members of the family are about 5 in (12 cm) long, though the largest, the Giant nuthatch *Sitta magna* of Burma is about 9 in (23 cm) long. Apart from three very brightly coloured southern Asian species, the upperparts are normally grey-blue with the underparts white, grey, red-brown or chestnut, often more richly coloured in the male. The wallcreeper resembles the nuthatches in build but the bill is slender and curved and the feet are weaker. The toes and claws are

long to aid climbing on vertical surfaces. Unlike woodpeckers and treecreepers the tail is short and not stiffened for use as a prop when climbing. Instead nuthatches climb obliquely, hanging from one foot, supported by the other. They are equally capable of progressing down a tree trunk head first; they and the treerunners being the only birds able to do so. The bill is strong and dagger-like, and may be used for hammering open seeds which are first wedged in crevices in the bark. The English vernacular name is derived from the ability of the European nuthatch *S. europaea* to open hazelnuts in this way. Some populations of the Brown-headed nuthatch *S. pusilla* in America are able to use flakes of bark as tools to prise off other flakes in the search of hidden prey.

All but two nuthatches nest in holes in trees, some of the small species excavating the hole themselves. Many of the Old World species reduce the size of the entrance hole by plastering it with mud, which may deter some of the larger potential nest-site competitors. Two species of *Sitta*, the Rock nuthatch *S. tephronota* and *S. neumayer*, have left the forest environment and inhabit rocky hillsides of southwestern Asia. These are the most industrious plasterers, walling up a rock cavity and constructing an entrance entirely of mud which may project 6–8 in (15–20 cm) from the rock face. None of the New World species uses mud though the Red-breasted nuthatch *S. canadensis* smears the edge of its hole with pine resin. Four to ten eggs, white with reddish spots, are laid in the nest, which may consist simply of bark flakes or be lined with moss or hair. Incubation lasts a fortnight and is carried out solely by the female, but the male assists in feeding the young which remain in the nest for a further three weeks before fledging. FAMILY: Sittidae, ORDER: Passeriformes, CLASS: Aves.   P.J.J.

NUTRIA, an alternative name, used especially in the fur trade, for the *coypu.

NYALA *Tragelaphus angasi,* an antelope of southeast Africa, related to the *kudu. The Mountain nyala *T. buxtoni,* is confined to the mountains of South Abyssinia.

NYMPH, a pre-adult stage in heterometabolous insects in which the young closely resemble the adult in structure but are sexually immature and lack wings. Metamorphosis is gradual and the development of adult features such as wings, if present, proceeds steadily through several successive instars.

European nuthatch bringing insect food to its nestlings.

O

OARFISH *Regalecus glesne*, a relative of the dealfishes, long, ribbon-like and unusual. If any one fish could be held responsible for stories of sea serpents it would undoubtedly be the oarfish. The body, which may reach 20 ft (6 m) in length, is thin, and the colour of polished silver. The dorsal fin is almost as long as the body. Starting just over the eye, the anterior rays are elongated into long plumes and these and the rest of the dorsal fins are bright red. The name of the fish derives from the scarlet pelvic fins, which are thin and elongated but expanded at their tips like the blades of an oar. The anal and caudal fins are lacking in the adult. The body is naked and the shining silver colour comes from guanine crystals deposited in the skin. Very few of these fishes have ever been seen alive but it is said that when one swims at the surface it lies on its side and undulates its body. Since the snout is short and the face a little horse-like, there are all the ingredients for a real sea serpent—a bright red mane, shining body, large size and humps (undulations when swimming).

In some areas this fish is known as the 'King of the herrings' (a name also given to the John dory). Pelagic eggs and some young stages have been found in the Straits of Messina, but almost nothing is known of the biology of the oarfish. FAMILY: Regalecidae, ORDER: Lampridiformes, CLASS: Pisces.

OATEN-PIPES HYDROID, colonial hydroids found at low-tide levels on rocks and seaweeds, particularly on the oarweed *Laminaria,* and especially common where the water flows strongly. Each polyp arises from a long stem originating in a mass of rooting stolons (horizontal stems). Each stem is surrounded by a protective, chitinous sheath or perisarc which ends below the head of the polyp. The polyps have two sets of long thin tentacles, one set around the mouth, the other at the base of the 'pear-shaped' body. These lower tentacles tend to droop. Between the two sets of tentacles are the reproductive bodies or gonophores, rather like bunches of grapes. Free living medusae are not produced, the eggs being fertilized in situ in the sub-umbrella cavity of the gonophore. The fertilized egg develops into a planula and then into an actinula larva, which is released. The actinula looks like a short stalkless polyp which creeps about, becomes attached and develops into a polyp. The polyps are rose-pink in colour with straw-coloured stems. They are often used in studies of regeneration, being able to regenerate tentacles and even a complete polyp head should this be detached. ORDER: Athecata, CLASS: Hydrozoa, PHYLUM: Cnidaria.   S.E.H.

OCEANIC ISLANDS, 'Nature has been exceeding sparing of her favours to this spot'. In these few words Captain Cook summed up the fauna and flora not only of Easter Island, which lies 2,300 miles (3,680 km) west of South America, but of most isolated oceanic islands. Man in his travels has, both inadvertently and deliberately, introduced so many animals and plants to such places that it is now often impossible to judge what the islands were originally like. However, Easter Island probably had only about 50 species of plants, and no land birds, mammals or even earthworms. In the Atlantic, 3,000 miles (4,800 km) from South Africa and 3,200 miles (5,120 km) from Brazil lies the Tristan da Cunha group of islands. These had a similar number of plants to Easter Island but more birds, including five land birds, five moths and butterflies and 20 beetles. Not all oceanic islands have impoverished faunas and floras. Hawaii has 2,000 plant species and no less than 77 endemic land birds, but in these cases many of the animals and plants have evolved within the archipelago from a few species which colonized the islands. Also, large islands usually have a varied range of habitats which can support many more species than small, usually more barren, islands.

Several factors influence what animals manage to colonize oceanic islands. In extremely isolated islands, such as Tristan da Cunha and Gough in the Atlantic, and Easter Island and many others in the Pacific, the distances from the nearest land masses are so great that it is not surprising that many groups of animals have failed to reach them. The chances of even a winged insect

Polyps of the Oaten-pipes hydroid *Tubularia.*

surviving a journey of several thousand miles are very small; for earth- or freshwater-bound mammals and amphibians they are virtually nil. A comparison of the invertebrates and vertebrates of various oceanic islands clearly shows what sort of animals reach these islands. Obviously those species which can fly, or even stay aloft, and so have the advantage of the prevailing winds, are the most likely to cross large expanses of sea. Even among birds some groups are more adaptable than others. Moorhens and rails (Rallidae) are found on most isolated islands where they frequently become flightless and evolve into new species. Island birds and invertebrates often have reduced powers of flight, as those which do fly are more likely to be blown off the islands than those which stay on the ground, and there are often few predatory species from which they have to escape by flight. Insects on the various islands of Micronesia are slightly smaller than similar species in other areas, presumably because the larger species, or even the larger individuals, are unlikely to stay airborne as long as the smaller ones and therefore fail to reach the more distant islands.

Some insect groups have forms which can 'climb' high in the air and are dispersed over wide areas. These are equivalent to the plankton in the sea.

The beetles of St Helena are mainly wood-borers or forms adapted for clinging to vegetation and bark and doubtless arrived on floating vegetation. Few oceanic islands have ever been connected to the continents by land bridges, so the only ways by which most animals could reach the islands are by swimming or on rafts of floating vegetation. Swimming is only possible for short distances and can be discounted for most islands. The few land mammals and reptiles on oceanic islands, for instance Giant tortoises *Geochelone elephantopus*, iguanas and Rice rats *Oryzomys* on the Galapagos, surely drifted there on large trees. Such voyages are perfectly feasible, as has been shown by the journey of the Kon-tiki. It must be conceded that only a few people have recorded large masses of trees and drift-wood in the open sea but written records cover only the last 400 years, a time so short as to be negligible when compared to the time available for colonization. Not only land animals face difficulties in crossing the open sea; an unbroken stretch of sea is just as much a barrier to sedentary or specialized marine forms, such as reef-living fishes, or marine invertebrates which do not have planktonic larvae. Various animals may have reached a single island by different means, e.g. Hawaii has a predominantly North American bird fauna but a Polynesian flora and invertebrate fauna.

Even if an animal manages to reach an island there are still many difficulties to be overcome before it can survive and multiply. As mentioned earlier island size is important, also the age of an island influences colonization, for as time passes there is less likelihood of a new arrival being able to settle on the island since most places will already be occupied by other species which will already have evolved to live very efficiently under the extreme or peculiar conditions on the island. The bananaquit *Coereba flaveola* is widespread in Central and South America and the West Indies, but does not breed on Cuba. It is inconceivable that the species has never reached Cuba so presumably all the niches are already occupied and the bananaquit cannot get a foothold on the island. On a smaller scale, Ireland has far fewer breeding birds than Britain though many of the missing birds occur there from time to time. St Patrick may have removed the snakes but one wonders why he did not like woodpeckers and other birds which do not breed there.

Many species colonize islands but for some reason always remain uncommon. As populations rarely remain stable, these small populations are very liable to be exterminated by chance. Such chance extinctions are known to occur frequently on islands, even only a mile or two off the coast of Britain. In the face of all these difficulties it is hardly surprising that these islands have few animals.

After his visit to the Galapagos Darwin remarked that 'the zoology of archipelagos will be well worth examination' and although studies are still in the descriptive stage his remarks on these islands, as on so many other things, have proved to be very true.

M.P.H.

OCEAN SUNFISHES, large disc-shaped oceanic fishes apparently lacking a tail which has earned them the alternative name of headfishes. The body is greatly compressed, the head large and the dorsal and anal fins prolonged into paddle-like structures. The most striking feature of these fishes, however, is the abrupt termination of the body behind the dorsal and anal fins so that they seem to be all head. During development the rear end of the vertebral column atrophies and there is a rearrangement of the small bones of the tail, somewhat as in a normal fish when the tail has been amputated at an early stage. The result is that the muscles of the body that should attach to the base of the tail no longer do so and instead they are attached to the bases of the dorsal and anal fins. This increases the power of these fins and they are the principal means of locomotion, the fish gently flapping them as it propels itself slowly along. Pelvic fins, as well as the swimbladder, have been lost. The skin is leathery and up to 3 in (7·5

cm) thick. The mouth is unexpectedly small and the teeth are fused together into a beak.

The Ocean sunfish *Mola mola* is the largest in this family. It can reach 11 ft (3·6 m) in length and weigh up to a ton. It is found in all oceans and even comes as far north as the British Isles. It derives its name from its alleged habit of basking on its side at the surface of the water on hot days, feeding on small crustaceans, jellyfishes and fish as they float by. It probably descends to lower levels in bad weather. Sunfishes swim slowly but are reputed to be able to squirt jets of water from the gills to give themselves an extra spurt. With their thick skins, they have few predators and they make little effort to escape when caught; the skin has been known to ward off rifle bullets.

Five species of sunfishes are known, placed in three genera. The Truncated sunfish *Ranzania truncata* rarely grows to more than 3 ft (90 cm) in length. The mouth in this species is apparently unique amongst fishes in that it closes as a vertical slit and not horizontally. In the earliest picture of a sunfish, published in 1613, this curious mouth is clearly shown. The Tailed sunfish *Masturus lanceolatus* is a rare species in which there is a small pointed tail.

Young sunfishes are nothing like the adults. They hatch at about $\frac{1}{10}$ in (2·5 mm) and at first resemble the larvae of any other

The Ocean sunfish *Mola mola*, head-on and side-view. The juveniles, like those of a related species *Masturus lanceolatus*, shown here, are quite unlike the adult in shape.

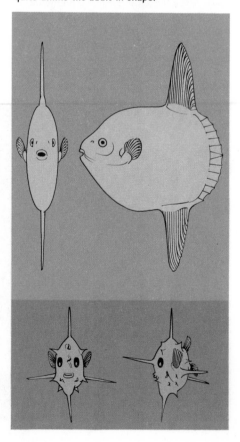

Boldly marked ocelot. The name is from the Mexican *tlalocelotl* or field tiger.

fish with a normal tail. These juveniles are the smallest free-swimming larvae of any large fish and in order to attain the full adult weight of one ton they must increase their body weight 60 million times. During development the larva's tail soon disappears and its body develops an impressive array of bony spines. When it is about $\frac{1}{2}$ in (1·2 cm) long the spines vanish and a new fringe-like tail appears, the body gradually changing in shape to resemble that of the adult. For many years the larvae were thought to represent a separate species of fish, which was named *Ostracion boops* (bo-ops meaning ox eye). It was only when intermediate stages were found that the true identity of the larvae was recognized. FAMILY: Molidae, ORDER: Tetraodontiformes, CLASS: Pisces.

OCEAN SUNFISH OIL. When the old-time Sperm whale hunters were having little success at finding whales, they would catch Ocean sunfish as they lay at the surface. The only valuable part of the fish was the liver which is very rich in oil. It was cut out of the fish's body and left in a barrel to rot in the sun until the tissues had decomposed leaving clear oil with a little solid matter at the bottom of the barrel. This oil was the finest available for softening and preserving leather and it was said to cure rheumatism.

OCELOT or Painted leopard *Panthera pardalis*, a medium sized South American representative of the Felidae. It is closely related to the Margay *Felis wiedi* and both are in the unfortunate position of having skins that are sufficiently attractive to be of inter-

est to the fur trade. The ocelot is a small but highly patterned cat of the general leopard type. It has a shoulder height of about 20 in (50·8 cm) and an overall length of some $4\frac{1}{2}$ ft (1·4 m) including the tail, which accounts for approximately one third of the total length of the animal.

As the patterning of the coat suggests, this is yet another member of the cat family that uses the variation of light and shade as concealment. The colouring is more varied than in the majority of cats, as the ocelot is a golden sand colour on the head and down the dorsal region, silvery on the sides of the body, and shading paler on the belly. The head and neck are marked with black longitudinal stripes, while the body line is broken by the presence of black spots that are arranged roughly in rows.

The ocelot is found from the southern part of Texas, at the north of its range, through the Isthmus of Panama and right down into Brazil and Bolivia. It is capable of pulling down and killing prey up to the size of a fawn of the smaller deer species, but for the main part it subsists on smaller animals and birds, and has developed the habit of living and hunting near villages and farms, where the domestic animals provide an easily obtainable supply of food. Apart from this predilection for domestic stock, the ocelot is no threat to man, and will usually avoid encounters with man and with dogs as well. It is not usually hunted for sport, but it may well suffer through its liking for domestic stock.

There is comparatively little known about the breeding habits of the ocelot, and it is thought by some that in the tropical regions of its range there is no fixed breeding season.

Ocelots in Texas produce their young in the autumn, while those in Mexico breed in January. The period of gestation is approximately 115 days, at the end of which time two kittens are born. The den usually consists of a small cave in the rocks or of a hollow log. The young are fully marked at birth, but are somewhat darker than their parents. Food is supplied by both the parents, and the pairs do not separate after the litter has been born. When hunting or near the den, the adult animals communicate with each other with a mewing sound.

The ocelot adapts well to captivity, and is to be found in a great many zoos. Several will live in harmony in the same area. They do not, however, make ideal pets, as they are easily excited and have formidable weapons with which to inflict damage upon their owners. It is unfortunate that because of their size and their supposed tractability there is a far greater demand for ocelots as pets than is sensible. FAMILY: Felidae, ORDER: Carnivora, CLASS: Mammalia.
N.J.C.

OCTOPUS, a mollusc whose most striking feature is the eight arms which encircle the mouth at the front of the head. On either side of the head are two large eyes enabling the animal to see all around itself. Behind the head is a sac-like body containing the viscera. Movement is either by 'walking' on the arms or by jet propulsion. Octopuses can change from almost white to dark reddish brown very rapidly, providing almost perfect camouflage. They have large brains and show considerable capacity for learning.

The suborder Octopoda includes three types one of which is the octopods without fins, to which the Common octopus *Octopus vulgaris* belongs. Eight families are included among these; they are all pelagic (free-swimming) except the family Octopodidae, which is benthic (bottom-living) and includes the octopus. Each of the eight arms, of about equal length, bears two rows of suckers in the octopus but only one row in the Lesser octopus *Eledone*. The arms are joined together for about half their length by the interbrachial web.

At the centre of the bases of the arms the mouth is found. There is a circular lip surrounding the chitinous beak, the upper half fitting into the lower one. Inside the mouth is a tooth-bearing ribbon, the radula. From the back of the mouth the oesophagus goes through the brain to the crop and stomach in the visceral mass.

The viscera are enclosed by the mantle muscle, which is free and forms a cavity below the viscera that opens just below the head. This is the mantle cavity into which the gills project. A locking mechanism, which consists of a cartilaginous stud or ridge fitting into a socket on each side of the mantle, seals

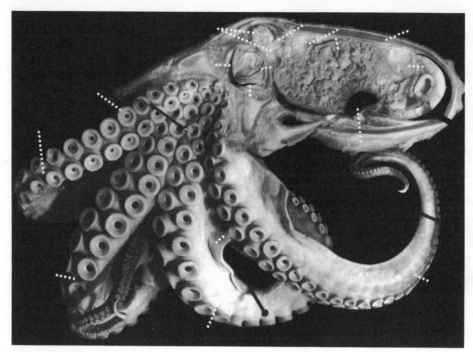

A half-section of an octopus to show the principle features of morphology.
The sessile suckers on each arm and the interbrachial web are indicated.
   The mouth, or buccal mass, occupies a large proportion of the head and behind it is the brain which surrounds the oesophagus. The hepatopancreas, where digestion takes place, forms a large part of the visceral mass.

The Common octopus is eaten in many parts of the world and is also widely used as a laboratory animal.

the mantle cavity while the exhalant jet of water is expelled through the funnel. During inspiration the lips of the funnel are drawn together so that water enters the mantle cavity and passes over the gills. The octopus can expel water forcibly through the funnel from the mantle cavity, and when it does so a locomotory jet is produced.

   The Common octopus is widely distributed, being found in tropical and temperate seas throughout the world. In the West Atlantic it can be found along the coast from Connecticut in the United States south to Brazil. It is found around the south and southwest coast of England and southwards as far as Africa. The Lesser octopus *Eledone,* has a wide distribution around the British Isles being found as far north as Scotland. The Common octopus is fished in the Mediterranean where it was observed and recorded by Aristotle in the 4th century BC. It is eaten in several Mediterranean countries including Italy, Greece, Spain and Tunisia, and also in Japan.

   The wide distribution of octopus is perhaps due to the planktonic, or floating, stage of its young. Once hatched the larvae swim towards the light and the surface of the sea where they remain floating with the current for one to three months. The larvae then settle on the bottom. Besides this change in habitat octopus also migrate seasonally, at least in the Mediterranean. They penetrate deeper water around the coasts as winter storms approach. In the spring they return inshore to mate, and then the female lays and cares for the eggs. Octopuses have been found in fairly large numbers within a small area by aqua-lung divers. Each animal has a home which it inhabits certainly for some weeks. These homes can often be recognized by the presence of mussel or other empty shells in so-called 'middens', which are found just outside the entrance.

   The sexes are separate although development of the reproductive organs occurs at different stages of the lifespan. In the male they mature when the animal weighs approximately 7 oz (200 g). In contrast the female usually weighs about $4\frac{1}{2}$ lb (2 kg) before the gonads are fully developed. The male is recognizable by two external features. One is the hectocotylus or specialized third right arm on the underside of which there is a groove running the length of the arm to the terminal spade-like portion. The spermatophores, or bundles of sperm, pass along the groove and are deposited in the mantle cavity of the female. The other feature is the presence, on the second pair of arms, of some especially large suckers which can be exposed as a display. Mating occurs close inshore from March until October in different parts of the world. As many as 50,000–180,000 eggs are laid in long strings and attached to rocks.

Lesser octopus *Eledone cirrhosa* showing the eight arms joined by the interbrachial web and bearing only one row of tentacles, as opposed to the two rows in the Common octopus.

The eggs are guarded and cared for by the female for three and a half to nine weeks. Meanwhile the mother eats little or nothing and once the eggs have hatched she dies.

Eggs of octopus are about $\frac{5}{32}$ in (3·5 mm) in length and the young, at hatching, are almost the same length. They increase rapidly in size and at two months are about $\frac{1}{2}$ in (1·2 cm) long. It is at this size that they settle on the bottom. By the end of a year they can reach a length of 30 in (75 cm). There are numerous tales of giant octopuses, but the largest ones caught recently in the Mediterranean have been about 22 lb (10 kg) although in 1851 one of 55 lb (25 kg) was reported. One species of octopus, *Octopus dofleini,* is, however, known to reach considerable size: up to a total length of $18\frac{1}{2}$ ft (5·6 m). In contrast, other species never grow large, and one of the smallest, *Octopus arborescens,* reaches an adult length of only 2 in (5 cm).

The octopus moves by jet propulsion, achieved by the expulsion of water through the funnel by contraction of the mantle muscles. Movement by this means is usually backwards, that is with the body in front of the head and the arms close together and streamlined behind the head. Forward movement is possible by ejecting the water towards the hind end of the body, indeed considerable accuracy in steering is possible by deflection of the funnel. Jet-propulsion is swift but

limited by the capacity of the mantle cavity and hence the size of the jet of water expelled. The octopus will also 'walk' on its arms and in this way travels quite quickly over the bottom.

The arms of the octopus are flexible and able to move with great delicacy while exploring amongst the rocks. The suckers on the arms can move independently and are richly endowed with nerves and muscles. It is the action of the suckers, with their complex musculature together with that of the arm, that provides the octopus with its great adhesive powers. Indeed an octopus weighing 2·2 lb (1 kg) can pull with a force of 39·6 lb (18 kg).

The octopus, like all other cephalopods, is a carnivore and its eyes are important in the search for food. The octopus will remain almost motionless in its home waiting until a crab moves across its visual field. A crab passing close to the octopus will be captured by an arm, but one moving some distance away will be attacked and enveloped by the arms and web. The crab is paralyzed with the poisonous secretion of the posterior salivary glands. The horny beak and radula are used to remove tissue from the crab. This is done with great delicacy as the exoskeleton of the crab is separated at the joints but not broken or bitten. Food passes along the oesophagus to the crop and then to the stomach to be

broken up into small particles. Digestion occurs largely in the 'liver', a structure quite unlike the organ in man or other vertebrates. Waste products leave the anus and are expelled forcibly through the funnel.

An important protective mechanism is the ability of the octopus to change its colour, by means of its chromatophores.

An adult has 1 –2 million such cells on its body, mainly on the upper surface. Each chromatophore consists of a pigment-containing cell with an expandable wall, to which is attached a number of radial muscles. These muscles are controlled by nerves from the chromatophore lobes of the brain. By the contraction and relaxation of these muscles the colour within the cell is more or less exposed. Two types of chromatophore are present, dark ones which have a colour range from black to red-brown and light ones which vary from red to pale orange-yellow. Below the colour cells is a layer of reflecting bodies, iridiocytes, giving green, blue or white depending whether the light is refracted or reflected. The activity of the chromatophores is controlled by the central nervous system.

The octopus can alter its bodily form and outline and make the skin appear rough by raising papillae. These variations in colour, body form and outline afford the octopus an excellent means of camouflage, making it almost impossible to discern amongst the

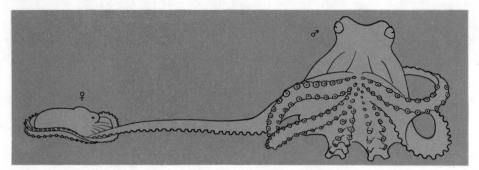

During copulation, the male *Octopus* uses the third (hectocotylized) arm to deposit spermatophores in the mantle cavity of the female in the end of the oviduct.

rocks and seaweed. The octopus excites interest, curiosity and often horror and indeed it is often called a devil-fish.

The soft body of the octopus makes it vulnerable to predators. Some protection is afforded by its home where the octopus sits, with its saccular body well protected, watching for prey. If attacked the octopus adopts a defensive posture exposing the suckers to the predator. In this position it is almost impossible, at least for man, to dislodge.

Another and quite different protective device is the ink. The ink sac contains a black pigment, melanin. The ink, or sepia, has been known and used for drawing for many centuries. The octopus will eject ink into the sea when disturbed, perhaps by a predator. The ink forms a black suspension from behind which the octopus can escape.

By comparison with other invertebrates the nervous system of cephalopods is very large and complex. The brain, protected by a cartilaginous cranium, forms a compact mass around the oesophagus. It consists of about 30 anatomically distinct lobes. The mass of brain below and at the sides of the oesophagus is largely concerned with motor responses such as movement of arm and mantle muscles, control of the chromatophores, and the circulatory system. The lobes of the brain above the oesophagus are

important in the control of eating and in the integration of information and memory. The largest of these are the kidney shaped optic lobes found behind the eyes, they are connected by a large number of optic nerves to the eye. The optic lobe is important in storing visual records. These complex connections between the eye and brain indicate the importance of the eyes in the life of the animal.

An octopus can learn to differentiate visually between two figures if food is given after it attacks one shape and punishment after attacking the other. For example it is able to distinguish between two rectangles when one is held with its long axis vertical and the other with the long axis horizontal, and also between black and white circles. Besides this ability the octopus, using information from receptors in the suckers on the arms, can distinguish between objects of varying degrees of roughness, for example balls with eight or 16 grooves. It can also distinguish different concentrations of chemicals. The capacity of the octopus to learn and store information is very considerable and has been demonstrated clearly during the past 20 years by Professor J. Z. Young, and others working with him at Naples. FAMILY: Octopodidae, ORDER: Dibranchia, CLASS: Cephalopoda, PHYLUM: Mollusca. M.N.

Common octopus propelling itself away from a rock. The funnel can be seen beneath the base of the arms.

OCTOPUS DANGER. Although the largest octopus reaches $18\frac{1}{2}$ ft (5·6 m) across the arms, most are much smaller and, being retiring creatures, they present little danger to man despite horrific stories of encounters with them. It is, however, quite possible for an octopus to hold a man underwater long enough to drown him, especially if the octopus is anchored and the man panics. There are also records of octopus-bite, with venom from the salivary glands causing a burning sensation and profuse bleeding. Such instances are rare and usually not serious, but there is a case of a young Australian apparently being killed by an octopus bite.

OESOPHAGUS, the part of the alimentary canal lying between the pharynx and the stomach. Except in animals with a well-developed neck, it is generally rather short and is often capable of considerable distention to permit the swallowing of large particles of food. In many animals its posterior or lower end is enlarged to form a storage organ, the crop. In mammals there is an interesting transition between voluntary muscles at the anterior end and involuntary muscles at the posterior end so that while the start of the swallowing process can be consciously controlled the remainder cannot.

OIKOPLEURA, a cosmopolitan genus of the tadpole-like marine animals known as *Larvacea. Barely visible to the naked eye some species of *Oikopleura* are nevertheless important as the food of young fish, especially of hake. The possession of a *notochord and gill-slits indicate the relationship of *Oikopleura* to the vertebrates.

OILBIRD *Steatornis caripensis,* in appearance something like a cross between a nightjar and a hawk, being some 18 in (46 cm) long with a chestnut-brown plumage barred with black and spotted with white and having a short but strong, hooked bill. The gape is surrounded by long bristles. The wings are long and pointed, the tail long and rounded and the legs very short and rather weak. The sexes are externally similar. It is the only species in the family Steatornithidae, the nearest relatives of which are thought to be the nightjars, Caprimulgidae.

The oilbird is found locally in mountain caves (sometimes in sea caves) in northern South America, from Peru in the west to the region of British and French Guiana in the northeast. The birds breed colonially in these caves, usually on high ledges. They only emerge from the caves at night when they fly out to feed on the fruits of certain forest trees, particularly of palms, which have a high oil content. Little is known of their behaviour but it seems that they return to the

caves with a stomach full of whole fruits and nuts (they have no crop) which are digested during the day. They are the only nocturnal fruit-eating birds.

The nest of the oilbird is a bowl of varying shape and dimensions made largely of a paste of regurgitated fruit which is mixed with seeds and the bird's droppings. Two to four white eggs are laid, at rather long intervals. Incubation (by both sexes) and growth of the young are also lengthy processes, taking around 33 days and up to 120 days respectively. Towards the end of that period the young are enormously fat, with a weight up to twice that of the adult, but this excess is lost with the growth of the feathers.

The fat deposits of the young oilbirds provide the explanation for the name of the species, for the practice continues—once a flourishing one—of taking young birds at the very fat stage of development and rendering down their fat. This results in a high-quality oil free of any unpleasant smell or taste which is used for cooking and lighting.

The specific name of the oilbird is derived from its original discovery by Europeans in a cave near Caripé in Venezuela when the area was visited by the explorers von Humboldt and Bonpland in 1799. The Spanish-American name for the bird is guacharo, apparently derived from an obsolete Spanish

Oilbird on its nest made of seeds, regurgitated fruit and droppings.

Okapi, a relative of the giraffe, only discovered in 1901, and originally thought to be a kind of horse.

word for one who laments or cries loudly, and referring to the very loud screaming calls of the birds, particularly when disturbed in the caves. In Trinidad the oilbird is known as the diablotin—a name also given to another West Indian bird, the Black-capped petrel *Pterodroma hasitata*.

The oilbird is one of the very few species of birds that uses echolocation. In the depths of the caves where they roost and breed there is not enough light for them to use their eyes effectively, even though they seem to be well-developed and used for night vision in the open. Instead they emit an almost continuous stream of short pulses of sound at a frequency of 6–10 kilocycles per sec which can be heard as a click and are presumably able to 'see' by the conformation of the echo. FAMILY: Steatornithidae, ORDER: Caprimulgiformes, CLASS: Aves.   P.M.D.

OKAPI *Okapia johnstoni*, with a build like a giraffe, but with foreshortened legs and neck, it is only found in the dense rain-forest areas of west central Africa, which explains why it was unknown to zoologists until 1901. Before that time okapi were hunted and trapped by Pygmies, but no other people were sure of its existence. Sir Harry Johnston, its discoverer, at first believed that this animal, with a 6 ft (2 m) head and body length and a tail of 17 in (43 cm), must be a type of horse, as he had seen pieces of its hide striped with black and white that reminded him of a zebra. However all the other known members of the horse family lived in open areas, not in forests. He

realized that it was a relative of the giraffe when he obtained several skulls. These possessed the lobed canine teeth and permanent horns partly covered by skin which are characteristic of the family Giraffidae. In the okapi, the pointed horns are present only in the males.

The distinctive skull and teeth of the okapi have been found in fossil beds 2 million years old in Tanzania, together with remains of extinct giraffes. No one knows if these two animals really shared the same habitat at that time. If they did, probably the more primitive okapi has changed its habitat since then moving out of the savannah areas into the less extensive rain-forest areas. Animals similar to the okapi had evolved by the Miocene, 25 million years ago, so this form is a very old one.

When people see the few captive okapi near giraffe in zoos, they seldom appreciate their close relationship as superficially there are striking differences. This is because the environments of the two species are so unlike. The forest habitat of the okapi has affected it in many ways. Its coat is a rich black shade with white markings on the thighs, legs and throat. This colouration serves to camouflage the animal in the dark forest. Its ears are large, to enable it to detect danger that may be close but unseen in the thick vegetation. It lives a relatively solitary life, because there is little advantage in herds when vision is so restricted; indeed the noise a number of individuals would make might drown the sounds of their chief predator, man. Like the

giraffe the okapi is not mute, but it seldom makes any vocal noises, at least in captivity which is the only place where it has been studied. Like the giraffe too, the okapi is entirely a browser.

Little is known of its breeding habits but the gestation period is 426 days. FAMILY: Giraffidae, ORDER: Artiodactyla, CLASS: Mammalia.   A.I.D.

OLD WORLD MONKEY, any member of the superfamily Cercopithecoidea of the Primate suborder Anthropoidea (higher Primates). The members of this superfamily are quadrupedal, unlike the related Hominoidea (apes and man). Most have external tails, a narrow thorax and legs somewhat longer than the arms. These features are unspecialized compared to those of the hominoids, but the dentition is highly specialized, with bilophodont molars (the cusps joined transversely in pairs, to make a very hard-wearing type of grinding tooth) and long, sabre-like canines with a sharp ridge up the back supported by a groove, which even extends up the root. These long canines, like the more robust, less fearsome ones of apes (except the gibbon), are restricted to males, the females having shorter ones. In the lower jaw the anterior premolar, against which the upper canine shears, is modified and ridged. It is known as 'sectorial' because it acts as a cutter together with the upper canine. The sectorial teeth of apes, like their canines, are not nearly so highly specialized as those of Old World monkeys.

All Old World monkeys are placed in a single family, Cercopithecidae; there are two subfamilies, the leaf-eating Colobinae with their complex stomach and digestive apparatus, and the omnivorous, often ground-living, Cercopithecinae, in which the stomach is simple but there are 'cheek-pouches', deep pockets in the tissue of the inside of the cheek in which food can be stored. The former include colobus and langur, the latter the common baboons, macaques, mangabeys, geladas, and guenons. They are the common Old World Primates of today, having attained this position, causing the decline of the apes, at the end of the Pliocene.   C.P.G.

OLIGOCHAETES, a group of worms which includes the earthworms (e.g. *Lumbricus*) and a variety of smaller, aquatic species (e.g. *Tubifex*). The class Oligochaeta is one of the three major classes within the phylum Annelida, the other two being the Polychaeta (lugworms and ragworms) and the Hirudinea (leeches). The body of an oligochaete is segmented and divided internally into a series of compartments each of which, in a generalized annelid, would be seen to contain a component of each of the major organ systems of the body. Oligochaetes show some divergence from this typical annelid condition, however, for example in the restriction of the reproductive organs to a few segments only. Other annelid features displayed by the oligochaetes include the spacious body cavity of the type known as a coelom, and the tubular excretory organs known as nephridia. In an earthworm the segmental coelomic spaces are separated from one another by transverse septa, and as each segmental cavity is filled with a relatively incompressible coelomic fluid the earthworm has a 'hydrostatic skeleton' on which its muscles act, for there are no hard skeletal elements such as a rigid external cuticle or a system of bones. The limits of the segments of an earthworm can be discerned externally as the familiar 'rings' or annulations.

Oligochaetes have a number of features which, taken together, serve to distinguish them from the other annelid classes. Certain individual features are, however, also possessed by the polychaetes or by the leeches. Chaetae, for example, are small bristle-like

The Spot-nosed monkey, of West Africa, one of several species of guenons with a distinctive patch of white or near-white on the nose.

Opposite: Special features of Old World or Catarrhine monkeys. Top left: male Rhesus monkey, note long canine teeth. Top right: female Rhesus with cheek pouches filled. Centre left: face of a baboon. Centre right: skull of gelada. Bottom left: Diana monkey and (below) Rhesus monkey leaping. Bottom right: the foot of monkeys is a grasping organ and is also used in locomotion when only the fingers are laid upon the ground.

M. Wilson

processes projecting from the body wall and found in both polychaetes and oligochaetes; but, as their names imply, polychaetes have many chaetae in each segment, whereas oligochaetes have relatively few. Furthermore, the number of chaetae in each segment of an oligochaete is not only small but constant. The earthworm *Lumbricus*, for example, has eight chaetae in each segment. They are used in locomotion, by providing a grip on the walls of the burrow as the worm moves along it. They can sometimes be felt if an earthworm is allowed to crawl over the hand. In the aquatic oligochaetes the chaetae are often longer and more slender than those of an earthworm. In a polychaete the chaetae are typically borne on flap-like extensions of the body wall, called parapodia, but in an oligochaete parapodia are absent.

The first few segments of an oligochaete are unspecialized and therefore similar in appearance to the rest of the body. The conspicuous eyes, tentacles and palps, commonly seen in polychaetes (for example, in the *ragworm) are not found in oligochaetes. This does not mean that the head region of an earthworm is insensitive, however, for it frequently possesses minute sense organs capable of appreciating such stimuli as light, chemicals, and touch.

Further points of contrast with the polychaetes concern the distribution of the reproductive organs. Polychaetes are unisexual, each individual bearing either male or female organs. whereas an oligochaete is hermaphrodite each worm carrying both testes and ovaries. These are few, occurring in only a limited number of the segments. In the earthworm *Lumbricus*, for example, there are only two pairs of testes (in the 10th and 11th segment), and one pair of ovaries (in the 13th segment). In the polychaetes, however, a pair of reproductive organs is present in almost every segment. In this respect, as in many others, a polychaete is a more generalized annelid, and it is likely that the oligochaetes evolved from polychaetes, or from a polychaete-like ancestral stock.

Oligochaetes are also characterized by having a variety of accessory reproductive structures. Sperm shed from the testes accumulate in sac-like seminal vesicles before being conducted to the exterior. When transferred to another worm during copulation the sperm are collected in specialized receptacles known as spermathecae. As oligochaetes are hermaphrodite the exchange of sperm between a copulating pair is mutual, each partner both donating sperm to the other and receiving sperm from it.

In addition to the seminal vesicles and the spermathecae, oligochaetes have a clitellum. This is a thickened, glandular region of the body which is an easily distinguished feature of an earthworm. The clitellum secretes three substances from three distinct types of gland: mucus, a viscous fluid which aids copulation; albumin, a nutritive fluid which surrounds and nourishes the developing young worms within the cocoon; and, thirdly, the material which forms the protective wall of the cocoon itself. Leeches also have a clitellum and produce a cocoon. Young earthworms develop within their cocoon without passing through a distinct larval stage. A similar situation occurs in leeches, but polychaete development is characterized by a free-swimming larval stage known as a trochopore. The loss of the larval stage in oligochaetes is doubtless one of the results of having adopted a primarily terrestrial way of life.

Oligochaetes have a world-wide distribution. Earthworms may be found in almost any soil, often in very large numbers, and sometimes reaching a great size (*Megascolecides*, of Australia, reaches 10 ft (3 m) or more in length). The commonest British earthworms are *Lumbricus* and *Allolobophora*. The aquatic oligochaetes, sometimes known as bloodworms because of their deep red colour, are smaller than earthworms and generally simpler in structure. Some are found in the intertidal zone, under stones (e.g. some species of *Enchytraeus*) or among seaweeds (e.g. *Lumbricillus*). But most of the aquatic genera are found in freshwater habitats, living, for example, in mud at the bottom of lakes (e.g. *Tubifex*). Such worms commonly have both anatomical and physiological adaptations which equip them to withstand the relatively deoxygenated conditions commonly found in such habitats. See earthworms, bloodworms. CLASS: Oligochaeta, PHYLUM: Annelida.   A.E.B.

OLIGOKYPHUS, a European genus of advanced *mammal-like reptile of Upper Triassic to Lower Jurassic age. Close relatives have been found in southern Africa, China, and North America. Together these forms constitute a group of 'near mammals' called tritylodonts. Although not directly on the mammalian line of descent they sit astride the reptile-mammal frontier as a collateral branch. Many of the features typical of mammals are present in tritylodonts such as a large braincase relative to skull size, specialized teeth for mastication, a bony secondary palate separating the nasal passage from the mouth cavity, and a lower jaw composed essentially of a single bone on each side. The tritylodont post-cranial skeleton also demonstrates many mammalian features. The particular tritylodont features concern the dentition. Behind the incisors was a gap in the tooth row, and there was probably a cheek pouch here as in modern rodents. The cheek-teeth are very diagnostic for each carries from two to four, depending on species, longitudinal rows of cusps. The tritylodonts were certainly herbivores and were descended from specialized *cynodonts. ORDER: Ictidosauria, SUBCLASS: Synapsida, CLASS: Reptilia.

OLINGO *Bassaricyon gabbii*, a South American procyonid closely resembling the *kinkajou *Potos flavus* in appearance and behaviour. It can be distinguished from this other carnivore, however, by its longer, non-prehensile tail. Further, while the slender olingo has a pointed nose and greyish head, the kinkajou is thick-set, with a yellowish, short-nosed face. Olingos are nocturnal and gregarious feeding mainly on fruit and eggs.

OLM *Proteus anguinus*, aquatic salamander living in a permanent larval or neotenous form and retaining three pairs of external gills throughout life. The single species from deep caves in Carniola, Carinthia and Dalmatia in Europe, grows to 12 in (30 cm) and is a uniform white except for the gills which are bright red. It lives in perpetual darkness and the eyes are concealed under the opaque skin. It seems the olm retains some sensitivity to light since when it is kept in the light in captivity it turns black. The olm is said to keep very well in captivity provided the temperature of the water is kept at about 50°F (10°C). The limbs are of moderate size and there are three fingers and two toes. Fertilization is internal and the eggs, laid singly, are fastened to the undersurfaces of stones and take about 90 days to hatch into larvae about 1 in (2·5 cm) long. It has been reported that sometimes the female retains the fertilized eggs in her body and the young are born alive. FAMILY: Proteidae, ORDER: Caudata, CLASS: Amphibia.

ONAGER *Equus hemionus onager*, a subspecies of the Asiatic wild ass. It is distributed from Iran to western India and in Turkmenistan, USSR. For further details see ass. FAMILY: Equidae, ORDER: Perissodactyla, CLASS: Mammalia.

ONTOGENY. The ontogeny of an animal is the whole course of its development and growth from fertilization to full maturity.

ONYCHOPHORA, a small but unusually interesting group of terrestrial animals occurring largely in the southern hemisphere. Their cylindrical bodies are velvety in appearance, from one to several inches in length, and they walk on 14–44 pairs of short wide legs, the number differing according to the species. They are nocturnal, spending the daytime in hiding, under stones, in soil crevices, deep inside decaying logs, under bark, in forested and open country, but in habitats which are never flooded by rain nor completely dry. Such habitats tend to be isolated by drier country, which forms impassable barriers, and the local colonies of Onychophora often differ in their species from those of neighbouring colonies.

At one time the Onychophora were thought to be intermediate between typical annelid worms and arthropods (crabs, spiders, insects, centipedes). But the whole of their structure, their mode of development from the egg to the adult, their basic leg movements and the relationship between habits and structure are most decidedly arthropodan in nature and utterly opposed to the worms. The group is no connecting link between worms and the armoured, jointed-bodied, arthropods. But many onychophoran features, such as the simple head, and the long series of similar limbs and some of the internal structure are undoubtedly primitive.

The Onychophora are equivalent in rank to the classes Crustacea, Arachnida and Chilopoda. There are but few onychophoran genera with probably 100–200 species. There is little range in structure within the group. Modern work upon comparative embryology and comparative functional studies of structure, aligns the Onychophora with the Myriapoda and Insecta (many and six-legged arthropods respectively) carrying surface stiffening of the cuticle. These three groups have much in common and must have evolved independently from the crustaceans and the arachnids (spiders, scorpions).

Head, feeding and defence. Onychophora are all carnivorous, able to find their prey in darkness. The head is provided with one pair of antennae, the sensory spines of which tap the ground in walking, as in many other arthropods, such as millipedes and centipedes, which all sense a path wide enough for the legs to follow. Simple small eyes are situated at the bases of the antennae, but they record only differences in light intensity and do not form a sharp image. Food is found by being stepped upon or touched by the antennae. The body is segmented, but the body wall is soft and shows no intersegmental boundaries on the head or trunk. Behind the first, or antennal, segment comes the jaw segment which bears a pair of stumpy short limbs with huge paired chitinous blades at the tip. The jaws are encompassed by a round, very flexible, lip which can close over the jaws, or can form a fold all round them, firmly adhering to the surface of a prey animal, such as a small arthropod, leaving the jaws to act within an oral cavity floored by the prey. Suction from the throat holds the prey, and the jaw blades slice into its body, cutting through soft membranes at the joints, and cutting up small portions, which are swallowed. Digestive saliva is also passed into the wound and this dissolves the internal tissues of the prey, which can then be sucked into the mouth of the onychophore. The jaws slice from before backwards by a movement essentially the same as that used by a leg in walking. Very strong muscles work the jaws,

Top: the velvety appearance of *Peripatopsis* is due to a covering of small papillae. Bottom: *Peripatopsis* 'spitting' jets of slime from its oral papillae. The jets solidify to form a network of silky threads.

and a skeletal rod passes from each jaw backwards through several segments, forming a long site for muscle attachments.

Behind the jaws the third segment carries a pair of reduced limbs, the oral papillae. They bear the openings of a pair of huge slime glands which pass along most of the body and bear many branches. The secretion from these glands forms the animal's only defence mechanism. When molested, a sudden contraction of the trunk musculature shoots out a jet of secretion, for a distance of up to 15 in

(38 cm). The material sets in contact with the air to form very sticky threads and droplets. Small would-be predators are entangled and immobilized by the sticky net. They are not eaten, and slime ejection is not used in pursuit of food.

The three segments carrying antennae, jaws and oral papillae constitute the head, a simpler head than that of most other arthropods in that there are fewer pairs of limbs both in front of and behind the mouth. During development the antennal rudiments shift from behind forwards at the sides of the mouth until they become preoral. In many arthropodan classes there is an embryonic preantennal segment, and another one in front of the jaws or mandibles which may or may not carry a second pair of antennae, or this segment may largely degenerate during embryonic life. It is unlikely that other arthropods ever passed through a stage when their head structure resembled that of the Onychophora. It is probable that from ancestral undifferentiated, segmented, animals the jaws were evolved on the second segment in the Onychophora and on the 4th in the Myriapoda, Insecta and Crustacea. The single pair of limbs (oral papillae) behind the jaws of the Onychophora is represented in many arthropods by several pairs of limbs used as accessory feeding organs. The Onychophora with one pair of limbs used in feeding have been called monognathan, the Pauropoda with two pairs are dignathan and the trignathan arthropods are very many, comprising Crustacea, centipedes, insects and others. But there is no reason to suppose that the monognathan state of the Onychophora is a primitive one that has been passed through by other arthropodan classes. More probably the mono-, di- and trignathan states have evolved independently and in parallel from animals possessing undifferentiated limbs. The heads and jaws of the Arachnida (spiders, scorpions) are quite differently constructed from those of the Onychophora.

The trunk and locomotion. The trunk region of the Onychophora bears paired legs of similar form on every segment except the last one or two where the anus and genital opening are situated. The surface cuticle which invests the body as a dead unwettable membrane, is very thin and does not stretch. But the body surface is abundantly furrowed and so extensive changes of shape can take place. The velvety appearance is due to rows of small surface elevations, each bearing a terminal sensory spine connected by nerves to elaborate receptors in each small papilla.

Such rich surface sensory perception is used by the animals in their habit of paramount importance, that of momentarily deforming the body extremely in order, without pushing, to squeeze through small cracks which lead into more commodious spaces, such as there are in a decaying log, through which large and predatory armoured arthropods cannot follow, because they cannot alter their shape. Exploration of crevices and holes is made by the antennae and the body then squeezes through, one leg at a time being flattened out until it reaches the other side, but no pushing is exercised by the delicate body surface. During squeezing, the transverse sectional area of the body may be reduced locally to $\frac{1}{5}$th, an achievement which no other arthropod with surface sclerites

(armour) can attempt. This great deformability of body, and its use in finding shelter, is a main standby for this group of animals. Their internal food reserves can last for a three months fast, so that under bad environmental or climatic conditions the animals can remain in hiding until outside conditions improve. The great survival value of this habit is clear, and it has been made possible by many structural features, which are noted below.

The body cavity of Onychophora, as in other arthropods, but unlike vertebrates, is filled with blood, and the coelomic cavities, present embryologically as in adult worms, are much reduced. It is by means of fluid (blood) pressure and flow that shape changes of the body are carried out, but the motive force is not the heart, which would not be strong enough. Movements are caused by the muscles of the walls of the body and legs, working against fluid pressure and controlled by internal sheets of muscles and a sufficiency of valves. The pressure changes, causing fluid flow and dilatation of parts of the body, can be minimal when the movements are executed slowly. If movements are fast and pressure changes great, then much energy is wasted by antagonistic muscle action. The desirability of minimizing changes in internal pressure is doubtless associated with the characteristic slowness of all onychophoran movements. And these movements are mediated by musculature which is almost entirely 'unstriated'. Such muscle fibres are capable of much greater changes in length than are the quickly contracting 'striped' muscles used for fast walking, running and flying in other arthropods and vertebrates. Unstriated muscles characterize the alimentary canals of vertebrates and the whole body of Sea anemones and coral polyps, where shape changes are great and the movements slow.

All muscles require sites for their insertion, either on sheets of connective tissue which do not stretch or onto exo- or endoskeletons (bones etc.). The muscles of Onychophora insert upon a cylinder of connective tissue fibres situated below the ectoderm (the outer layer of living cells). This layer of fibres is thickest dorsally and becomes thinner over the legs. It is the 'skeleton' of the body, but is flexible and deformable in any direction owing to the lattice arrangement of the fibres. The fibres themselves do not stretch. Moreover, this thick connective tissue layer is not unique among arthropods (as at one time supposed). In all of them the muscles are inserted below the ectoderm onto basement membrane or thin sub-ectodermal layers of connective tissue fibres, and these membranes or fibres are anchored by 'tonofibrils' which pass through the ectodermal cells to the surface cuticle (exoskeleton). Onychophora and the hard-bodied arthropods are not fundamentally different in the construction of

their body walls as has been claimed. They are fundamentally alike. Muscles are abundant in the body walls of caterpillars, the thorax of barnacles and in regions where there is little surface sclerotization (hardening) on centipedes and others. The onychophoran peculiarities of thick subcutaneous connective tissue and unstriated muscles, the furrowed cuticle, the surface sensory system, are all correlated most precisely with the habit of life of enormous importance to the survival of these animals. Again they are not necessarily primitive in the sense that other arthropods passed through a similar stage, although some groups may have done so.

The legs in walking swing forwards and backwards. A pair of terminal claws grip the ground when it is slippery, but more usually the claws are held up and the leg walks on a sub-terminal pad of short spines. Each leg changes in length during stepping so that it is outstretched at the beginning and end of the step and shorter when half way through the backstroke. Each leg is put on the ground just after the one in front is raised. Stable rhythms of leg movement are maintained along each side, but the cross coordination is various and not mechanically important. Antagonistic muscles in the walls of the leg and muscles passing from the leg into the trunk which fix onto the connective tissue cylinder, work the legs, but always in conjunction with internal fluid pressure. The muscles alone, if all contract fully, can reduce a leg to a small wart-like lump on the body. There are sufficient internal arrangements which can isolate each leg hydrostatically from another and so assist in the differential movement of each.

This onychophoran leg movement differs fundamentally in general principles from that of the limbs (parapodia) of worms, where a central stiff rod or rods (acicula) push out or pull in the limb, so altering its length during stepping. The jointed limbs, which characterize the Arthropoda, could readily have been derived from a 'lobopodium' limb such as is possessed by the Onychopora, but the jointed limbs have nothing in common with the parapodial limbs of worms. It is probable the onychophoran limbs are primitive in that they represent in essentials the lobopodia of the segmented animals which must have given rise to the arthropods.

Just as a horse can walk, canter or gallop, so can an onychophoran employ different gaits, and they are certainly primitive compared with those of other arthropods. A range of gaits is used in the Onychophora, but none is extreme. Their slow types of gait have been exploited by the millipedes in giving much motive force for head on pushing used in burrowing, which is generated by many legs pushing against the ground at one moment. The faster type of gaits of the Onychopora are exploited by the swift running centipedes where speed is gained by the use of a very quick backstroke; and this means that very few legs will be in contact with the ground at one moment, most of them being in the recovery forward swing. The extremely fast and the slow strong leg movements become mutually exclusive, and each is made possible by a mass of structural specializations which are entirely absent in the Onychophora. These animals have no need of great speed in catching small prey in crevices. They do not push against the substratum, their primary need is slow deformability of body and this is incompatible with great speed of running.

Breathing, digestion, excretion and reproduction. Onychophora breath air by means of minute, largely unbranching tubes or tra-

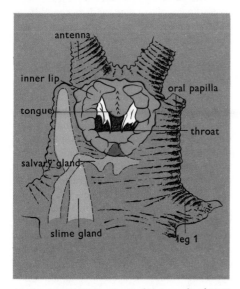

Underside of the head end of the onychophoran *Peripatopsis sedgwicki*, of southwest Africa, showing the mouth with lips distended.

cheae, which pass inwards from tiny pits in the body surface, many on each segment, and then spread out, carrying air to all tissues of the body. Similar unbranched, narrow, tracheal tubes are also found in certain centipedes, where changes in internal fluid pressure are utilized for various purposes. Tracheal tubes of small diameter (0·002 mm) are deformed by pressure changes much less easily than the larger, branching, ones of most air breathing insects.

The dry, unwettable cuticle on the outside of the onychophoran body is a protection against desiccation, and every land animal must be able to avoid drying up. But the greater danger to small land animals is that of water absorption after rain, an osmotic uptake which may blow up an organism if it cannot keep the water out. The unwettable cuticle is of most importance in keeping water out. The perforation of the cuticle by numerous external openings of the tracheal tubes does not let water in, but does permit loss of water vapour from the body, and in con-

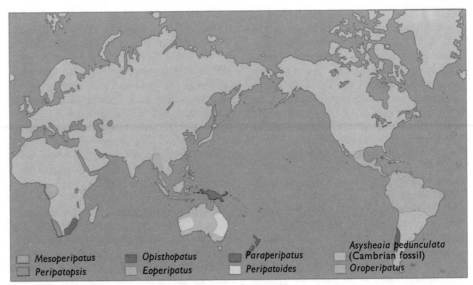

Map showing the distribution of the genera of Onychophora.

☐ *Mesoperipatus*
☐ *Peripatopsis*
■ *Opisthopatus*
☐ *Eoperipatus*
■ *Paraperipatus*
☐ *Peripatoides*
Asysheaia pedunculata (Cambrian fossil)
☐ *Oroperipatus*

sequence onychophores can only live in damp places.

Food when swallowed is digested in a simple straight alimentary canal. The need to conserve water on land is associated with the elimination of nitrogenous waste material in the form of uric acid crystals, and not as the more soluble urea or ammonia. The uric acid crystals are formed daily on the inner surface of the alimentary tract and are got rid of in a tiny tube of cuticle, which collects up the indigestible materials as well. Uric acid excretion has been evolved independently also by snails, birds, insects and others, as an adaptation to land life.

Reproduction of Onychophora is remarkably geared to terrestrial life. Fertilization is internal, and some species lay isolated heavily yolked shelled eggs out of which a fully formed onychophoran emerges after more than a year. Others retain the egg with plenty, little, or no yolk, and it develops internally until, in about 13 months, living young are born, nourishment being absorbed from the maternal oviduct. In New World species the eggs are minute and nourishment is transmitted to the embryo in part by a uterine placenta-like structure. The giving birth to miniature adults instead of laying shelled eggs is an adaptation towards life on land which has also been aquired by a few amphibia, reptiles, snails and insects, besides the mammals. The vast majority of land invertebrates lay protected shelled eggs, and it is surprising to find an advanced character, such as viviparity, in Onychophora which show so many primitive features. Growth is slow, four years or more is needed by African species to reach full size. Increase in size is intermittent, as in all arthropods, occurring just after the periodic moults of the surface cuticle.

The discontinuous distribution of Onychophora, scattered over the southern continents with a few species spreading into India and the Malay Archipelago, is suggestive of

survival of a once more widespread group of animals. But the fossil record tells us nothing about the origin of the terrestrial arthropods because of the scarcity of suitable fossiliferous deposits of the right ages. Scorpions first appear in Silurian deposits, well differentiated millipedes (Diplopoda) in the Devonian and Carboniferous, and wingless hexapods (insects) in the Lower Permian. Millions of years earlier, when the land was scarcely habitable to animals, an apparently marine deposit of Middle Cambrian Age has yielded remains of *Aysheaia,* a creature which looked remarkably like the present day Onychophora, but this has now been shown to be probably a primitive cnidarian (see Xenusion). In any event, there was no convincing evidence that this animal was really related to the modern Onychophora. CLASS: Onychophora, PHYLUM: Arthropoda. S.M.M.

*O-O-AA *Moho braccatus,* insectivorous honey-eater. found in Hawaii where it climbs trees in search of food, using its tail feathers for support, as in woodpeckers. It is one of a number of honey-eaters which have diverged from the family's principal method of feeding, i.e. licking up nectar from flowers. FAMILY: Meliphagidae, ORDER: Passeriformes, CLASS: Aves.

OOLOGY, the study of birds' eggs, particularly the scientific study of dimensions, colour pattern and other features of individual eggs, clutch size, and comparison between races. Oology has contributed to the general progress of natural history as a scientific subject, but a minority of oologists have been more interested in amassing collections than in study of their finds and have contributed to the decline of rare species. In many countries the collecting of eggs of most wild birds is now restricted or prohibited by law.

OPAH *Lampris guttatus,* a large deep-bodied oceanic fish placed in a family of its own but related to the oarfish, chiefly on the basis of the structure of the mouth. The opah derives its common name from the name given to it on the Guinea coast of West Africa. It is, however, also called the moon-fish, sunfish and kingfish. It is found mainly in the warmer waters of the Atlantic and Indo-Pacific but nowhere is it common. The body is oval and compressed, the pectoral fins are sickle-shaped and there are fairly long dorsal and anal fins. The colour is quite spectacular. The back is bluish and the lower flanks are red, the whole body being covered with large silver spots. The fins are bright vermilion. The opah has no teeth and feeds on cuttlefish, crustaceans and possibly octopuses. It grows to a length of 6 ft (1·8 m) and a weight of 600 lb (270 kg) and the flesh is said to have an exquisite flavour. Although usually recorded from tropical waters, it has been caught as far north as Newfoundland and Iceland and fishermen in the Orkneys usually catch several specimens each year. FAMILY: Lampridae, ORDER: Lampridiformes, CLASS: Pisces.

OPALINA, a flagellate protozoan found in the large intestine of amphibians. It is large, flat and oval, and possesses many nuclei and many flagella which make it look like one of the ciliates with which it was previously classified. However, the fact that when division occurs it is between the rows of flagella and not across them, and that the nuclei do not represent macronuclei and micronuclei, separate *Opalina* from the ciliates and place it in the flagellates. *Opalina* reproduces asexually and forms cysts and when the frogs are spawning these pass out on the surface of the spawn. Tadpoles become infected by swallowing the cysts when they nibble at the spent envelopes of spawn and a sexual process with the formation and fusion of gametes occurs. ORDER: Opalinida, CLASS: Mastigophora, PHYLUM: Protozoa.

OPISTHOCOELA, amphibians with opisthocoelous vertebrae, that is, the centrum of each vertebra is flat or concave in front and convex behind. The South American and African members of the group are tongueless and belong to the well-known family *Pipidae. One of these, the African clawed toad *Xenopus laevis,* has been widely used for pregnancy tests since it was discovered that urine from a pregnant woman injected into an unmated female toad would cause it to lay eggs, whereas urine from a non-pregnant woman would not.

The European and Asian opisthocoelans form the family Discoglossidae. These have disc shaped tongues and include the Fire-bellied toad *Bombina bombina* which turns a fiery orange colour on its undersurface when disturbed. Closely related to it is the Midwife

toad *Alytes obstetricans,* the male of which cares for fertilized eggs by attaching them to his legs. ORDER: Anura, CLASS: Amphibia.

OPOSSUMS, North and South American, generally carnivorous and arboreal, marsupials of the Family Didelphidae. The name 'opossum' has also been applied to Australian marsupial *phalangers which are herbivorous and arboreal. The latter are now usually called possums to distinguish them from American forms. The opossums are the most primitive living marsupials and are distinguished from the phalangers by having the substantially unmodified carnivorous dentition of their remote ancestors. They are described as being polyprotodont (see marsupials) because of the large number of teeth—five upper and four lower—on each side of the jaws. The opossums are also didactylous, having the second and third digits on the hindfeet separate, whereas the phalangers are syndactylous, with the second and third digits fused. The opossums thus most resemble, amongst the Australian marsupials, the dasyurids (marsupial 'cats') which are also polyprotodont, syndactylous and carnivorous.

All opossums are quadrupedal with five digits on each foot, the first toe of the hindfoot usually being opposable to the remainder. The tail is usually prehensile. In size the opossums range from mouse-like to forms a little larger than domestic cats. They are crepuscular and nocturnal, occurring from northern USA to Patagonia in South America and on some West Indian Islands.

The pouch, or marsupium, is well developed in some kinds of opossums, but vestigial or absent in others. The Virginian opossum *Didelphis marsupialis virginiana* has a well developed pouch usually containing thirteen teats although there may be as few as nine or as many as seventeen. The teats are usually disposed in a horseshoe pattern with the open end towards the pouch opening. The occurrence of an uneven number of teats is unusual in marsupials; all Australian species have an even number consisting of one, two, three or four pairs.

The Mouse opossums *Marmosa* of South America are pouchless and with seven to fifteen teats. Mostly the teats are arranged on the posterior region of the undersurface (abdominal and inguinal regions) but in some species some teats are farther forward, in the pectoral region. All opossums produce a large number of very small young often in excess of the number of teats present so that some newborn young, which cannot find teats, die.

The Virginian opossum breeds at least twice in each year throughout its extensive range. After conception the fertilized eggs, often 25 or more in number, develop for 13 days in the uterus. There they are nourished by a placenta consisting of vascularized and

non-vascularized parts of the yolk-sac. The young at birth are minute and weigh $2\frac{1}{2}$ gr (0·16 gm). They are suckled in the pouch for about 80 days before they emerge to ride the mother's back.

The Virginian opossum is the only form occurring in North America to which it migrated from South and Central America in comparatively recent geological times. Within recorded history the Virginian opossum has rapidly extended its range and is now found in parts of southern Canada. It is about the size of a house cat with grizzled grey pelage, white head, black legs, unhaired ears and scaly, naked, prehensile tail. The clawless great toe of the hindfoot is held at right angles to the other toes. Opossums live in woodchuck burrows, natural cavities in rock piles, tangles of low vines and, more rarely, in natural cavities in trees. Although it is an adept climber the opossum's natural habitat is on the ground where it feeds on fungi, various parts of green plants and fruit, insects and other invertebrate animals, frogs, reptiles, birds and small mammals. Climbing is the opossum's first means of escape but it has a remarkable facility for 'playing possum' or appearing to be dead by entering a state of tonic immobility. The nest is made of dried leaves and grasses gathered by mouth and passed under the body to be grasped by the curved tail and carried to the nest site.

There are about 60 species of opossums of various sorts native to Central and South America. Allen's opossum *Philander opossum* has spots of light-coloured fur above the eyes and is often called the Four-eyed opossum. About 40 species of small opossums are included in the genus *Marmosa;* arboreal animals with grasping digits and prehensile tails which eat insects and fruit. *Marmosa robinsoni* is about the size of a House rat but is distinguished from this rodent by its large mouth, large eyes, naked ears, prehensile tail and feet with five distinct toes. Other species of *Marmosa* are well known as animals frequently included accidentally with a cargo of bananas on boats leaving South America.

The opossum 'rats' of South America are neither opossums nor rats but a unique group of six species of marsupials placed in the superfamily Caenolestoidea. They are didactylous marsupials, as are the opossums, but have a pseudo-diprotodont type of dentition; the anterior pair of lower incisor teeth being enlarged and directed forwards as in the Australian diprotodont marsupials. The opossum rats were known in some degree for more than 30 years before their marsupial nature was discovered. They are shrew-like, pouchless, quadrupedal animals with five digits on both fore- and hindlimbs. The first digit of the hindfoot is not opposable to the remainder. The caenolestoids were presumably derived from the basic marsupial

Mouse opposum snowing its strong prehensile tail. It usually wraps it loosely around a twig as it walks and sometimes hangs by its tail alone.

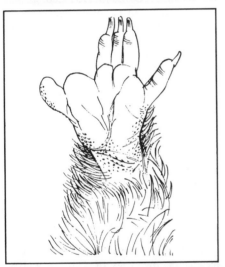

Above: Virginian opossum, the only member of the family to live in North America, where it is spreading northwards into Canada.

Left: Foot of opossum: the first toe is clawless and opposable to the others in grasping.

stock very early in its evolution for they were highly evolved by the Paleocene epoch 55–70 million years ago. The living forms are a remnant of a much greater diversity of species. All are ground dwelling or, at most, climb a little way up the trees and are insectivorous and perhaps egg eating animals. Several species of *Caenolestes* inhabit mainly high altitude areas in cool forests not far from the upper altitudinal limit of trees in northwestern South America. *Lestoros inca* occurs in Peru at an altitude of about 14,000 ft (4,200 m). *Rhyncholestes raphanurus* inhabits temperate forest on Chiloé Island. Little is known of the breeding and, indeed, few specimens have been collected alive. There are four or, in the case of *Rhyncholestes,* five teats the fifth being placed in a median position as is the unpaired teat in many opossums. FAMILIES: Didelphidae, Caenolestidae, ORDER: Marsupialia, CLASS: Mammalia.   G.B.S.

OPOSSUM SHRIMPS, small transparent crustaceans mostly less than 1 in (2·5 cm) long, with some oceanic species attaining a length of about 6 in (15 cm) and coloured red. All species live in marine or estuarine (brackish) water except *Mysis relicta,* which lives in freshwater lakes, and two species of *Antromysis.*

The body is similar in many ways to that of the crayfish and lobster. The cephalothorax is the head and thorax fused together and is covered by a shield, the carapace. The thoracic legs have outer and inner branches, that is, are biramous, and are used for swimming and feeding. In front of the thoracic legs are the mouthparts which filter particles of food from the water and can tear small animals such as copepods to pieces and render them more easily digestible. A pair of pleopods, the swimming feet, occur on each of the first five abdominal segments but some species of females may have all and some species of males may have one or two pairs not fully developed. The third and/or fourth pair of pleopods of some species of males are greatly elongated and are used during mating to hold the female. The eyes are on stalks and are movable, shallow water species having hemispherical, usually black, eyes; some species living in deeper water have golden or red-brown eyes and others bright red eyes and in some the eyes are very much reduced in size and altered in shape. The females carry their young in a pouch (marsupium), and the young are miniature adults when they are released from the pouch.

A balancing organ (statocyst) is present at the base of each of the two inner uropods of the tail fan of the majority of the 650 known species of these animals; about 40 species,

Baby opossums in their mother's pouch where they are attached firmly to the nipples. They leave the pouch when 11 weeks old.

Opossum shrimps

many from the deep sea, have no statocysts. Consequently, the presence of statocysts makes the majority of these animals readily identifiable as Opossum shrimps.

Species of Opossum shrimps occur in most sandy bays and among the seaweeds on rocky shores throughout the world. They often occur in large shoals in brackish water areas and are most easily found at the water's edge at low tide. The incoming tide spreads the populations throughout the intertidal area and the outgoing tide concentrates them at low water. Most mysids live close to the bottom and nets on sledges that are towed over the seabed are usually required to catch species that live in deeper areas. Many Opossum shrimps migrate vertically from the seabed to the surface of the sea at night but swim back down to the seabed at sunrise; many species of plankton perform this migration, the phenomenon being known as a diurnal vertical migration. The freshwater species *Mysis relicta* lives in lakes in North America and Europe, including Ireland and Lake Ennerdale in England. The two species of *Antromysis* are restricted to caves in Yucatan and crab holes in Costa Rica.

Opossum shrimps probably mate at night and the spermatozoa are shed by the male so that they enter the marsupium; the female then lays her eggs into the marsupium where they become fertilized. The embryos develop inside the marsupium and two to three weeks later miniature adults are released into the sea. Breeding takes place throughout the year in many of the species of Opossum shrimps so far investigated but the number of individuals breeding in the population varies seasonally. In some of the British species, and probably other species as well, there is an

Marine Opossum shrimp showing the brood pouch where eggs are fertilized and embryos develop.

outburst of breeding in the spring and a 'spring generation' is produced. These young grow in the following two months and breed during the early summer to produce a 'summer generation' which in turn develops to form an autumn breeding population which produces a generation that lives throughout the winter and the major portion of which does not mature sexually until the following spring. Individual members of this over-wintering population probably have a natural life-span of between 5 and 8 months while members of the spring and summer generations probably have a life-span of nearer 4 months. Some of the species living in

deeper water, 300–600 ft (100–200 m), may live longer, up to one year, and have one breeding season (sometimes during the autumn) but few data are as yet available on the breeding of these species. Females of some shallow water species produce several broods of young, the new brood being laid into the marsupium within 24 hours of the release of the previous brood, and this leads to immense increases in the sizes of the populations of these animals, increases that can almost be described as 'population explosions'. The numbers of young produced per brood vary between 20 and 60 in the spring and summer, depending on the species, size of the females and temperature of the water, but decrease to between 1 and 20 during the winter.

The food of these animals is varied, many feeding on fragments of seaweeds and on small animals found on the seabed but they also eat organic material carried by rivers or streams from the land into the sea. Some are voracious carnivores feeding almost exclusively on small copepods.

Several species caught in shallow bays or at the mouths of rivers or streams (for example, *Neomysis*) are very easily kept in a small aquarium and will feed on bits of meat, *Artemia* eggs and larvae, or small copepods; some minced seaweed or cultures of algae should also be supplied.

The shoals of mysids are eaten by some of the larger marine invertebrates, by fish, birds and marine mammals. They are also harvested by fishermen in certain areas and used as bait, and in India and parts of Asia they are used for human consumption. ORDER: Mysidacea, SUPERORDER: Pericarida, SUBCLASS: Malacostraca, CLASS: Crustacea, PHYLUM: Arthropoda.   J.M.

Opossum shrimp showing the marsupium or brood pouch and the statocysts.

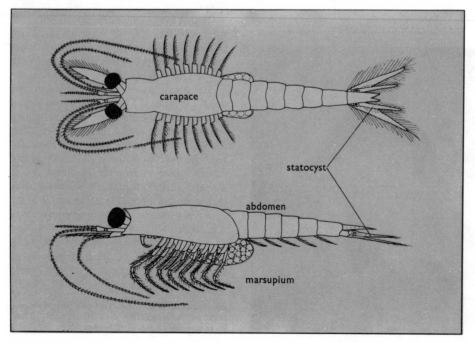

OPTOMOTOR REACTION. When we watch the passing countryside through a train window our eyes may follow trees, houses and the like quite involuntarily until the objects pass out of sight past the back edge of the window. Our eye movements keep the images relatively still on the retina, a reflex tendency only subdued by fixation on a particular object. Similar optomotor responses occur in many animals; they have been studied most carefully in insects.

The eyes of insects are fixed in their heads and therefore they must move either their heads or the whole of their bodies to keep pace with the moving patterns. This is of great use to the investigator because such movement shows that an insect is perceiving a moving object and so can form the basis of a test for visual acuity. A screen of equally spaced black stripes can be drawn past an insect to see whether it produces an optomotor response. The stripes are then reduced in thickness until the insect is unaffected by their movement. At this point one can say that the stripes are too narrow to be perceived, so the smallest angle subtended by an object which can be distinguished by the insect is estimated.

The most important use of this response under natural conditions is to keep an animal stationary in a moving current of water or of air. A fish or an insect, like the backswimmer *Notonecta*, swims against the current just fast enough to keep images of water weeds and so forth in a constant position on its eyes. In the dark these animals cannot prevent themselves from being swept away because they cannot see any landmarks to help maintain position. Similarly a flying insect reacts to the movement of images of objects on the ground. Mosquitoes *Aedes aegypti* were flown in a small wind tunnel, on the moveable floor of which stripes were painted. When there was no air current and no movement of stripes the insects flew in all directions, but as soon as a gentle current was moving they orientated themselves upwind; at various speeds of wind they adjusted their ground speed to about 17 cm/sec. When the wind was too strong to allow them to make headway, they landed. If the wind had started to blow them backwards the images of the stripes would have begun to move from behind forwards. Moving the stripes at various speeds, while keeping the wind at a constant velocity, showed that it was this stimulus which caused them to land. If the stripes move across the eye from one side to the other the insect turns to orientate itself according to that movement. Under normal conditions this response would reinforce any sensation coming from perception of the movement of the air stream.

In terms of the mechanism of perception the optomotor response is of the greatest interest for if an insect moves images of objects in its surroundings will move over its

The female orang-utan lacks the fleshy cheek flanges of the male but has a gular pouch like a monstrous double chin.

eyes and yet this image movement does not evoke an optomotor response. The question still remains, however: how does the animal distinguish between the results of the movements of objects in its surroundings and those of its own bodily movements?   J.D.C.

ORANG-UTAN *Pongo pygmaeus*, large anthropoid ape related to the chimpanzee, gorilla and man. Two subspecies have been described: the Borneo orang-utan *Pongo pygmaeus pygmaeus*; and the Sumatran orang-utan *Pongo pygmaeus abelii* but differences between them are not great enough to make it easy, even for an expert, to identify a captive live orang-utan whose origin is not known, as coming from Sumatra or Borneo. Members of the Sumatran subspecies tend to be larger and lighter coloured than those from Borneo.

The name 'orang-utan', commonly used hyphenated, is derived from two separate Malay words: 'orang', meaning 'man', and 'utan', meaning 'jungle'. In west Borneo, the native term 'Maias' is nearly always used, as it is by Malays.

The orang-utan is a large animal with marked sexual dimorphism, males growing to double the weight of females. The coat has coarse, long and shaggy hair, especially over the shoulders and arms, where it may grow up to 18 in (45 cm) long. It comes in shades of orange to purplish or blackish brown and is generally darker with increasing age. Infants and sub-adults have a shock of hair standing up from the crown of their heads which becomes short and flattened in adults, falling in a slight fringe over the forehead. The face and the gular pouch are bare, except for a fringe of hair on the upper lip and chin, growing strongly orange-coloured,

in adult males. The skin is tough and papillated, dark brownish to black in colour with irregular, wide patches of blue and black shining through the hair, especially on the abdomen. A large gular pouch and prominent cheek flanges of fat and tissue placed at the side of the face are the most striking features of heavy, adult males—but many males have them poorly indicated, especially if they are lean or in poor health. The face is somewhat concave, like a dish, with projecting mighty jaws and slightly pronounced eyebrow ridges. The eyes and ears are small, the latter pressed close to the skull. The arms, a principal asset in arboreal locomotion, are extremely long—the longest and strongest of all apes—with spans ranging between 7 ft and 8 ft (2·1–2·4 m). Similarly the hands are longer than those of either the gorilla or chimpanzee and are extremely powerful, except for the thumb which is small. The legs are relatively short and weak. Nails on hands and feet are strongly curved. The nail of the first or big toe is frequently missing in Bornean orangutans. There is no tail.

The impression of huge size is gained mainly when an adult male is seen with arms extended, moving arboreally. However, owing to its short legs, when standing up, the animal may only reach about 4 ft 6 in (1·3 m) in height; a female is about 3 ft 6 in (1·1 m). Males may weigh between 165–220 lb (75–100 kg); females between 75–100 lb (35–45 kg), depending on their age and state of health, and the food supply in their range, which varies with the seasons. Captive orang-utans in zoos, especially adults, tend to be heavier than free-ranging animals and obese (for instance: 'Andy' in New York, aged 19, was 330 lb (150 kg); 'Jiggs' in

Detroit, father of three, weighed 414 lb (188 kg) owing to lack of exercise combined with optimum food.

The skull is domed and in a majority of adult males, bears a sagittal crest. A nuchal crest is present in all. The mandible is massive, with a broad ascending ramus and simian shelf. The deciduous dentition develops from the fifth month after birth and the first permanent molars in the fourth year. The rest of the permanent dentition starts by the end of the fifth year and is complete, with canines and third molars growing last, after attaining maturity, in the 12th to 15th year. The orang-utan has the typical pongid pattern with 32 teeth. The main cusps of the molar teeth have secondary wrinklings of the enamel by which they can be distinguished from the chimpanzee and gorilla. Supernumerary molars are a common feature of the orang-utan.

The animal lives in confined tropical rain-forest areas, usually within river boundaries or mountain ranges over 6,500 ft (2,000 m) high which it is unable to cross. Orang-utans are mainly found in the province of Atjeh, north of the Wampe River and along the Simpang-Kanan and Peureulak Rivers of northern Sumatra, as well as between Menlaboh and Singkel on the east coast of the island. Uninhabited and protected forests of Sarawak and Sabah (East Malaysia) and Kalimantan (Indonesian Borneo) contain several areas of its Bornean range, mainly along both sides of the political border dividing Sarawak and Kalimantan in northwest Borneo, in pockets between the Sadong and Batang Lupar Rivers of Sarawak and others much further to the north and east in Sabah's interior, including the Mt Kinabalu National Park. The largest and least disturbed areas are inland from Borneo's eastern coast, in the Sandakan district, along the Lokan River and tributaries of the upper Kinabatangan and upper Segama Rivers. Their range also extends downwards to the south from here, across the political border into Kalimantan. The main parts of southern Borneo are not inhabited by orang-utans.

Free-ranging orang-utans number approximately 5,000 at present, with little more than half of that number distributed in Bornean areas, mostly as scattered, smallish groups.

There are indications that adult orang-utan males may fight for the possession of a female at mating time. Males caught in nets as adults in the early decades of this century for export to western zoos had numerous healed scars on face and neck, missing fingers or digits and torn noses and lips, probably indicating hostility with other males. A peculiar prelude to mating on the part of the male is the so-called 'singing', a prolonged vibrating burr starting low, and increasing in volume to a deep roar before

decreasing again and finally ceasing. Pairs may play prior to mating: wrestling, slapping with hands, mock-biting round the neck and face, accompanied by low grunts. Mating takes place in trees and in a hanging position, usually face to face. The animals can mate on flat surfaces with the female supine or crouching on her belly, but zoos providing high cages with hanging facilities and ample room for two adults to move in extensively, have been more successful in breeding than others.

The female's menstrual cycle is about 29 days, with a slight flow lasting three to four days. There is no periodic sexual swelling, except during pregnancy which takes roughly eight months (255–275 days). The infant is born weighing between $2\frac{1}{4}$ and $3\frac{1}{8}$ lb (1·1 and 1·6 kg) and clings to mother's fur from the start. But it is necessary for the mother to carry and hold the infant as well, which she usually does over her hip with one arm, leaving three limbs free for locomotion and feeding in trees. She nurses her baby with gradually decreasing quantities of her milk for two or three years, but already during the first year, she starts feeding it supplementary food in the form of masticated fruits and vegetables which she pushes with her lips right into the baby's mouth. The baby starts taking an independent interest in food at about six months old, nibbling and picking leaves as far as its hands and feet can reach, while the mother is at rest; or it takes food out of the mother's mouth and hands. The infant starts to move separately and in the close vicinity of its mother at the age of one year, and emits high-pitched screams should she move any distance away. At about four years old, a youngster is able to look after itself and move independently within a known range. At that time also, he associates with others of his own age, roaming but keeping in touch with his mother who now becomes ready to mate again.

Orang-utans grow very slowly. They reach maturity at about ten years or more and may live to about 35 years old. Infant mortality is very high, so is the chance of a life cut short through disease (pneumonia, malaria and other infections), through poaching by man or other accidents. Of about five babies born to a free-ranging adult female during her lifetime, only an average three have a chance of surviving to adulthood and themselves having offspring.

Like all the great apes, the orang-utan is essentially a quadrupedal climber. Though able to move on the ground, it is also the only truly arboreal ape, spending most of its life in trees. It walks up trunks using irregularities in the bark to give a firmer grip for fingers and toes and usually proceeds in the middle stories of the forest, cautiously and silently. The orang-utan walks quadrupedally along branches or bipedally with arms

holding on above, its powerful, far-reaching 'hook grip' bearing its main weight. It progresses, balancing and swinging slowly, using its body weight on trees and branches to bend them in a desired direction. Occasionally the orang-utan brachiates for short distances, legs freely dangling, specially in moving from one tree to another and in a quick flight. It does not jump. Descending a tree is a reversed climb or a jerky glide.

The middle stories of the rain-forest, where slender-stemmed, dense-growing trees push up into the canopy, are especially suitable for horizontal travel. Thick stems of old giants cannot be gripped so well, especially by youngsters. But here, vines hanging down from the crowns, or similar growth attached to the stems, are used for climbing nimbly upwards, right into the top for feeding and rest.

The normal ground gait is quadrupedal, the weight being borne by the clenched fists and inverted, clenched feet. The walk is similar to that of dogs, that is two diagonally opposing limbs advance while the other pair carries and propels the body forward. Quadrupedal locomotion is sometimes alternated with rolling head over heels—specially if the animal speeds to a near gallop on sloping ground free of vegetation. It may also playfully roll over from a squatting position, to cover a few feet of ground.

Orang-utans may sit, recline or hang in a variety of positions, including suspended from both feet with head and arms dangling down, or from one hand or one foot, without further support.

Captive orang-utans commonly adopt bipedalism to the extent of standing erect, supporting themselves with one or both hands, or of walking a few staggering steps with slightly spread legs, hands thrown up and rotating above shoulder level.

While moving and at rest in trees, the orang-utan continually manipulates vegetable and animal matter within its reach, testing them as food. It specializes in many kinds of jungle fruit and eats or chews an infinite variety of buds and leaves, flowers, bark, epiphytes, canes, roots, even mould and humus. It forages at leisure, alternately squatting and climbing, nibbling, masticating and rejecting through its lips the shells and seeds of fruit and portions of the vegetables tested. It picks and plucks its food with cupped hands; if the material is small it uses the side of the index finger in an interdigital grip. It may use its feet in a similar way or lock one or both of them into vegetation in order to secure its arboreal position.

The orang-utan has a 'thoughtful' expression, although it is not justified to equate the facial expressions of monkeys with those of man.

Indo-Pacific Ocean. Their shell has only one valve and the animal has no operculum. It is characterized by the very shallow spire and a line of five or six holes in the shell. These holes are obliterated at the posterior end by the addition of nacre, or mother-of-pearl, on the inside of the shell and new holes are formed at the front shell margin as the animal grows. The animal ventilates its gill by passing a current of water through these holes and it is very susceptible to lack of oxygen, so ormers are almost impossible to keep in marine aquaria.

Ormers crawl, like many molluscs, by pedal waves which pass along their flat muscular foot. If, when crawling, the animal becomes dislodged it can right itself by extending and twisting the foot and, when this is gripping the substrate, powerful muscles connecting the foot to the shell are contracted and the animal rights itself.

Ormers are herbivores and make periodic excursions to feed on red seaweeds. They will also feed on detritus. When crawling they are very sensitive to touch and give a powerful escape reaction with starfish, which seems to suggest they are preyed on by these animals. I have found the Common ormer *Haliotis lamellosa* drilled by a carnivorous proso-branch, possibly the Sting winkle *Ocenebra erinacea*. Certain *Pea crabs are commensals with these animals and are found sheltering inside the ormer shells.

Ormers are either male, or female, the males releasing clouds of sperms into the sea with the exhalant water from the mantle cavity. The presence of sperms in the water stimulates the females to release eggs which are fertilized externally. A free swimming trochophore larva is produced which is the dispersal phase of the animal's life-cycle. ORDER: Archaeogastropoda, SUBCLASS: Prosobranchia, CLASS: Gastropoda, PHYLUM: Mollusca.   P.F.N.

ORNITHOLOGY, HISTORY OF.

If ornithology is the scientific study of birds and, if as T. H. Huxley said, science is organized commonsense, then the history of ornithology must have had as long a development as man's emerging mind. Man has certainly always been interested in birds, for to catch them for food necessitates an interest in their habits, and such an interest is best pursued methodically. Yet a methodical interest may be not enough to qualify as ornithology; perhaps some kind of deliberate record of an interest in birds is needed. In which case the earliest known ornithologists were, perhaps, the Aurignacians of the Old Stone Age who portrayed birds, among other animals, on the walls of their Pyrenean caves, 17–18,000 years ago. They were followed by the Magdalenians, who figured birds in the round as well as graphically. When these people spread north with the retreat of the ice, about 8,000 years BC, they were replaced by a Neolithic culture the people of which have left us Spanish cave drawings executed about 5,000 BC of at least ten species of birds.

Such peoples must have given some serious thought to the study of the birds they portrayed, as was surely the case with the Sumerians who, before 3,000 BC, used doves, eagles and geese in their decorations, and the Egyptians who were painting geese of recognizable species in their frescoes at about the same time. From this time on a recorded interest in birds is more and more evident, with birds becoming common in the art of Egypt and Greece, for example.

The person who has the first real claim to the title of ornithologist is Aristotle 384–322 BC. The evidence that remains to us suggests that he knew, or knew of, some 170 species of birds, though only 126 of these are recognizable from his descriptions. Aristotle's material is in fact largely physiological, though he does refer to certain ecological matters, including territory. He also classified birds in eight groups, but his classification employs little of the natural grouping which we use today. Aristotle of course relied much on information from contemporaries and predecessors, as have all who followed him; followed him, that is, in an objective interest in the true facts of natural history. Pliny the Elder, 23–79 AD, next to Aristotle chronologically, relied to a considerable extent upon the information handed down from his eminent predecessor and authorities differ as to the importance of Pliny's contribution to ornithology. But there followed about 1,000 years of stultification of natural history when religious dogma and bigotry ordered mens' thinking and the only accepted natural history was that of fable, bestiary and anecdote. This darkness only began to clear in the 9th century when Arabian science, based on the Greek writings, flourished particularly at the University in Cordova and in Baghdad.

The most important of these Arabic scientists and philosophers, indeed the most important natural philosopher of the Middle Ages, was Averroes (Abu'l Welid Muhammad ibn Rushd al-Maliki), 1126–1198, who brought Aristotle to the notice of the Church in France and northern Italy.

Towards the end of this age of darkness there is one European of note, Emperor Frederick II, 1194–1250. He attracted savants from east and west to his kingdom in southern Italy. He had Aristotle's work re-translated—a translation which was to form the basis of the studies of scientists of the later Middle Ages—and himself wrote an important work on falconry: *De Arte Venandi cum Avibus*. This not only dealt with hunting, but also displayed a critical understanding of Aristotle's work in avian anatomy and some knowledge of bird behaviour, including migratory movements. It is unfortunate that after Frederick's death ecclesiastical reaction blocked much of the progress he had initiated.

The Renaissance emergence from ecclesiastical despotism was of no less importance to ornithology than to any other endeavour, and with Konrad Gesner, 1516–1565, we begin to see the importance of the freeing of the mind. Gesner was a prodigious worker and, among other publications, brought out in Zürich a *Historia Animalium* in four volumes totalling some 3,500 pages. The second volume was on birds but would not interest us here if it were not for the fact that Gesner was careful to acknowledge the sources of his material and was the first to use illustrations in support of his text.

In the same year that Gesner's bird book was published (1555) Pierre Belon, 1517–1564, published in Paris his *Histoire de la nature des Oyseaux*. Belon had a greater practical knowledge of birds than Gesner and his work contained more original material; and it was outstanding in one particular—it contained the first published exercise in comparative anatomy. This was in the form of a careful textual and diagrammatic comparison between the skeleton of man and bird, the human standing and the bird in a corresponding position. However, in his general skeletal work Belon only shortly anticipated Volcher Coiter, 1554–1590, whose treatises on the general internal structure of birds and the osteology and myology (study of bone and muscle respectively) of certain selected types were published in Nuremberg in 1573 and 1575 respectively. Coiter also was probably the first to draw up a classification of birds, with a key to their identification. It was to be more than 200 years before these advances were taken up again by Buffon, to be improved upon later by Cuvier.

At this point in our history we are well into the Renaissance and the age of print, when published works were proliferating rapidly. As we proceed with our story therefore, the studies mentioned represent a steadily decreasing proportion of the total amount of work achieved. The next landmark and one of the most important of all is the work of John Ray, 1627–1705, and Francis Willughby, 1635–1672, who, by their joint efforts firmly cemented the foundations of scientific ornithology. Some authorities regard Ray as the finest field naturalist of all time; it is certain that from the travels, studies and collections made with Willughby arose a series of works which were to change natural history completely. Much of Ray's genius is centred upon his unification of the scientific approach with field study. This is shown particularly by his botanical work, which is even more important than his ornithology. Nevertheless, the *Ornithologia* (commonly known as Willughby's Ornithology) published in Latin in 1676 and in English, with many amendments, in 1678 and the *Synopsis Methodica Avium* published in 1713, after Ray's death, had the greatest influence upon the work of others. Ornithologically, both Linnaeus and Buffon were dependent upon Ray and the whole school of British ornithology has built upon and been inspired by his labours.

Though Linnaeus, 1707–1778, largely followed Ray in his classification of birds, his binomial system whereby each separate species has a scientific name (either Latin or Greek) of two words only has been of enormous value to science, making it possible to deal with vast numbers of species without confusion. His terseness of description however, particularly with birds, has sometimes made it difficult to recognize the species to which he is referring. Nevertheless, some 500 of his 564 species of birds are accepted as true species today. And, of course, modern classification begins with the tenth edition of his *Systema Naturae*, 1758.

While the *Systema Naturae* was going through successive editions Mark Catesby published in London his *Natural History of the Carolinas*, which contained coloured plates of birds of Florida and the Bahamas as well as the Carolinas. This was the precursor of the later expensive illustrated ornithologies.

The next ornithological landmark is Buffon, 1707–1788. He instigated the publication in Paris in 1765 of *Planches enluminées d'histoire naturelle*, by the younger D'Aubenton. This appeared in 42 parts up to 1780, with 1,008 coloured plates, mostly of birds. But he seems to have regarded this only, or largely, as a preliminary to his own publications, principally his *Histoire Naturelle* in 15 volumes, beginning in 1749. When the first of the nine volumes on birds appeared in 1770 it was perhaps the first occasion on which birds were the theme of a man with literary ability. Buffon could write extremely well and he became justly popular.

In Britain at this time natural history was flourishing and a number of ornithological lights were shining brightly. Thomas Pennant, 1726–1798, gave a strong impetus to zoology in general and ornithology in particular. His *British Zoology* of 1766, *Genera of Birds*, 1773, and *Arctic Zoology*, 1785–1787, were all authoritative and influential.

Perhaps the most brightly shining, yet most unassuming of the British naturalists of this, or any other, time was Gilbert White, 1720–1793. Born in the vicarage of Selborne in Hampshire, where his grandfather was vicar, and dying there as curate, White was a quiet comfortable countryman who, nevertheless, had a genius for the observation, description and interpretation of nature. His

Natural History of Selborne has gone through more editions and influenced more people than any other single work in natural history or ornithology. Apart from the charm of his writing, which has made 'Selborne' a classic, and his picture of 18th century country life, White left us the richer for his first published recognition of the Lesser whitethroat and the distinction between the three species of Leaf warbler, his suggestions as to the principles of protective colouration, and his thoughts on territory, the origin of domestic pigeons, the agricultural importance of earthworms and even bird migration. He anticipated modern thinking in ecology, evolution and ethology to a degree remarkable for his time.

Of greater popular appeal was the work of the Northumberland wood-engraver Thomas Bewick, 1753–1828, whose most famous publication, *A History of British Birds* appeared in two volumes: *Land Birds* in 1797 and *Water Birds* in 1804. The cuts of the birds which Bewick knew in life are claimed by some to be second in excellence only to those of Dürer. The popular appeal of Bewick, the universal charm of White, and the academic excellence of Ray, almost in themselves, explain the widespread interest in ornithology, particularly in Britain, which shows no abatement even today.

While we must mention in passing the work of Georges Cuvier, 1769–1832, in comparative anatomy and paleontology, and that of Chevalier de Lamarck, 1744–1829, in general biology, we now turn to the greatest naturalist and biologist of all time, Charles Robert Darwin, 1809–1882. Standing head and shoulders above all others, Darwin was as important an influence on ornithology as on any other branch of natural science, probably more so, for ornithology was advanced enough to be able to test and demonstrate the validity of Darwin's theory of evolution by natural selection of the 'fittest' variants in a population.

Probably the most important period for Darwin was when, as naturalist on the long voyage of *H.M.S. Beagle*, 1831–1836, he was able to sample the world's fauna and flora, past and present. His ornithological notebooks of this period are crammed with observations of behaviour as well as morphology, of ecology as well as distribution. On the Galapagos he was able to observe in detail an isolated group of oceanic island birds, since named Darwin's finches, which were in effect a living demonstration of his half-formed theory. That he had begun to develop his theory on the voyage is apparent from his notebooks, although he was not to draw up his first sketch of the theory until 1842, and the *Origin of Species* was not in fact published until 1859. Even then he had to be urged to publish.

Among the friends and colleagues who supported him in his work the most important was T. H. Huxley, 1825–1895, self-styled 'Darwin's bulldog'. He it was who by his eloquence and authority forced people to appreciate the commonsense of Darwin's theory. But he was also responsible for some fine ornithological work himself, notably on the use of the avian palate in classification, and on the features of birds aiding the tracing of descendants of a reptile stock.

By this time the output of ornithological publications was gathering momentum, partly as a result of a great multiplication in the number of books produced, and partly because of the establishment of numerous learned and semi-learned societies many of which issued periodicals dealing with their specialized interests. It would now be impossible for any one person to read all published work in ornithology as it is produced; recourse has to be made to reviews and bibliographies.

One definite trend to be seen via the medium of this ever-increasing ornithological literature is the gradual incorporation of Darwinian thinking into taxonomy, so that now we have a classification of birds which, we believe, is a fair reflection of their evolutionary history. Another trend has been a decrease in the proportion of general works produced, presumably because of the great increase in ornithological knowledge and the difficulty of keeping it all in view. At the same time the number of monographs published has greatly increased. 'Every kingdom, every province, should have its own monographer' wrote Gilbert White. He would surely be impressed with the present monographic coverage, not only of areas, but of species, groups of species, anatomical and physiological systems and behavioural and ecological specializations. He would be amazed at the proliferation of popular weekly and monthly magazines which, dealing partly or even entirely with birds, impressively illustrated with colour photographs, reach millions of people through the newsagents and bookstalls.

This general interest in birds is also reflected in the continued production of illustrated ornithologies, even to this day, if we allow the illustrations to depict general ornithological matters in addition to the variety of species. In 1802 Audebert and Vieillot produced *Oiseaux dorés ou a reflets metalliques*, with gilded plates. Several other large works were published around this time, but the most famous of all was undoubtedly the *Birds of America* by John James Audubon, 1770–1851. His principal work was the original edition of four folio volumes, with 435 plates, printed in Edinburgh and published in London between 1827 and 1838.

1832 saw the beginning of the illustrated ornithologies of John Gould, with the first of

An oropendola, one of several South American species of the family of New World Orioles that have strange displays and songs.

the five volumes of his *Birds of Europe*, completed in 1837. By 1873, he had published over 40 folio volumes, with more than 3,000 colour plates. Though the latter are of varying quality and were executed by several different artists, many of them are excellent, and the works as a whole have had considerable influence. The only real challenger to Gould, in artistry and influence, was Archibald Thorburn, whose *British Birds* was first published, in four volumes, in 1915. Some consider Thorburn to be the best bird artist of all, with the ability to capture the 'jizz' (essence of character) of a bird better than anyone.

The contributions of all those we have mentioned and, to a lesser degree, of a thousand we have not, have been responsible, in divers ways, for the gradual development and current health and strength of the serious study of birds. In countries throughout the world, individuals, clubs and societies, have built upon the solid foundation of the past an edifice of such varied perspective, such vigorous activity, and such actual and potential benefit to all those interested in natural history, that the founders of ornithology would be both gratified and amazed.   P.M.D.

ORNITHOMANCY, the practice of divination based upon the behaviour of birds such as the direction of flight or the time of the seasonal appearance. In certain parts of the world the pattern of human communal activities, such as agriculture, has been influenced or even governed by bird movements. In Borneo birds are still powerful omens. The English words 'auspice' and 'augury', from the Latin *avis*—bird, have their origin in ornithomancy.

OROPENDOLA, the common name for 12 species of social birds of the family of New World *orioles. They have a very wide distribution in the Americas from Mexico, throughout Central America and south to northern Argentina.

Oropendolas are rather large birds, somewhat larger than a jackdaw, and in all species the male has brighter plumage and is considerably larger than the female. They live the whole year round in flocks, feeding, nesting and roosting in groups. They are to be found among the trees in forests, forest edges, along forest-fringed rivers and some species at least are also common in plantations and in groups of trees in open country.

Among the best known is the Crested

oropendola *Psarocolius decumanus* which has a very wide distribution, occurring from Panama south through Colombia, Venezuela, Ecuador, Peru, the Guianas, Brazil, Bolivia, Paraguay and northern Argentina. It is largely glossy black, the lower back, rump and lower underparts are chestnut and in the rather long tail the middle feathers are black and the outer ones, yellow. The strong bill is pale yellow and the eyes a very fine pale blue. Males vary in weight from 10–10½ oz (280–290 gm), but females are only 5–6 oz (145–170 gm). The male has a few long and narrow feathers on the head forming a crest. It feeds partly on fruits and, as it takes cultivated fruits, such as mangos, papayas and citrus, it can do a lot of damage in cultivated areas. Insects also form a large part of its diet and it captures flying termites on the wing.

Crested oropendolas nest in colonies, preferring trees that tower over the surrounding vegetation, for instance the huge cottontrees or palms, although colonies in quite low isolated trees are also known. The nest is a wonderful structure, a long, pendent purse about 3 ft (1 m) in length with the entrance right at the top. The nest-chamber is at the end and the bottom is lined with dry leaves

Nests of Crested oropendolas dangling from the fronds of a palm tree.

on which the eggs rest. It is entirely constructed of long stripped leaf-fibres and is fastened at the very end of a branch, very often at a considerable height. Nests move freely in a strong wind and during storms they sometimes break off and fall to the ground. It takes between 9–25 days to complete the nest. Owing to their inaccessibility the contents of the nests are difficult to examine without first cutting off the branch to which they are attached. Nest-building, incubation and the feeding of the nestlings is confined to the female.

The size of a colony varies from two to more than 40 nests. Isolated nests are also known but are apparently never used. The eggs, one or two in number, are pear-shaped and white with varying numbers of purple dots, blotches and lines. The incubation period is from 17–18 days and the nestlings stay in the nest for a period of 31–36 days. The female roosts in the nest covering the nestlings for 23–26 days. The nesting season is rather extended and in Surinam the earliest date for young birds on the wing is 8 February and the latest 20 July. After the nestlings have left the nest they wander about in noisy flocks, constantly uttering their begging cry and frequenting fruit-bearing trees where they are fed by the accompanying females for what seems to be a long period.

The males are present during the nesting period in the colonies where they apparently hold a definite territory. They have a very remarkable display during which they utter strange notes which can be considered to be their song. When displaying they sit on a branch and start by bending forwards until the head is well below the feet, the bill pointing down. All the time they ruffle their feathers and bring the extended wings almost together over their backs. The ruffling and trembling feathers make quite a loud rattling noise. While extending their wings, the tail is brought forward over the back making an angle of about 90°. During this display strange, and not very melodious, notes are uttered which are impossible to describe.

Through careful field studies made in Venezuela and on Trinidad the life-history of this particular species is now quite well known and, with a few minor exceptions, can be considered as typical for all the oropendolas.

A near relative of the Crested oropendola, the Green oropendola *Psarocolius viridis,* which is olive green and chestnut, has the same display but in bending downward it goes even further, the bow being so deep that the bird almost seems to tumble over, looking as if it is hanging upside down by its feet.

Many of the colonies of oropendolas, especially the Crested and the Green species, are parasitized by another member of the Icteridae, the Giant cowbird. Female Giant cowbirds are often present in colonies of oropendolas and they are, where possible, chased away from the latter's nests. They, nevertheless, manage to smuggle their eggs into the nests, where they are incubated by the oropendolas. The nestlings of the cowbirds grow up together with those of the host. Some colonies are very heavily parasitized. FAMILY: Icteridae, ORDER: Passeriformes, CLASS: Aves.   F.H.

ORTOLAN *Emberiza hortulana,* a bunting found in Europe and western Asia, formerly regarded as a delicacy. It was netted alive in very large numbers and sometimes fattened for the table. In France the term ortolan has been used for all buntings and the term has become extended in other parts of the world to cover all small birds considered to be delicacies, such as the bobolink *Dolichonyx oryzivorus* of North America. FAMILY: Emberizidae, ORDER: Passeriformes, CLASS: Aves.

ORYX, a medium- to large-sized antelope, one of the most typical inhabitants of Afro-Arabian desert. The nearest relatives are the Sable and Roan antelope and the addax; together these antelopes form the tribe Hippotragini, which according to Fritz Walther are essentially larger, more heavily built relatives of the gazelles. Oryx are distinguished from their relatives by their straight or slightly backcurved horns, which are slender and closely ridged, and placed immediately behind the eyes; by their predominantly light colouration; and by their face-pattern, which is a modification of the gazelle type, there being a dark eye-stripe, a dark nose-patch and often a separate dark forehead-patch. The three may unite to form a kind of bridle pattern.

The largest and most widely distributed species of oryx is the gemsbok *Oryx gazella.* This species is about 48 in (120 cm) high. It is fawn above with a black dorsal stripe and a black flank-band separating the fawn from the white underside, which is often continued back to make the thighs black. The forelegs have a black garter above the knees, and are white below this, as are the hocks. The ear-tips are black, as is a line down the throat and chest. The black nose-patch and eye-stripes often unite to form a girdle round the muzzle.

The gemsbok has a disjunct distribution: in the Kalahari (from northwestern Transvaal through western Rhodesia, Botswana, northern Southwest Africa into Angola as far north as Benguela), and again in the Somali arid zone along the northern coast of Tanzania into Kenya, portions of Uganda and the Sudan, Ethiopia and most of Somalia. The Kalahari race is the true gemsbok *O. g. gazella.* It has a thick black flank-band which continues back onto the thighs. The dorsal stripe extends to the tail-tuft; the nose-patch and eye-stripe unite on the nose to form a girdle round the muzzle; the black throat-fringe may be elongated to a tuft halfway down; and the forelegs are black from the shoulders to the knees. This strikingly handsome race is scarcer than formerly, but is well protected in reserves, and in the Kalahari Gemsbok National Park.

The northeastern subspecies of *O. gazella* are less strikingly marked: the nose-patch is either not united to the eye-stripes or only very narrowly. There is no throat fringe and the flank band is narrower and does not extend to the thighs. The dorsal stripe ends on the rump. The two subspecies are, however, quite clearly different. The Beisa oryx *O. g. beisa,* found northeast from the Tana River and Uganda, is tawny (less grey than the gemsbok) with a black patch on the front of the lower forelegs and the nose-patch does not unite with the face-stripes. The Tufted or Fringe-eared oryx *O. g. callotis* is found south of the Tana to the Kilimanjaro district, and west to the Rift valley. It is redder in colour, with long black ear-tufts. The light face-marks are fawn, not white and there are no black patches on the front of the forelegs. The black eye-stripe is sometimes narrowly joined to the nose-patch, and sometimes extends back under the lower jaw to join with the throat-stripe.

The second species is the Arabian or Beatrix oryx *O. leucoryx.* This is smaller than the previous species, only 40 in (1 m)

A group of Tufted or Fringe-eared oryx found widely over the open parts of East Africa. They are antelopes of the species *Oryx gazella*, also called gemsbok.

high. It is white with brown limbs, blackish frontal and nasal patches and eye-stripes which expand below and unite under the lower jaw, being continued back as a throat-stripe. The horns in this species are often at least as long as the animal is tall. Formerly found all over the Arabian peninsula and north into Syria and Iraq, this species has been drastically reduced in numbers and in range. It has always been hunted because of the believed connexion between killing an oryx and virility. Recently oil-rich sheikhs have led large hunting-parties into the desert which have mown down great numbers with automatic rifles and machine guns from fast cars and even from aeroplanes. An expedition from Qatar into the Rub' al Khali in 1963 accounted for over 300—at that time thought to represent more than three-quarters of the surviving stock. Accordingly in 1964 the Fauna Preservation Society mounted 'Operation Oryx' under Ian Grimwood, which captured two males and a female to form the nucleus of a breeding herd in Phoenix Maytag zoo, Arizona, against the probable extermination of the species in the wild. This expedition focused world attention on the plight of the species. The London zoo contributed its female, and both the Sheikh of Kuwait and the King of Saudi Arabia revealed that they possessed private herds in captivity, out of which each generously donated animals to the Phoenix pool. A number exist in a zoo in Ta'iz, Yemen, and David L. Harrison has recently

obtained evidence of the animal's continued existence in the wild. The Phoenix herd has now increased to 19 (as of 1969), and there is every hope that the species has been saved.

The third species of oryx is rather different from the other two by virtue of its predominantly red and white colour, and its curved horns. This is the Scimitar oryx *O. dammah*. It is 4 ft (120 cm) high, weighs 440 lb (200 kg) and has horns up to 40 in (1 m) long, which are lightly backcurved, but more strongly so than in the other two species. It lives in the southern Sahara; east of the Nile it lives in Nubia; west of it, as far west as Senegal and Rio de Oro. In the dry season this animal migrates as far as 15°N; in the rains, it returns north into the Sahara proper. It has reddish face-markings, both eye-stripes, nose-patch and forehead-patch, though these may be partly obliterated. The neck is light reddish also, and this colour may extend as far back as the hindquarters. The amount of the backward extension of the red is individually variable. Although decreasing in numbers, recent estimates place the total population of this species at about 10,000. Both this species and the Arabian oryx are alternatively known as the White oryx.

Oryx live in small herds, from half a dozen to several dozen head, mainly cows; some bulls live solitary lives. Oryx are extremely wary and keen-sighted. Like their relative, the Sable antelope, they have a

reputation for being dangerous when approached too closely: the long rapier-like horns of a gemsbok can transfix a lion—as a matter of record—and a recent expedition to relocate some oryx, from the Namib desert to the Kalahari Gemsbok National Park, was charged repeatedly and its lorries speared.

A recent investigation has shown that oryx can tolerate unusually high temperatures—104°F (40°C) and above—without significantly increased water loss; moreover it feeds at night when the dry desert plants on which it lives, containing only 1–2% water by day, absorb moisture so that they then contain 40%. To compensate for the reduction of sweating, the brain is protected from overheating by a rete mirabile, or network of closely approximated arteries and veins, so that the arterial blood is cooled by venous blood from the nasal cavity.

During the rutting season, which varies in different parts of the oryx's range, the bulls fight very viciously, although there are usually no fatalities. The horns are crossed and there follows a wrestling match, head to head. For protection, the bulls have considerably thickened skin over the shoulders. In courtship, too, there is an aggressive element. Male and female spar in the same fashion as two males, the male pushing the female round in a circle. When they have circled a few times, they break and a chase ensues; the male mounts the female, clasping her loins with his forelegs, with head and neck held up. Between the sparring and the mounting occurs the 'laufschlag': the male, after rubbing the female's hindquarters with his cheek, lays his head on her back, raises his foreleg horizontally and strokes the outside of the female's back leg, or between her back legs. The male is stretched stiffly upwards, the female lowers her head. Laufschlag is repeated several times, they circle again and then the chase ensues.

Inter-male fighting differs from male-female fighting in that the partners stand farther apart and their heads are stretched up; the male and female in courtship stand close together 'with heads low. If the female does not wish to mate she tries to 'defeat' the male in this sparring and will circle as many as 20 times; she breaks, and the male pursues her. If they are enclosed, the female will run to a wall, the farthest she can reach, and the male in the heat of his excitement may stab her.

Arabian oryx, the most desert-adapted species, retire into the dunes when alarmed. In the heat of the day they dig into the sand for shade. They are less aggressive than gemsbok and they run with a slower, more cumbersome canter, without the twists and turns that gemsbok make. FAMILY: Bovidae, ORDER: Artiodactyla, CLASS: Mammalia.
C.P.G.

OSMOREGULATION, the means by which organisms regulate the concentration of their body fluids. Osmosis is the process by which water flows from a medium of low solute concentration to one of high concentration across a membrane permeable to water but not to dissolved subtrates. Animals which have a permeable body surface and which maintain their blood concentration at a level differing from that of the medium in which they live tend to gain or lose water accordingly.

Life probably began in the sea and, reflecting the evolution of the basic biochemical mechanisms in this environment, the functioning of most modern cells is dependent upon their being bathed by a medium which, like sea water, contains a high proportion of sodium chloride and lesser amounts of potassium, calcium, magnesium and sulphate. Both the total concentration and the concentration of the individual chemical constituents of the blood have to be maintained within certain limits. The degree to which salinity change in the medium can be tolerated varies widely, however. Animals which do not survive more than a small change are said to be stenohaline. Those which tolerate a wide range are termed euryhaline.

The blood of most marine species of invertebrates and that of the hagfish (*Myxine*) is relatively similar to sea water both in concentration and composition. Since the osmotic pressure (a function of the concentration) of the blood is the same as that of the media, these animals require no special means to restrict water flow across their body surface and in general the permeability is quite high. If such forms are transferred to a more dilute medium, water enters the body by *osmosis, salts are lost in the urine and across the body surface and the blood concentration falls. Few sub-littoral marine species tolerate a prolonged drop in blood concentration of more than about 30%. A greater degree of tolerance of dilute media is shown by some inshore and estuarine species such as the Common mussel *Mytilus edulis* and the lugworm *Arenicola marina*. These animals cannot maintain the concentration of their blood above that of the medium but they tolerate dilutions down to about one-third of that of the sea water. Since the blood concentration falls until it is the same concentration as the medium, survival is due to the ability of their cells to adapt to the altered conditions. Cellular adaptation requires that the internal osmotic pressure of the cells be matched to that of the blood in order to avoid gross water shifts across the cell surface. Adaptation involves two components: first, regulation of the ionic composition and second, control of the amount of small organic molecules in the cells.

About $\frac{1}{3}$ of the osmotic pressure of the cells of a species such as the Shore crab *Carcinus maenas* is accounted for by inorganic ions: potassium is the dominant ion with sodium, chloride and magnesium also contributing to a lesser extent. On dilution of the blood from the level present when the animal is in sea water a loss of ions from the cells assists towards the reduction of cell osmotic pressure. Limitations are placed on the participation of potassium in the loss, however, since this ion is concerned in the maintenance of electrical potential across the cell surface. As a consequence much of cell osmotic adjustment is dependent on changes in the amount of small organic molecules such as free amino acids, trimethylamine oxide and betaines. (Amino acids are the small nitrogen-containing molecules from which proteins are built up. When the blood concentration falls in a euryhaline form the amount of free amino acids in the cells is reduced. Conversely, a rise in blood concentration is followed by an increase in cell free amino acids. The amino acid level is determined by the individual cells and not by hormones circulating in the blood, since similar changes can be effected even when the cells are isolated from the body. Probably the factor controlling the rate of formation or breakdown of amino acids in the cells is the action of inorganic ion levels on the enzymes (organic catalysts) regulating amino acid synthesis.

The degree to which cell osmotic pressure can be varied is limited and euryhaline forms which can live in dilute brackish water or in freshwater must supplement the cellular regulation by maintaining the blood concentration at a level higher than that of the medium. This involves the active uptake of sodium and chloride to replace the ions being lost by diffusion and in the urine. The active transport of ions requires the expenditure of energy and there has therefore been pressure on the colonizers of fresh and brackish water to decrease the rate at which ions are lost from the body. Theoretically, restriction of loss can be achieved in three ways; by reduction in the permeability of the body surface to ions and water; by the production of urine more dilute than the blood; and through decrease in the gradient between blood and medium. The emphasis placed on these methods varies in different groups of animals. Molluscs and worms living in freshwater have rather permeable body surfaces but maintain a smaller gradient of concentration between blood and media than do the less permeable forms such as Crustacea and fishes. Within the Crustacea there is a marked tendency for species living in freshwater and brackish water to have lower permeabilities than marine species. Production of urine more dilute than the blood assists in the removal of water taken in by osmosis without excessive ion loss. The ability to produce such hypotonic urine occurs widely in freshwater animals, for example in Pond snails, worms, crayfishes and fishes. However, a few species such as the Chinese Mitten crab *Eriocheir sinensis* and the African Freshwater crab *Potamon niloticus* can only produce urine of the same concentration as the blood.

Replacement of ions lost from the body is the function of active transport systems. Ions such as sodium and chloride can be taken up across the body surface of most aquatic animals in the direction opposite to that in which they are tending to move passively. Parts of the surface specialized as respiratory organs are usually also the site of active transport. Thus sodium uptake occurs at the gills of freshwater fishes and crustaceans and across the anal papillae of mosquito larvae. The rate of active transport can be regulated by the individual to meet its ion requirements. If the blood concentration falls below normal the rate of transport is increased. Conversely, the rate of uptake is decreased if the blood concentration rises above normal. This control over the rate of uptake is necessary to counteract the effects of various physical and chemical factors on the loss and uptake of sodium and chloride. Since fishes and invertebrates are poikilothermic (cold-blooded) their body temperature varies with that of the medium. The various processes involved in the loss and uptake of ions are affected to different degrees by temperature variation so that any change in temperature produces a change in blood concentration. Any alteration in blood concentration, however, automatically initiates the processes which lead to compensating variations in the rate of active ion uptake at the body surface. This *feedback system ensures that temperature alteration produces only minor variations in blood concentration.

The concentration of the medium can also affect the rate at which ions are transported. The maximum transport rate remains more or less constant down to a given concentration, but declines in still more dilute solutions. The effectiveness of the ion 'pump' in dilute solutions, therefore, depends on the concentration of the medium necessary to permit the maximum transport rate to be achieved. Freshwater animals are physiologi-

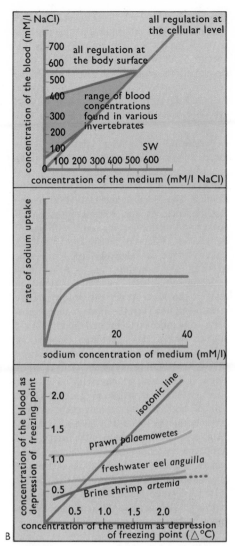

cally specialized in this respect and have 'pumps' capable of transporting at the maximum rate in more dilute media than those of related brackish-water and marine species.

In general, freshwater animals are no more tolerant of raised salinities than marine species are of diluted media. Most die when exposed to salinities more concentrated than their normal blood concentration. There is evidence, however, that some of the animals now inhabiting the sea are derived from ancestors which lived in freshwater or brackish water. These include some prawns, the majority of marine fishes, Marine iguanas, Sea snakes, whales and seals. All these animals have a blood concentration less than that of sea water. Various physiological mechanisms have been adapted by different animals to assist in the maintenance

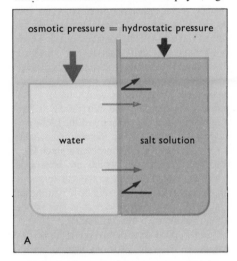

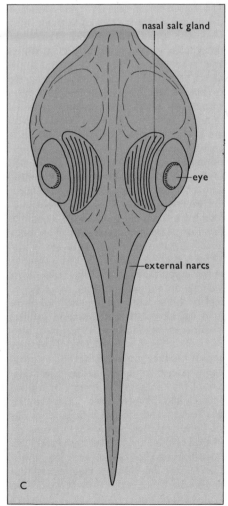

A. When a semipermeable membrane separates solutions of different concentrations, water will diffuse through from the weaker to the stronger solution. In the example shown here, diffusion will stop when the hydrostatic pressure (weight of extra water on one side) equals the osmotic pressure (tendency for water molecules to diffuse out of the other side). B.1. The relation between osmotic regulation at the body surface and at the level of the general cells of the body

in brackish-water animals maintaining various gradients of concentration between their blood and the medium. B.2. The relationship between the concentration of the medium and the maximum possible rate of sodium uptake by the freshwater race of the isopod crustacean *Mesidotea entomon*. B.3. The relationship between blood and medium concentrations in three animals able to maintain the blood hypotonic to the medium when the latter is concentrated.

C. Dorsal view of the head of a black-headed gull showing the position and size of the nasal salt glands. D. The approximate blood concentration in various marine vertebrates. Only the elasmobranchs and the hagfish have blood isosmotic with the medium. Urea (white) makes a major contribution to the total concentration of elasmobranch blood.

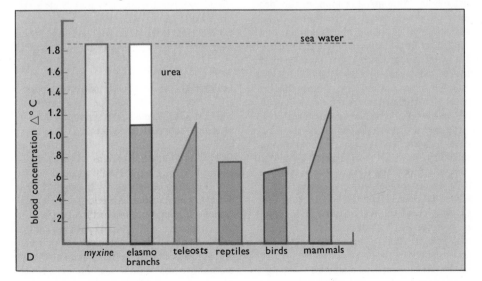

of this low blood concentration in the face of the tendency for water to be withdrawn from the body by osmosis and for ions to penetrate down the gradient from sea water.

Teleosts, prawns and Brine shrimp Marine teleosts, that is to say the majority of fishes in the sea other than the sharks, rays, coelacanths and sturgeons, have blood which is only about $\frac{1}{3}-\frac{1}{2}$ the concentration of sea water. To replace water lost by osmosis they drink the medium and take up the salt and water from the gut. In those fishes where the drinking rate has been measured the amount drunk is about 10–40% of the body weight per day. In addition to the salt taken in from the gut, more also enters across the body surface. The kidneys of fishes have never developed the capacity to produce urine with a higher concentration than the blood so they do not contribute to the elimination of the excess salt entering the body. Instead sodium chloride is removed by secretion across the gills back into the medium. The euryhaline prawn (*Palaemonetes*) and the Brine shrimp (*Artemia*) regulate their blood in a similar manner when in sea water though, like migratory fishes, such as the eel and salmon, they can also maintain the blood at a higher concentration than the medium when in dilute media. The Brine shrimp is so effective at regulating its blood in highly saline media that it can even tolerate saturated brine from which the salt is crystallizing out.

Elasmobranchs The blood of sharks and rays contains approximately the same amount of salt as that of marine teleosts but the excretory product urea $[CO(Nh_2)_2]$ is retained to such an extent in the blood that the total osmotic concentration of the body fluids slightly exceeds that of sea water. There is thus no gross tendency for water to move across the body surface and these animals do not need to drink sea water to replace losses. Salts entering the body in the food and down the concentration gradient from the medium have to be removed, however, and, as in the teleosts, the kidney cannot produce urine with a salt concentration greater than that in the blood. Elimination of the excess salt is assured by a gland opening into the rectum and not by the gills. The rectal gland secretes a fluid which has the same total concentration as the blood but which contains about twice the blood's salt concentration. The rate of secretion is variable to suit the animal's requirements but can reach 2cc/kg body wt/hr in the dogfish *Squalus acanthias*.

Coelacanths Very little is known of the means by which coelacanths osmoregulate but the blood of *Latimeria*, like that of the elasmobranchs, contains a high concentration of urea.

Amphibia There are no truly marine amphibians, although the Indo-Chinese Crab-eating frog *Rana cancrivora* tolerates salinities of the order of 80% sea water. Independently of the coelacanths and the elasmobranchs this species (and the toad *Bufo viridis*) have developed the capacity to raise the blood concentration by retaining urea. Other toads, such as *Bufo bufo,* which do not tolerate high salinities, lack the ability to retain this substance.

Freshwater Amphibia eliminate water taken up by osmosis by producing dilute urine and replacing lost salt by active uptake across the skin, particularly that of the belly.

Reptiles The blood concentration of marine reptiles such as the Marine iguana, Sea snakes and turtles is comparable with that of the teleosts. They are air breathing and the body surface is relatively less permeable to water and salt than that of fishes, thus reducing water loss. Sea water is drunk to replace the loss. As in the group already mentioned, however, the kidneys cannot produce urine more concentrated than the blood and so excess salt has to be disposed of extra-renally. In reptiles the organ responsible is an orbital gland which secretes saline 'tears'. These tears, which are the basis of the dubious tale that turtles cry because of the pain of egg-laying when they come ashore, may contain as much as 1,000m E/1 chloride and 900 m E/1 sodium in the Loggerhead turtle. Such a concentration is almost twice that of sea water and allows the excess salt to be eliminated with little wastage of water.

In freshwater reptiles there is some uptake of water across the skin and this is removed by the formation of urine more dilute than the blood. The way in which crocodiles replace salt loss is not yet known, but freshwater terrapins can take up sodium through the skin of the pharynx after taking water into the mouth.

Birds Since they are warm-blooded with a high metabolic rate birds tend to lose considerable quantities of water in the respired air. Maritime birds replace this by drinking the media. Although the kidneys can produce urine with a salt concentration higher than that of the blood, the maximum concentration of the urine is lower than that of sea water. So, again, recourse must be made to an extrarenal secretory organ for the removal of salt. In the case of birds this is a nasal gland located above the eyes and opening on the bill. These glands are present in all birds but are much larger in marine birds than in terrestrial species. The maximum secretory rate is considerable, Humboldt penguins producing fluid at a rate of up to 0·36 cc per minute with a concentration of 800 m E/1 Na. Given this ion level then for every 3 cc of sea water drunk 2 cc would be excreted and 1 cc of pure water would be available to replace respiratory water loss and so maintain the blood concentration.

Mammals Most marine mammals maintain a blood concentration which is a little above that of the terrestrial members of the group; thus the depression of freezing point (a function of concentration) is 0·83°C in a dolphin and 0·7°C in the Sperm whale, as opposed to 0·57°C in man and 0·56°C in sheep. Osmoregulation in the sea poses less severe problems to the members of this group than to the birds for several reasons: mammals are normally largely submerged thus preventing evaporative water loss across the surface; the metabolic rate is less than in birds and so the loss of water in the respired air is proportionally small, and the kidneys can produce urine with a total concentration greater than that of sea water. However, the chloride concentration of sea water is higher than the concentration of chloride found in the urine of marine mammals and it would appear, therefore, that marine mammals cannot readily replace their respiratory water loss by drinking sea water and secreting excess salt in the urine. This consideration is borne out by the fact that seals do not appear to drink in the sea; their water intake is derived solely from the food. Since their diet consists largely of teleost fishes which have a low blood concentration the salt intake is low and well within the capacity of the kidney to excrete the excess. The Whalebone whales have somewhat greater problems since they feed on invertebrates which are isosmotic with sea water but even so the salt intake is much less than in an equivalent volume of sea water since only about $\frac{1}{3}$ or less of the volume of invertebrates is blood.

Man himself cannot survive if he drinks undiluted sea water. Various factors are involved of which two are of primary importance: the high concentration of magnesium in sea water irritates the gut and causes gut water loss, and secondly the chloride concentration in sea water is higher than the maximum possible concentration of the urine so the blood concentration starts to rise. As a rise in blood concentration causes thirst followed by more drinking a vicious circle is set up. Death occurs when the blood concentration rises from its normal level of 156 m M/1 NaCl to about 200 m M/1 NaCl.

A.P.M.L.

OSMOSIS, the movement of solvent molecules from a weak solution to a stronger solution of the same solute separated from it by a semi-permeable membrane.

OSPREY *Pandion haliaetus,* a large, fish-eating bird of prey, the only member of its family but found regularly throughout the world except for South America where it only occurs on migration. In North America it is known also as the Fish hawk. Measuring up to 24 in (61 cm) long, the osprey is unusual among birds of prey in being almost wholly dark above and white beneath. It has a white

An osprey landing at its nest of sticks. Note the long, sharp talons with which it grasps slippery fish.

head with a dark streak through the eye, a barred tail, and angled wings with a dark patch beneath at the angle.

The osprey feeds very largely on fish and occupies both freshwater and marine areas where there is sufficient food. It hunts by cruising above the water at heights up to 200 ft (60 m) and takes its prey by plunging in a shallow dive. The talons are brought forward to strike the prey just as the osprey hits the water and it sometimes completely submerges. The feet are very strong, the claws long and sharp and the toes bear spiny tubercles on their undersurfaces to give a good grip on a slippery fish. Furthermore, the outer toe is large and can be moved to face backwards as in the owls. The grip following a good strike is so efficient that the bird may not be readily able to let go, and there is at least one record of an osprey striking a very large fish and being dragged under the water. After a successful strike the osprey rises from the surface, shakes the water from its plumage, arranges the fish head-forwards and carries it to its young or a suitable feeding place. In addition to fish, ospreys take mammals, birds, Sea snakes and even large Sea snails. In some regions they are frequently robbed of their prey by eagles, such as the American Bald eagle *Haliaetus leucocephalus*.

Ospreys usually nest in trees or on cliffs, though they also nest on the ground. In some regions, particularly eastern North America and northeast Africa, they nest in large colonies. The nests usually command a clear view of the fishing grounds, and are built of sticks, grasses or any other available material. They are often used year after year and may have material added to them annually. Ospreys usually mate for life, which may be 20 years or more. Two to four, usually three, eggs are laid and incubation, largely by the female, begins with the first egg. The eggs hatch after about 35 days. For five or six weeks the young are fed by the female with food brought by the male. Then, when the young can deal with the food themselves, it is dropped to them by both parents. The losses of eggs and young are high but successful young leave the nest after 8–10 weeks.

Ospreys have suffered considerably from shooting, reduction of their habitat and pesticides. The colony on Gardiner's Island off Long Island, New York, contained around 300 nests early in this century. Now there are only about 20 and the hatching success of these birds has dropped by a third. In Britain the osprey ceased to breed in 1908 but in the 1950s it attempted to re-establish itself in Scotland. The first nest was found in 1955 and with increased protection the first young were reared in 1959. The efforts made by the Royal Society for the Protection of Birds, to make it possible for this important species to re-establish itself have resulted in one of the success stories of conservation. At the time of writing the Scottish ospreys have nested for 10 successive years and in 1969 there were four nests with eggs.

The future of the osprey, however, remains in doubt. Like many other animals, particularly birds of prey, the osprey suffers from a combination of misfortunes. The widespread use of chlorinated hydrocarbon pesticides such as DDT, which do not break down in the soil or in animals and accumulate as they progress up a food chain, are particularly dangerous to primary predators such as the osprey. FAMILY: Pandionidae, ORDER; Falconiformes, CLASS: Aves.   P.M.D.

OSTARIOPHYSI, a superorder containing the majority of freshwater fishes, comprising two large orders, the carp-like fishes, Cypriniformes and the catfishes, Siluriformes.

The cypriniform fishes include three major groups of families:

1 Characoids (characins) with 16 African and South American families.

2 Gymnotoids (Electric eels and knifefishes) of South America, three families.

3 Cyprinoids (carps, suckers, loaches, Hillstream fishes), six families.

The siluriform fishes include 31 families of catfishes from almost every part of the globe.

The common factor that links all these many and varied forms is the possession of the Weberian apparatus, a series of small bones modified from parts of the first four anterior vertebrae and serving to link the swimbladder to the inner ear. This arrangement clearly affords much greater sensitivity of hearing but it seems unlikely that this fact alone would have been responsible for the incredible success of the group in the freshwaters of the world though not in the sea. The problem still awaits a satisfactory solution.

The Ostariophysi embraces at least 6,000 species of fishes showing an extraordinary diversity in both form and habit and living in the freshwaters of every continent except Australia and Antarctica. A few members, such as the Sea catfishes, are found in salt water.

OSTEOLOGY, the study of the form, structure and development of bones. Vertebrate bones have been especially studied since the early days of zoology because they reflect the general organization of the animal to which they belong, and so are useful in comparative and evolutionary studies; a knowledge of the osteology of living forms is essential to paleontology; and bones, being easily prepared and stored, are easy subjects for study.

OSTRACODA, one of the subclasses of Crustacea characterized by the possession of a bivalved shell which encloses the head, trunk and limbs. The shell is a complex structure. It is hinged at the top, so that the valves can be opened to allow various limbs to protrude. A muscle runs across the body from the middle of one shell valve to the other. Contraction of this muscle draws the two valves closely together, protecting the limbs. Some parts of the internal organs extend into the wall of the shell. A tube with a blind end extends from each side of the gut and enters the wall of the shell. In the intact ostracod this extension of the gut can be seen as a line running obliquely across the shell valve. In the female the ovary can often be seen running parallel to the gut extension.

A further characteristic of ostracods is the possession of very few limbs. There are two pairs of antennae, which act as feelers and are also often used in swimming. Behind the antennae there are only five pairs of appendages. The first of these are the mandibles, which are concerned with feeding. Behind the mandibles the remaining four pairs of limbs show great variation in different ostracods. In some forms a filter of fine setae is developed on the appendages next to the mandibles. Water is pumped in at the front edge of the shell and out at the back. Small particles carried by the current of water are trapped on the filter, and combed off by setae from the next pair of limbs, which project through the filter and push the particles towards the mouth. Other ostracods are either scavengers or predators which seize other small animals.

In some ostracods the last pair of legs do not protrude through the opening of the shell, but are bent back alongside the trunk and are used as a 'toilet foot', keeping the inside of the shell free from debris. At the end of the body there is usually a caudal furca, consisting of two branches or rami. Each ramus is elongated and provided with two or more claws at the end. Muscles attached to the bases of the rami can flex them forwards to clear out the spaces between the front limbs.

The ostracods are world-wide in occurrence, in both freshwater and the sea, from the polar regions to the tropics. They have also adopted a wide range of habits. Many are scavengers on the bottom of the sea, or in lakes and pools. There are also planktonic species, swimming continuously, many of them using a filtering method to obtain their food. One of the planktonic species, *Gigantocypris mülleri,* is the largest known ostracod, reaching the size of a cherry. It is a predator, and specimens have been found with their gut packed with copepods and small shrimps. Most ostracods are much smaller than *Gigantocypris* and only reach a length of 1–2 mm.

Some species of freshwater ostracods have been dispersed around the world with the rice plant. During one study of the ostracods in the rice fields of northern Italy 13 species were found, of which only four were common European species. The others came from Asia, Australia, South America and Africa.

Members of the genus *Mesocypris* have become terrestrial in habit. They live in the damp forest floors of South Africa and New Zealand. The limbs of *Mesocypris* are more stoutly constructed than those of their aquatic relatives and they can move quite quickly over dead leaves and debris.

The reproductive habits of ostracods are varied. Some species lay their eggs on the surfaces of plants, others carry the eggs inside the shell for several days before they hatch. There is nothing particularly unusual about the structure of the female reproductive system but that of the male is one of the most remarkable in the whole animal kingdom and occupies a large part of the body. The first remarkable feature is the size of the sperms. They are sometimes more than twice as long as the male that produced them, and they are much bigger than the sperms of many larger animals. Another remarkable feature is a pair of structures known as Zenker's organs. These form part

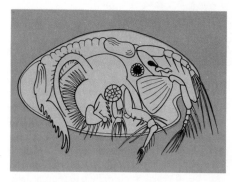

A typical ostracod with the valve on the right side removed to show the limbs and antennae as well as the internal anatomy.

of the duct leading from the testes to the outside. Each consists of a central tube with wreaths of chitinous spines at intervals. Numerous tiny muscles link the spines of each wreath together and also link adjacent wreaths. The whole is enclosed in a thin transparent membrane. The only known function of this complex structure is to pump the sperm out of the body. Perhaps such a structure is necessary for very large sperms. The penis of an ostracod is also very complex and no one has yet satisfactorily explained the way in which it functions.

The eggs of an ostracod may hatch within a few days, or they may remain dormant for several months, or even years if the pond dries up. The young emerging from the eggs have a bivalved shell, but only three pairs of appendages. These are added to as the young ostracod moults seven times before reaching the mature state, after which it does not moult again. This means that for most species there is a fairly sharply defined upper size limit. The precise time taken to reach maturity varies with temperature and other ecological factors, such as the availability of food. Some species can become mature in

two weeks when kept in good conditions.

Numerous fossil ostracods are known, dating back to the Ordovician, and some of these are useful in analyzing the stratigraphy of oil bearing rocks, particularly those in non-marine deposits. CLASS: Crustacea, PHYLUM: Arthropoda. Ja.G.

OSTRACODERMS, a term used for the fossil members of the Agnatha or jawless fishes, the living members (lampreys and hagfishes) being formerly termed cyclostomes. See jawless fishes and fishes, fossil with its accompanying classification table.

OSTRICH *Struthio camelus,* the largest living bird, is flightless and is the only member of the family Struthionidae. At one time found in large numbers in many parts of Africa and southwest Asia, the ostrich is now common in the wild only in parts of East Africa. There are also considerable numbers in ostrich farms in South Africa and domesticated birds have become feral in South Australia.

Like most other *ratite birds the ostrich is well adapted for a terrestrial life, being able to run well. The legs are very long and strong and with the long neck make up a considerable part of the ostrich's height, which in a large male may be 8 ft (2·5 m). Such a bird would weigh up to 300 lb (135 kg). Typically the colour of the male is black with white wings and tail and that of the female greybrown. The female is smaller but in both sexes the head appears small in proportion to the rest of the bird. The head and most of the neck are almost bare, being sparsely-covered with down and bristle-like feathers. The legs also are almost bare and the skin of the neck and legs is greyish or reddish according to subspecies. Well developed eyelashes are present.

The ostrich has only two toes on each foot—the original third and fourth digits. The third is much the larger. This is an adaptation to a predominantly running and walking mode of life, giving greater strength and thrust to the foot, as in the reduction of the horse's foot to one strong digit. The ostrich, with its long neck and keen eyes is able to see long distances and its long strong legs make it capable of speeds up to 40 mph (64 kph) so that it can outpace most pursuers. It is commonly found, therefore, in open country with little cover and is very difficult to approach except in nature reserves where the birds have become accustomed to vehicles. In some areas however vehicles have brought about the ostrich's downfall for in combination with high-powered rifles they make it possible for the birds to be hunted successfully by man. It is almost certain that the reduction in numbers of the ostrich in many parts of its range has been due to excessive human predation.

One of the six subspecies of ostrich, the Arabian ostrich *S. c. syriacus,* is now extinct. It was fairly common in the deserts of Syria and Arabia until about 1914, but none has been seen since 1941. It was ruthlessly hunted for its plumes and for sport. The southern form, *S. c. australis,* was once widely distributed through southern Africa but is now largely restricted to parts of Southwest Africa and Angola. This is the form which was first successfully domesticated for its plumes. The northern subspecies, *S. c. camelus,* formerly much more widely distributed, is now found in steppe country south of the Sahara from the Niger in the west to Ethiopia in the east. Further to the west in Mauretania and Rio de Oro a fourth form has been described, *S. c. spatzi.* This is separated largely on the grounds of size, though the validity of the distinction has been disputed. However, it seems that this population still exists in small numbers. The fifth and best known form is the Masai ostrich *S. c. massaicus* of southern Kenya and Tanzania, found largely in open plains. The Somali ostrich *S. c. molybdophanes,* a bird of the bush country, is found from northern Kenya to Ethiopia and Somalia.

Ostriches are found in the open country of eastern and southern Africa, where they feed on a variety of plants and animals.

Ostriches often live in groups and can be seen feeding alongside game animals such as zebras and wildebeest.

Ostriches are omnivorous, though the bulk of their food is usually of plant origin. They take a variety of fruits and seeds and also the leaves and shoots of shrubs, creepers and succulent plants. A variety of invertebrates and smaller vertebrates, such as lizards, are also eaten. Quantities of grit and stones are swallowed, aiding digestion by assisting in the grinding of resistant foods. The succulents provide a certain amount of moisture and they obtain more from some fruits and animals, which has probably given rise to the supposition that ostriches can survive for long periods under desert conditions without water. This is not the case; they must either obtain water from their food or else have access to drinking water. They also bathe when they have the opportunity.

All ostriches are polygamous. Varying numbers of females are recorded as forming the harem of a single male but this may be the result of differences in the availability of females rather than racial differences. The nest is a shallow pit dug in sandy soil and in this the eggs of all the females of a particular male are laid. Varying clutch sizes are recorded, from 15–60 eggs. It seems that each female lays from six to eight eggs, usually

An ostrich squatting, showing the almost bare neck and legs.

one every other day. The eggs vary in surface texture in the different subspecies, some smooth, some pitted, and there is also a certain amount of variation in size. The average egg is around 6 in (15 cm) long and 5 in (13 cm) wide, with a weight only 1·4% of that of the laying female. This is an unusually low figure for such a large bird.

The incubation period is around 40 days, rather short compared with other ratites, possibly a development resulting from the considerable amount of predation to which ostrich nests are subject. The male bird incubates at night but one or more of the females takes over for much of the day. A large proportion of eggs fails to hatch. An 'injury-feigning' distraction display may be performed by either or both of the sexes if danger threatens the eggs or young and, as in other birds, this is more frequent around the time of hatching. The young are precocial and can follow the parent as soon as they are dry. They can run as fast as the adult when they are only one month old.

Ostriches are usually seen in small groups, a male being accompanied by the females of his harem and a number of young. Groups of 5–15 are common, though single birds may be seen and also parties of 50 or more. In some areas ostriches may accompany mammals such as zebra and wildebeest. It may be that, as in other cases of bird-mammal association, the ostrich is better able to detect danger visually, while the mammal may pick up a dangerous scent before the danger is visible. The association is consequently to the mutual advantage of both animals.

Ostriches have been farmed for their plumes in Cape Province in South Africa since the 1850's. In the early part of this century there were over 700,000 birds in captivity and ostrich farming enterprises had also been started in North Africa, the USA and various European countries, as well as South Australia. But the First World War almost eliminated the industry and now there are only about 25,000 birds in captivity in South Africa, principally for the production of high-quality leather.

The story of the ostrich provides a good example of the influence which man has on other species. Although in its natural state the ostrich is well-protected, seldom being approached closely or being cornered and, when cornered, being able to kick very effectively, man's activities have placed the species in considerable danger. If it were not for the domestication of ostriches and the development of conservation programmes since the Second World War, the ostrich would be a rarity, if not extinct, outside zoos. FAMILY: Struthionidae, ORDER Struthioniformes, CLASS: Aves.　　　　P.M.D.

OSTRICH NAÏVITY? The ostrich's proverbial habit of burying its head in the sand to escape danger, on the principle that if it cannot see it cannot be seen, dates back to classical times. In the version recorded by Pliny the ostrich pushes its head into a bush. The probable explanation is that when an ostrich is sitting on its nest its reaction to disturbance is to lower its head with the neck held out straight. The head may then be hidden behind a hummock or clump of herbage, while the body, although inconspicuous, is still visible. The ostrich's habit of swallowing indigestible materials, from nails to beer bottles, is also exaggerated.

OTOLITHS or ear-stones, three small limy concretions in the inner ear of fishes (see hearing in fishes). The largest otolith in most fishes is the sagitta lying in the sacculus or lower portion of the inner ear chamber. In the lagena or sac-like extension of the sacculus lies the second otolith, the asteriscus (sometimes larger than the sagitta). The third otolith, the lapillus, lies in the utriculus or upper part of the inner ear chamber. The otoliths touch sensory 'hairs' and so stimulate them when the fish moves and they thus relay information on momentum and direction. The otoliths have such a characteristic shape in each species that new fossil species have been described solely on the basis of the form of the otoliths. They have also been of great value in ageing fishes since their concretionary layers, like the rings of a tree, can be related with seasonal events. This method of ageing fishes can be used both to check the conventional method using the scales and on its own for fishes that lack scales.

Otoliths grow by the deposition of lime on their outer surfaces. The lime is obtained from lime salts taken in with the food just as in us layers of bone are laid down by the lime salts in the body. Many of the plankton animals, on which fishes feed, have limy shells. The deposition of the lime is continuous but the rate at which it is laid down varies with the season. In summer when the fish is feeding heavily and growing rapidly there will be a greater amount laid down as compared with the winter when the fish is relatively inactive and feeding is low. Growth lines can be seen, with the aid of a lens or a low-power microscope, as a series of alternately light and dark concentric rings similar to the annual rings across the trunk of a tree.

Otoliths are irregularly shaped. They are usually somewhat flat, perhaps concave on one side, more or less oval, with the surface marked with grooves and ridges that vary with the different species of fishes. They have a pearly lustre and are aesthetically pleasing to the eye and at least one dealer in gem stones took to collecting fish otoliths because of their beauty; and from that took to studying them scientifically. By contrast the otoliths of the fishes known as drums (Sciaenidae) are very large and in former times were worn on a string around the neck as a preventive and cure for colic.　　M.B.